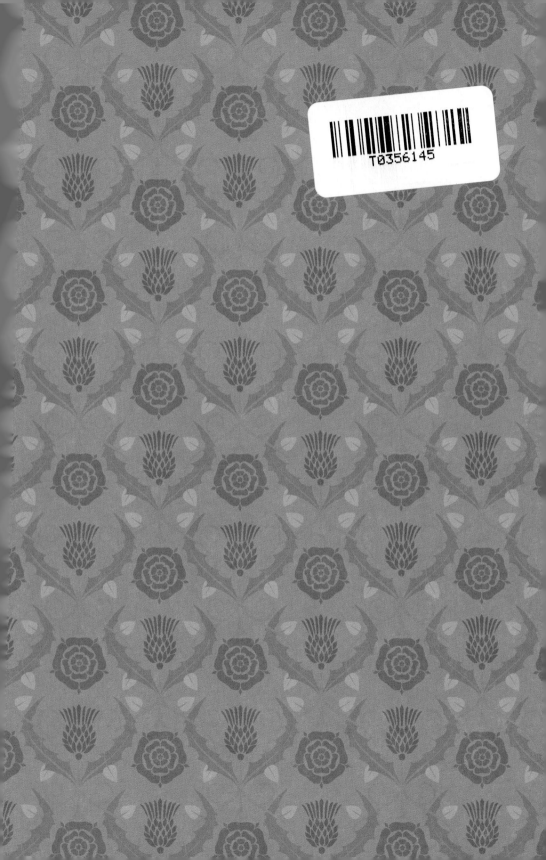

CAPTIVE QUEEN

CAPTIVE QUEEN

The Decrypted History of
MARY, QUEEN OF SCOTS

JADE SCOTT

PEGASUS BOOKS

NEW YORK LONDON

CAPTIVE QUEEN

Pegasus Books, Ltd.
148 West 37th Street, 13th Floor
New York, NY 10018

ISBN: 978-1-63936-801-3

10 9 8 7 6 5 4 3 2 1

Printed in the United States of America
Distributed by Simon & Schuster
www.pegasusbooks.com

For Stewart

Contents

Dramatis Personae

ROYALS

Mary, Queen of Scots, 1542–1587

Sent to the French court at age five; Queen of France 1559–1560; personal reign in Scotland 1561–1567; forced to abdicate in 1567; flees to England in 1568 and spends the remainder of her life in captivity.

Henry Stuart, Lord Darnley, 1546–1567

King of Scotland following his marriage to Mary, Queen of Scots in 1565. Murdered in February 1567 at Kirk o' Field in Edinburgh.

James VI of Scotland, 1566–1625

Son of Mary and Henry Stuart, Lord Darnley; ascends to throne of England in 1603 on the death of Elizabeth.

Elizabeth I of England, 1533–1603

Becomes Queen of England in 1558 and remains on the throne until her death in 1603.

Henri II of France, 1519–1559
King of France from 1547 until his death following a jousting accident in 1559. Mary's father-in-law.

Catherine de' Medici, 1519–1589
Wife of King Henri II of France and mother-in-law of Mary, Queen of Scots. Acted as Regent of France for her son Charles IX from 1560 until 1563.

Francis II of France, 1544–1560
Mary's first husband who reigned as King of France from 1559 to 1560, dying from an ear infection which led to meningitis.

Charles IX of France, 1550–1574
Mary's brother-in-law and King of France from 1560 until his death, possibly from tuberculosis, in 1574.

Henri III of France, 1551–1589
Mary's brother-in-law and King of France from 1574 until his assassination in 1589.

Philip II of Spain, 1527–1598
Inherits a huge kingdom encompassing Spain, Spanish Netherlands, and the colonized territories in the Americas from his father, Charles V, in 1556; husband of Queen Mary Tudor of England from 1554 until her death in 1558.

Don Juan of Austria, 1547–1578

Illegitimate half-brother of King Philip II of Spain; governor of the Spanish Netherlands from 1577.

POPES

Pope Pius V, 1504–1572

Head of the Catholic Church from 1566 until his death in 1572; issues the bull of excommunication against Elizabeth.

Pope Gregory XIII, 1502–1585

Head of the Catholic Church from 1572 until his death in 1585.

CONSPIRATORS

Charles Paget, c. 1546–1612

Catholic conspirator implicated in Throckmorton Plot of 1583 and Babington Plot of 1586 who lived in exile in Paris from 1581; secretary to Archbishop James Beaton from 1582; alias Wattes.

Thomas, Lord Paget, c. 1544–1590

Elder brother of Charles Paget; also a Catholic implicated in Throckmorton Plot; fled into exile in Paris in 1583.

Francis Throckmorton, c. 1554–1584

Warwickshire gentleman and Catholic conspirator; became a letter bearer for the Spanish ambassador while in the Low Countries and was central to the Throckmorton Plot of 1583.

Dame Margery Throckmorton, d. 1591
Mother of Francis Throckmorton; devoted Catholic; sheltered priests in her household.

Cicely Hopton, d.1625
Daughter of the Lieutenant of the Tower of London, Sir Owen Hopton; Catholic convert and messenger of Throckmorton brothers while in the Tower.

Henri, Duke of Guise, 1550–1588
Mary's cousin; son of Francis, Duke of Guise; close friend of King Henri III of France; military commander; leader of the Catholic League from 1576; nicknamed Le Balafré (Scarface).

Anthony Babington, 1561–1586
English Catholic nobleman implicated as a leader of the final plot that saw Mary tried and executed for seeking to assassinate Elizabeth.

Thomas Morgan, 1546–1601
Welsh secretary of George Talbot, Earl of Shrewsbury; later cipher clerk for Mary, Queen of Scots.

Thomas Howard, 4ᵗʰ Duke of Norfolk, 1536–1572
Leading noble in England who was executed for his involvement in the Ridolfi Plot and his attempts to marry Mary, Queen of Scots without Queen Elizabeth's permission.

Thomas Percy, 7ᵗʰ Earl of Northumberland, 1528–1572

Supporter of Mary, Queen of Scots who openly rebelled against Elizabeth in 1569 before fleeing to Scotland; returned to England in 1572 and executed at York; older brother of Henry Percy.

Anne Percy, Countess of Northumberland, 1536–1591

Wife of Thomas Percy, 7ᵗʰ Earl of Northumberland; a committed Catholic who led forces during the rebellion of 1569; was a supporter of Mary's cause and continued to agitate for the restoration of Catholicism while in exile on the continent.

Henry Percy, 8ᵗʰ Earl of Northumberland, 1532–1585

English nobleman; gained the title of Earl of Northumberland upon the execution of his older brother Thomas Percy in 1572 after his failed rising to free Mary Queen of Scots; Catholic conspirator; died in the Tower in 1585, likely by suicide.

DIPLOMATS AND COURTIERS

Michel de Castelnau, Sieur de la Mauvissière, c. 1520–1592

French soldier and scholar; diplomatic envoy to Scotland in 1559, 1561 and 1564; ambassador to England from 1575 to 1585.

William Cecil, Lord Burghley, 1520–1598

Elizabeth's chief advisor and Lord High Treasurer from 1572 who was convinced Mary, Queen of Scots was a threat to Elizabeth's safety and the security of the realm.

Sir Francis Walsingham, c. 1532–1590
Queen Elizabeth's chief spymaster, experienced diplomat and principal secretary; led the hunt for evidence against Mary, Queen of Scots during her later years of English captivity.

George Talbot, 6ᵗʰ Earl of Shrewsbury, c. 1522–1590
Acted as Mary, Queen of Scots' custodian for the longest period, hosting her at his properties in Staffordshire and Derbyshire.

Sir Francis Knollys, c. 1511–1596
First custodian of Mary, Queen of Scots when she arrived in England in 1568.

Sir Ralph Sadler, 1507–1587
Custodian of Mary for a brief period between 1584 and 1585.

Sir Amyas Paulet, 1532–1588
Final custodian of Mary, Queen of Scots until her execution in 1587.

Thomas Randolph, 1523–1590
English ambassador to Scotland 1559–1566, 1570–1571, and intermittently special envoy between 1578 and 1586.

Henry Killigrew, c. 1528–1603
English diplomat and special envoy to Scotland at various times between 1566 and 1586.

Paul de Foix de Carmain, 1528–1584

French prelate and diplomat with suspected Huguenot sympathies; ambassador to England 1561–1565; ambassador to Rome from 1579 until his death.

Bertrand de Salignanc de la Mothe-Fénelon, 1523–1589

French ambassador to England 1569–1575; ambassador to Scotland 1582–1583.

Guillaume de L'Aubespine, Baron de Châteauneuf, 1547–1629

French ambassador to England 1585–1589.

Don Bernardino de Mendoza, c. 1540–1604

Spanish military commander and diplomat; ambassador to England from 1578 until his expulsion in 1584; ambassador to France 1584–1591.

Antonio de Guarás, 1520–1579

Spanish ambassador to England from 1571–1578.

John Leslie, Bishop of Ross, 1527–1596

Representative of Mary, Queen of Scots during the commissions of 1568 and her ambassador to England during her captivity.

James Stewart, 1st Earl of Moray, 1531–1570

Half-brother of Mary, Queen of Scots and Regent of Scotland following Mary's forced abdication in 1567. Assassinated in 1570.

James Hepburn, 4th Earl of Bothwell, c. 1534–1578

Third husband of Mary, Queen of Scots who fled Scotland after the Battle of Carberry Hill in 1567 and died after being imprisoned in Denmark.

James Beaton, Archbishop of Glasgow, c. 1517–1603

Mary, Queen of Scots' ambassador to France from 1561 to her death in 1587; Catholic Archbishop of Glasgow 1551–1571 and once again 1598–1603.

Matthew Stewart, 4th Earl of Lennox, 1516–1571

Father of Henry, Lord Darnley, grandfather of James VI, and husband of Margaret Douglas, Countess of Lennox. Regent of Scotland 1570–1571.

John Erskine, 1st Earl of Mar, d. 1572

Regent of Scotland 1571–1572 and custodian of James VI following Mary, Queen of Scots' abdication.

James Douglas, 4th Earl of Morton, c. 1516–1581

Final Regent of Scotland during James VI's minority 1572–1578. Executed in 1581 for his role in the murder of Henry Stuart, Lord Darnley.

William Maitland of Lethington, 1525–1573

Mary's principal secretary throughout her personal reign, he continued to act in her interests after her abdication though he also negotiated with the leaders of the party supporting James VI. Arrested in 1569, he died in Edinburgh in 1573, possibly at his ownhand after the castle was taken by English forces.

George Seton, 7th Lord Seton, 1531–1586

Devoted supporter of Mary, Queen of Scots; travelled to the continent to seek aid for her cause.

John Maxwell, 4th Lord Herries of Terregles c. 1512–1583

Supporter of Mary, Queen of Scots; followed her into England in 1568 before acting as her representative and courier in Scotland and England.

John Fleming, 5th Lord Fleming, 1529–1572

Supporter of Mary, Queen of Scots who followed her into England in 1568, returning to Scotland in 1569 and holding Dumbarton Castle in her name until April 1571. Briefly exiled in France before returning to Scotland in 1572; dying during the defence of Edinburgh Castle.

Claude, Lord Hamilton, 1546–1621

Son of James, Duke of Châtellerault and leader of the Hamilton family's support for Mary, Queen of Scots. Commander of her vanguard troops at the Battle of Langside in 1568, he travelled with her into England. Implicated in the assassination of James Stewart, Earl of Moray and Regent of Scotland.

Robert Boyd, 5th Lord Boyd, c. 1517–1590

Supporter of Mary, Queen of Scots, appointed one of her commissioners after her arrival in England in 1568. Declared allegiance to the young James VI and his regents in 1571.

William Kirkcaldy of Grange, c. 1520–1573

Opposed Mary's marriage to Bothwell and a close supporter of James Stewart, Earl of Moray and Regent of Scotland; led the Regent's forces at the Battle of Langside. However he switched allegiance to Mary after Moray's assassination in 1570 and held Edinburgh Castle in her name until it fell in 1573, whereupon he was hanged.

Augustine Raulet [Rallay] d. 1574

Mary's French secretary from 1571 until his death in 1574.

Claude Nau, d. 1605

Mary's French secretary from 1575 until her execution in 1587.

Gilbert Curle, d. 1609

Mary's Scottish secretary throughout her English captivity from 1568 until her execution in 1587. Previously a valet from 1567, he travelled with her into England. Curle married Barbara Mowbray, one of Mary's attendants, at Tutbury Castle in October 1585.

WOMEN IN MARY'S LIFE

Marie de Guise, 1515–1560

Mary's mother, wife of King James V, and Regent of Scotland from 1554 until her death in 1560.

Antoinette de Bourbon, 1494–1583

Mary's grandmother and the matriarch of the Guise family.

Mary Seton, 1542–1615

Mary's most devoted attendant from her childhood, through her English captivity until her retirement to France in 1585. One of the 'four Marys' who travelled with the Scottish queen to France when she was a child.

Mary Beaton, c. 1543–1597

One of the 'four Marys' and a cousin of Mary's ambassador James Beaton, Archbishop of Glasgow.

Mary Livingston, 1541–1582

One of the 'four Marys', sister of William Livingston who followed Mary into England with his wife Agnes Fleming.

Mary Fleming, 1542–1584

One of the 'four Marys', Mary was from a family of supporters of the Scottish queen. She married William Maitland of Lethington in 1567.

Agnes Fleming, Lady Livingston c. 1535–1597

Sister of Mary Fleming, she and her husband William, Lord Livingston, followed Mary into England; she acted as a spy and courier for Mary after her return to Scotland in 1572.

Jean Scott, Lady Ferniehurst, c. 1548–c.1593

Wife of Thomas Kerr of Ferniehurst and a close supporter of Mary, Queen of Scots during her English captivity, maintaining a coded correspondence network.

Margaret Douglas, Countess of Lennox, 1515–1578

Daughter of Margaret Tudor and Archibald Douglas, 6th Earl of Angus, she married Matthew Stewart, 4th Earl of Lennox in 1544. Mother of Henry Stuart, Lord Darnley and grandmother of James VI and Arbella Stuart.

Annas Keith, Countess of Moray and Argyll, c. 1540–1588

Wife of James Stewart, 1st Earl of Moray and Regent of Scotland until his assassination in 1570. She remarried Colin Campbell, heir to the Argyll Earldom in 1572.

Margaret Erskine, Lady Lochleven, c. 1510–1572

Mistress of King James V of Scotland and mother of James Stewart, 1st Earl of Moray and Regent of Scotland. She cared for Mary during her imprisonment at Lochleven Castle.

Elizabeth Talbot, Countess of Shrewsbury (Bess of Hardwick), 1521–1608

Wife of Mary's custodian George Talbot, Earl of Shrewsbury, Bess and Mary spent a great deal of time together embroidering but fell out after several years of living in close quarters.

Arbella Stuart, 1575–1615

Granddaughter of Margaret Douglas, Countess of Lennox and of Elizabeth Talbot, Countess of Shrewsbury. She was cared for by the Countess of Shrewsbury after her mother's death in 1582 and spent time with Mary, Queen of Scots.

Elizabeth [Bess] Pierrepont, 1568–1648
Daughter of Henry Pierrepont and Frances Cavendish and granddaughter of Elizabeth Talbot, Countess of Shrewsbury. Part of Mary's household and implicated in Babington Plot of 1586.

Barbara Mowbray, 1556–1616
Niece of William Kirkcaldy of Grange, she was an attendant on Mary during the 1580s and married Mary's Scottish secretary Gilbert Curle in October 1585.

Geillis Mowbray, dates unknown
Niece of William Kirkcaldy of Grange and sister to Barbara Mowbray, she was an attendant on Mary, Queen of Scots from late 1585.

Elizabeth Curle, dates unknown
Sister of Mary's Scottish secretary Gilbert Curle, she was an attendant on Mary in England and was with her at her execution in 1587.

Jane [Janet] Kennedy, d. 1589
Attendant on Mary, Queen of Scots and with her at her execution in 1587. She was a relative of Gilbert Kennedy, 4th Earl of Cassilis, a supporter of Mary.

Christian Hogg, dates unknown
Attendant on Mary, Queen of Scots and wife of her servant and musician Bastian Paget.

Decoding Mary's Letters

*Not willing to send thither anything of
importance until I am sure that you have
received the alphabet here enclosed to serve
henceforth between us, for this one has passed
through too many hands to be trusted.*[2]

C OMING ACROSS A letter from Mary, Queen of Scots in
the archives is a thrilling experience. No matter how
many times you've seen that iconic signature, the heart
still skips a beat when you realize it is right there in front of you.
You can reach out and touch it, trace the ink from her pen. It is
like she is reaching out through time. Despite all my efforts to
remain professional and keep my historian hat on, there is no

denying that letters have a visceral impact. There is something innately human about this type of source. We might not write letters as often today, but communication remains at the heart of our modern lives. We email, text, WhatsApp, Snapchat, tweet, put things on Instagram… Sometimes we are speaking to one person, sometimes we have an audience we are performing for. We are expert curators of our own brands; we want certain people to see us in a particular light. The messages we send to our best friend are not the same as the ones we put on our social media platforms, but the impulse is the same: we seek connections with other people. People in the past experienced this same need, it is just that their main way of communication, especially at a distance, was via letter. Mary, Queen of Scots used her letters in similar ways: for both personal conversations and as tools. Letters were one of the very few means through which she could be active in her own contemporary portrayal and later memorialization. Though just as we can find our digital messages become misconstrued or even wilfully twisted, Mary's correspondence has been used by admirers and by adversaries over the centuries. As she herself warned: 'People may make things appear different from what they were.'[3]

Mary's letters have been crucial for her biographers for centuries. The Scottish humanist scholar George Buchanan, who very much sought to portray Mary as a murderous tyrant, used her alleged correspondence with James Hepburn, 4th Earl of Bothwell, as evidence in his attack against her in his book *Ane detectioun of the duinges of Marie Quene of Scottes* (1571). Similarly, John Leslie, Bishop of Ross, Mary's representative and supporter, framed his *Defence of the Honour of Marie, Queene of Scotland* (1569) with evidence from letters. Letters continue to inform more recent biographies, but, like Buchanan and Leslie, it can be easy to allow our own biases and agendas to influence how we read Mary's words.

How can we even agree that a letter is in fact Mary's own words? Early modern letter-writers, especially those of elite status, relied on secretaries to write their letters. Royals were not expected to write all their correspondence themselves; they had a small army of clerks to perform these tasks. Letters were often written collaboratively, going through a process of composition (whether written or dictated to another), drafting, editing and copying. Beyond letters written entirely in her hand, of which there are examples in French and Scots, there are hundreds of Mary's letters in which the main text was penned by a secretary but that she signed in her own hand. She often added postscripts too. Signatures, then, are important markers of her authorship.[4] But what about when the letters themselves are cloaked in disguises?

Turning to the archives to look at the contents of one of Mary's letters and finding that it is in a strange blend of letters, numbers and symbols brings you up short. I've examined hundreds of coded letters between Mary and her friends and supporters over the years now, and each one remains as exciting and frustrating as the first. Even when we have deciphered copies telling us roughly what the letter says, we can never be entirely sure of the details. We can attempt to decode these letters ourselves, if the key survives or other examples are available for us to analyse, and some historians have undertaken this excruciating but amazing work with other prolific letter-writers, including Mary's granddaughter Elizabeth Stuart.[5] But until recently, scholars have tended to rely on contemporary deciphering, especially when such huge numbers survive.

Mary's ciphered letters have come down to us in one of three ways: the original letter written in code no longer survives, but contemporary agents tried to decipher it while it was intercepted and so we have their interpretations; the original ciphered letter has been preserved alongside a contemporary translation; we have only the original, or a copy of the original, letter in cipher and it has never been decoded. These are tantalizing documents that continue to seduce researchers. What if the agents who copied and interpreted the letters at the time got it wrong? What if we could somehow break the code and see inside these undeciphered letters for the first time?

Recently a remarkable project did just that: some of Mary's letters have been decoded and the public has been given new access to these coded documents. A team of scholars from across different disciplines – George Lasry, Norbert Biermann and Satoshi Tomokiyo – deciphered fifty-seven letters by Mary for the first time since their composition more than four hundred years ago.[6] The letters date from 1578 until 1584, when she was being held captive in England, and are preserved at the Bibliothèque nationale de France in Paris. They had been catalogued as enciphered messages, but because the sender and the recipient were unknown, they had been archived alongside other manuscripts that related to Italian affairs. It is only through this new decipherment by George Lasry and his colleagues that we know the letters were from Mary, Queen of Scots.

Exhilarating enough that these newly decoded letters have been attributed to Mary for the first time, what else might be hiding among the libraries, archives and private collections just waiting for their author to be revealed? We've always known that innumerable copies of Mary's letters did not survive – either because they were destroyed at the time or because they were lost over the centuries – but the Lasry team's extraordinary new research opens the possibility of adding even more examples to the catalogue of her correspondence. If ever we needed a reason to thank curators and archivists for making sure manuscripts are preserved for the future, this is it. These coded texts were opaque; they had held on to their secrets for hundreds of years. However, because they were cared for as historic documents, valuable in their own right because of their age and the evidence for early modern cryptography they offered, new technologies were able to revolutionize our knowledge.

The decoding project relied upon a combination of manual research and computerized cryptanalysis. Programmes developed were able to identify the plaintext language as French, and from there a series of increasingly complex decipherment was achieved, moving from recognizing single letters of the alphabet through to identification of prefixes, words and individual names.

The symbols used to refer to Queen Elizabeth, her chief spymaster Sir Francis Walsingham, King Philip II of Spain and Pope Gregory XIII were revealed. Figures central to the schemes of the 1580s to free Mary from captivity were also illuminated, including eager young gentlemen such as Francis Throckmorton, Thomas Morgan and Charles Paget. These extraordinary deciphers by Lasry and his team, further confirm that Mary was intricately involved in the schemes to free her – for example, as we will see, she knew about the Throckmorton Plot of 1584 from its earliest incarnation, despite her public protests to the contrary.

The contents of these newly deciphered letters are a mix of political discussion and personal complaint, a theme we see across all of Mary's correspondence. As in many of her letters, she was scathing about those she viewed as enemies. She warned that Walsingham was not to be trusted and that the Puritan faction at court in England were plotting against her. She wrote often about negotiations for her release, based upon her willingness to give up claims to the English throne. This change in approach from the late 1570s onwards, which she had long fought against, seems in part due to the deterioration of her personal circumstances; her finances were becoming more difficult to access, meaning she was struggling to reward servants and supporters, while her health suffered from lack of exercise, poor ventilation in her rooms, and recurrent bouts of physical and mental illness.

Importantly, the newly deciphered letters tell us how Mary maintained links with supporters through her correspondence even during the intense surveillance of her captivity. In one of the newly decoded letters from May 1578, Mary complained that she had been without any letters for more than seven months; but in another from eighteen months later, she was thrilled to have a new way of conveying her letters secretly.[7] As the schemes and plots swirling around Mary grew, the surveillance she was subject to increased accordingly. Her letters were intercepted by English agents who combed through the contents looking for any suggestion of conspiracy or foreign support. By the time Mary reached her tenth anniversary of captivity in 1578, she recognized that the ciphered letters were not enough. She needed to somehow get past the interceptors of her letters and find a route that was kept hidden from Walsingham.

The newly decoded letters show us just how Mary managed this. Many of the fifty-seven coded letters were sent to Michel de Castelnau, Sieur de la Mauvissière, a longstanding ally of Mary's. Mauvissière had first met Mary when she was a young woman at the French court, before her marriage to the dauphin, Francis II, in 1558. He later travelled with her during her return to Scotland in July 1561. The two seemed to have become especially fond of one another at this point. When Mauvissière left Scotland in October of that year, along with the rest of the French entourage, Mary organized a masque to be performed in his honour. The masque may have been an early performance of George Buchanan's *Apollo et Musae* (it was held before he turned against Mary) and it absolutely infuriated John Knox, the Protestant preacher and leader of the Scottish Reformation, who deplored the lascivious entertainments put on for the French. When Mauvissière was posted back to Scotland in 1564, during the negotiations for a marriage between Mary and King Charles IX of France's youngest brother, Francis, Duke of Alençon and future Duke of Anjou, Mary once again showed her affection for him.[8] She confided in him that she was more interested in a match with King Philip II of Spain's eldest son, Don Carlos, though she admitted that she knew such a match would displease Charles's mother, Catherine de' Medici, who was loathe to have Mary align herself openly with Spain. Although Mauvissière didn't pass this intelligence on to Catherine, he nevertheless noted Mary's defiance, reporting that she was insulted by the offer of marriage to Anjou, believing that he was beneath her station. Mary had, after all, been Queen of France.

His credentials and unwavering personal support secured, in 1575 Mauvissière became perfectly positioned to set up a secret channel of communication between Mary and the outside world. He was appointed as French ambassador to England and was based at the French embassy, Salisbury Court, in Fleet Street, London. Letters sent to Mary from her supporters would be delivered to the embassy, where trusted couriers would carry them on to her and, at the same time, pick up letters from Mary in return, taking these to the French embassy for their onward journeys. The embassy was an ideal cover for this secret communication route – Mary's letters to recipients in France and beyond including Spain and the Vatican could be smuggled out inside the diplomatic bag of correspondence, which was unlikely to be searched at the English ports. Mary used both channels, the 'ordinary way' and the 'secret way', at the same time, depending on the content of her letters. On occasion, she even sent letters using the official postal route while sending a letter on the same day through the secret channel.

The secret route maintained by Mauvissière has long been known, but the newly decoded letters show us for the first time how successful this channel was. As one historian put it: 'it was kept so secure that none of it has survived and we therefore do not know what was in it.'9 Or at least, we didn't know until Lasry and his colleagues decoded the letters that ended up in Paris. Prior to 1583, the network had been so secure that we can be sure that several letters to and from Mary were able to travel as intended and their contents are, frustratingly for us, but thankfully for Mary, now lost. From late 1582, however, Sir Francis Walsingham had the French embassy under surveillance. Mary sent a ciphered letter to Mauvissière in February 1584, which Walsingham received from his inside man. The mole added a note in his own hand requesting that Walsingham 'keep all this as secret as you possibly can so that Monsieur the ambassador [Mauvissière] does not realize'.[10] This mole has variously been identified as Claude de Courcelles and Jean Arnault de Chérelles, both Mauvissière's secretaries at different times. More recently, John Bossy proposed that the most likely suspect, based on the handwriting and dates, was Laurent Feron, a clerk in the embassy.[11] He had access to the secret correspondence, was familiar with the ciphers and was also trusted to deliver correspondence from the embassy to Walsingham, a convenient cover for him to slip in some unexpected extra letters.

The decoding project let to renewed interest in Mary's coded correspondence. Using hundreds of Mary's letters and those sent to her we can now take a new look at Mary's captivity, at the plots and schemes for her freedom, and ask ourselves: how far was she really willing to go for her liberty?

Key locations from Mary's personal reign in Scotland

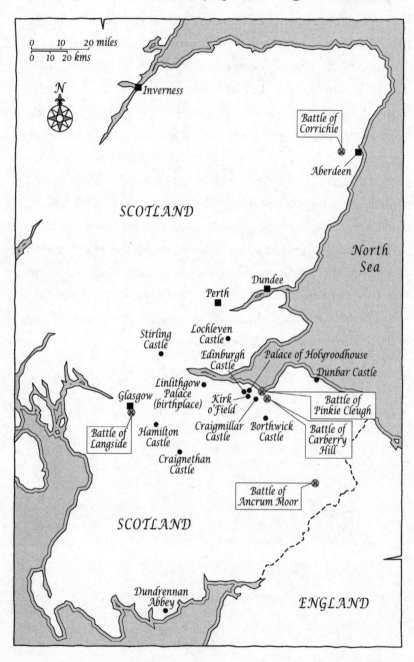

Key locations from Mary's captivity in England

'In My End Is My Beginning'

1

I am sorry that my letters bring you nothing but continual complaints and grievances, but still the circumstances I suffer – which I pray God brings to an end one way or another – force me to use all possible means, since all my proposals were, against all reason, rejected and it does not please you to grant me yourself what I deserve.[2]

DISMISSING HER SECRETARY *and reassuring her ladies that they, too, could leave the room, Mary Queen of Scots pulled the paper towards her. She dipped the nib of the goose-feather quill, one of the better-quality ones she had managed to get hold of, into the pot of dark ink on the plain but sturdy writing desk. She had insisted they let her bring this battered piece with her when she was moved from Sheffield to Tutbury. Funny how she had hated its simple style and dull surface when she was first given it all those years ago. And now here she was, leaning upon it for the thousandth time, as the winds roared against the shutters of her chamber and the chill seeped in through the cracks, bringing the sour scent of the moat that not even a gale could blast away.*

God, how she hated Tutbury. It had been a few years since she was last trapped here, but now, in September 1585, she was back. Pausing briefly, she considered jumping right in, letting the words rush from her onto the page. Instead, she penned, 'Madam, my good sister,' at the top of the page. Then, leaving it on its own line to draw the eye, she carefully began to write. She wrote until the page was filled to the edges. After refilling the ink, she signed her name with the usual sentiment, 'Your very affectionate and good sister, Marie R'. She never forgot that 'R' for Regina, meaning queen. One of the few devices she had left to her: a symbol of her royal status.

She folded the page carefully. No need for an address; the bearer would know who this was meant for. Besides, the letter would be read cover to cover before it ever left this house. Still, she gathered a few of the black threads her maid had left over from tending to her night-cloak. Folding them tightly together, she pressed the bundle on the page before quickly holding a cube of red wax over the candle flame. Trapping the floss in the melted wax, she added the final touch, pressing her ring into the puddle. Signed, sealed, and now to be delivered. Perhaps this time Queen Elizabeth would reply?

———————————∽◦∽———————————

MARY, QUEEN OF Scots spent eighteen years as a captive in England, from 16 May 1568 until her execution on 8 February 1587. She was moved between properties and passed between jailers, kept to the northern and midland reaches of the kingdom, never coming any closer to the English court than Fotheringhay Castle in Northamptonshire. She rarely had any say in where she would be accommodated, though on occasion her dogged persistence succeeded in gaining temporary relief – being removed from her most hated prison at Tutbury Castle in Staffordshire to more comfortable properties nearby or travelling to take the mineral waters at the spa in Buxton. By reconstructing her movements during these captive years, we can watch the ever-changing periods of acute crisis and tedious inaction that characterized her life. As plots were hatched – and foiled – we see Mary being shunted to more remote locations, far from any potential rescue attempt. We share in her frustrations as she was left to linger for weeks and months on end, in gloriously gilded cages. And in her last captive years, as both Mary and her enemies determined to bring things to an end one way or another, we watch as she was brought south, much farther than she had been permitted before. Brought suddenly south, to her end.

During her captivity in England, letters were a lifeline for Mary.

She wrote endlessly to family and friends in France, to supporters in Spain, to allies in Scotland and to her adversaries across England. She pleaded to be allowed to discuss her situation in person. She railed against the conditions of her captivity. She cajoled and flattered and threatened. Letters became her weapons, her armour, her battle strategy. Sometimes she would pen letters in her own hand, filling pages and pages with her neat handwriting, squeezing words into the margins of the paper. At other times, she would dictate letters to her secretaries, who would copy down her words, or else she would leave notes for them to polish into fully formed texts, which she would cast an eye over before signing her name at the bottom of the page. A speaker of several languages, her letters were multilingual – she wrote in French, English, Scots, Latin and Italian.

Several thousand letters to and from Mary, Queen of Scots survive, scattered in archives and collections across the world. They enthral and entice us. When the last letter Mary ever wrote was put on public display at the National Museum of Scotland in Edinburgh in February 2017 to commemorate the anniversary of her death, the crowds were so big that additional viewings had to be organized.[3] We thrill to see her signature there on the page: a letter of hers with a postscript in her own hand came to market in 2022 and sold for £32,500, more than double the asking price.[4] Mary's letters were prized during her lifetime too, though for different reasons. Her letters were gathered as evidence against her at her final trial in 1586, held up as proof of her involvement in plots that sought to depose and even assassinate Queen Elizabeth I of England. Her signature was the golden prize – if Mary had signed a letter with her own hand, then she was understood to have authorized the contents within. So, while she was able to send and receive letters throughout her years as a captive in England, her correspondence was always subject to surveillance by English courtiers. William Cecil, Lord Burghley, the Lord High Treasurer of England and Elizabeth's closest advisor, and Sir Francis Walsingham, principal secretary and chief spymaster, managed this surveillance network, regularly intercepting Mary's letters. Sometimes letters would be held up en route, with a copy made and the original letter sent on with a replica wax seal attached. The recipient might never suspect anything untoward, so expert were these intelligencers. As Mary would discover at her final trial in 1586, letters of hers that were intercepted could also be altered by these agents, making it appear that she had given instructions that she herself would later deny.

As her captivity went on, with diminishing hopes of a diplomatic agreement in her favour, and ever more dramatic schemes drafted in response, Mary's access to the outside world was incrementally curtailed. Diplomatic correspondence and letters regarding her finances were still transmitted using official postal channels that were supervised by Sir Francis Walsingham. Mary referred to this official route as 'the ordinary way' or more archly as 'Walsingham's way' in recognition of his close monitoring. So intense was Walsingham's surveillance that Sir Ralph Sadler, ambassador to Scotland and respected courtier during Elizabeth's reign, was once forced to explain what some odd-looking marks were on the back of a letter he was sending on from Sheffield Castle, where he had been guarding Mary for a while; in a postscript, he clarified that they were not hidden messages but simply pen marks where his young secretary had scribbled on the page before scraping them away when he realized his mistake.[5]

Mary was well aware that her letters were read by third parties, which was problematic when she wanted to convey information of a more sensitive nature. If she wished to correspond with supporters without Walsingham's spies poring over the contents of her letters, she needed a disguise. She began to compose more and more letters in cipher, using coded symbols to hide names, places and dates. Eventually entire letters were written in cipher, but we are unsure whether Mary actually penned them in her own hand – naturally, she did not sign ciphered letters. Usually, Claude Nau, her French secretary, would write letters in French, while those that were to be translated into Scots or English would be drawn up by her Scottish secretary Gilbert Curle. Each would usually then transcribe the letter text using ciphers, with multiple levels of obfuscation: individual people and places, as well as dates, would be given a unique symbol; letters of the alphabet would be disguised; red herrings would be added; words or letters would be doubled unnecessarily; and phrases would be added indicating to the reader that the previous word was to be deleted. The ciphers themselves were a mix of graphical symbols and alphabetic letters drawn from Greek and Arabic.

Codes and symbols were routinely used in the period to disguise information and could range in complexity. Mary relied upon multiple different ciphers in her letters: more than seventy different combinations survive, with specific versions brought into action depending on the person she was communicating with.[6] She also made sure to keep changing the ciphers, either to avoid unwanted readers potentially breaking them, or because she realized that examples had been intercepted. Coded correspondence relied on both parties having access to a key, which would allow the hidden text to be revealed. If keys were discovered, then the cipher had to be adapted; her principal secretary back in Scotland and lead supporter during her English captivity, William Maitland of Lethington, wrote to her attendant and friend Agnes Fleming, Lady Livingston, warning Mary against using their usual code when he realized it had been lost after a loyal messenger was arrested and was now 'known to their adversaries'.[7] Mary's letters are therefore peppered with references to 'alphabets' and at various moments of crisis – usually when a new plot was being planned or a conspirator had been taken by her enemies – she would be forced to change the codes used.

At the same time, Mary used less high-tech means of disguising her letters. Whereas normally letters would be carried in packets or bundles, occasionally they would be hidden in unusual places. She would have letter bearers hide them under stones for her servants to go and collect later, without the watchful eyes of her jailors. Or they would be slipped in between the pages of books or rolled up in fabrics sent for making clothes.[8] Her ladies-in-waiting were also able to slip letters under the sleeves of their dresses, especially when they were folded up into tiny little packets. Towards the end of Mary's captivity, her jailors were so suspicious that they forced her male servants to strip so that the lining of their clothing could be searched for secret letters. Though her ladies were not subject to such undignified behaviour, she had her own laundry women removed from her and local women brought in to strip her bed and clean her linens. It was suspected that Mary's own washerwomen had been hiding messages in the mounds of sheets, which were overlooked as they left her chambers.[9] Each time these hidden methods of communication were discovered, Mary would seek out new channels. Letters were the only way she could ever hope to escape her English prison; she could not afford to let herself become cut off. She would maintain this persistence until the very end.

MARY HAD INITIALLY pursued a non-combative policy with her English jailors. She was certain that she would not be in England long and would undoubtedly secure Elizabeth's support either to return to Scotland to face her rebellious subjects or to travel onward to France where she could be sure of a warm welcome. The first worrying sign that things would not go according to her plan was the establishment of the commissions of October and December 1568. The commissions, guided by Cecil and leaning heavily in favour of the Scottish nobles who had deposed Mary in 1567, aimed to prove whether she had been responsible for the murder of her second husband, Henry Stuart, Lord Darnley, in 1566, which had precipitated the civil war in Scotland and led to her forced abdication in 1567. Irate and insulted though Mary was, she was unable to prevent these commissions from going ahead. And though they never came to a conclusive verdict, the commissions shocked Mary into realizing that she was not an honoured guest but was being held against her will in England. She was, in fact, a captive.

Mary then drew up various alternative strategies to secure her freedom. She was implicated in a brief uprising of disaffected Catholic nobles, the Northern Rebellion of 1569, but this first foray into violent resistance was half-hearted. She was much more enthusiastic about securing her liberty via marriage and launched eagerly into negotiations with Thomas Howard, 4th Duke of Norfolk, the chief nobleman in England at the time, speculating that marriage to an English Protestant lord would appease Elizabeth. When this, too, was stymied, she changed tack once more and focused her efforts and attention on her foreign allies. Family ties were called into action in France and religious affinities were emphasized with supporters in Spain. At the same time, she navigated potentially joining forces with her son, James VI, to rule Scotland jointly, though James soon decided he would rather reign independently and changed his mind about this proposal. After several years of these diplomatic negotiations came to nothing, Mary was resolved to take more direct action. She learned of several plots that were being developed and hitched her wagon to them. The first was planned in liaison with her cousin Henri, Duke of Guise, for an invasion force to land in England and spirit her away. When the Throckmorton Plot, as it came to be known, was foiled, Mary was determined to continue this new combative path and was quickly drawn into another scheme. The Babington Plot, a scheme infiltrated from the start by Walsingham's agents and designed to finally trap Mary in agreeing to the assassination of Elizabeth, would end up being her last attempt to break free of her English captivity.

MARY'S YEARS AS a captive in England have been studied in great detail.[10] Historians and biographers seek access to her lived experience, to the day-to-day realities of her confinement. They search insatiably for insight into her mind and her heart during the plots and schemes. We want to know what she knew. We want to feel what she felt. Mary stirs our blood – we either adore her, romanticize her and idolize her or we detest her, denigrate her and demonize her. We might try hard these days not to pick a side, to see both the good and the bad, but Mary has always been forced to play roles: she is either innocent, naïve, open or she is cunning, manipulative, deceitful. She is the victim, betrayed by her family and her people, cast aside unjustly and thus righteous in her pursuit of restoration, her quest for liberty. Or, she is the adulterer, the tyrant oppressing her people, above herself, pursuing an English throne she was never entitled to.

When you think of Mary does she come to mind alone? Or do you find yourself conjuring a shadowy twin? Another woman, powerful and iconic. A woman in opposition. It is hard, regardless of what your own thoughts on Mary might be, not to compare her to this shadow twin, her 'sister queen', Elizabeth I of England. Elizabeth and Mary have always been set in opposition to one another. For a short time though, it seemed that Mary would be victorious. Mary was of undisputed royal blood. She was the granddaughter of Henry VIII's sister Margaret Tudor and King James IV of Scotland. She was born of a legitimate marriage between the royal Stewart line and the pinnacle of French nobility – King James V of Scotland and Marie de Guise. Elizabeth, on the other hand, was burdened by the schism created by her mother Anne Boleyn's marriage to Henry VIII – to some Elizabeth could never be the rightful heir to the throne of England because her father had unlawfully cast aside his first wife, Katherine of Aragon. To some, she would always be the child of an adulterous relationship. Mary then went on to marry the dauphin, Francis II, heir to the throne of France. Elizabeth refused to marry. By the time Mary gave birth to her son James on 19 June 1566, she had performed what contemporaries believed to be the duty of a woman and a queen in a way that Elizabeth never would – she had secured the safety of her kingdom by giving them a legitimate heir.

And yet, within two years these advantages had disintegrated. Mary's second marriage, to Henry Stuart, Lord Darnley, had been disastrous. The marriage had drawn the ire of Elizabeth because Darnley was a potential – though unlikely – claimant to the English throne through his mother, Margaret Douglas, Countess of Lennox, who was herself the daughter of Margaret Tudor. Two Tudor descendants marrying was problematic and unacceptably close for comfort. More pressing to Mary however was the problem of Darnley's own character. He had been overindulged and spoiled by his doting parents, Matthew Stewart and Margaret Douglas, Earl and Countess of Lennox. He was convinced that upon marriage, Mary should have deferred to him as King of Scotland in his own right. Mary, and several of her leading nobles, refused to countenance such action.

Unpopular though he was, the scandal of Darnley's assassination at Kirk o' Field in Edinburgh on 10 February 1567 was disastrous for Mary. The property he was staying in was blown up, but Darnley's body was found outside with marks suggesting he had been strangled or smothered while trying to escape the building.

It quickly became evident that there had been a cover-up, with the death originally meant to have looked like an accident. As suspicions flew, Mary's own behaviour was scrutinized. She was slow to react, going along with events planned before the murder took place. Crucially, she didn't set up a legal court until April of that year, several months after Darnley had been killed, and only then after being forced into action by an outcry from Darnley's parents and supporters.

Most shockingly to contemporaries, Mary eventually married the man accused of her husband's murder at this delayed trial – James Hepburn, 4th Earl of Bothwell. Though he was quickly acquitted, Bothwell had certainly been involved to some degree in Darnley's death, having been part of a conspiracy agreed by several Scottish noblemen that the tiresome King consort had to go.[11] He had been a keen ally and supporter of the queen during her marriage troubles and whispers had been growing that he sought to marry Mary himself. On 24 April 1567 he met Mary while she was travelling from Linlithgow Palace, the place of her birth, following a visit to Stirling Castle where her son was being cared for, back to Edinburgh. Claiming that she was to be attacked in Edinburgh, he convinced her to travel instead to his own property at Dunbar. While there it is likely that Bothwell raped Mary and certainly played upon her vulnerable state to force her to marry him. They were wed on 15 May 1567. Darnley had been dead for only a little more than three months.

Mary's marriage to Bothwell condemned her and continues to do so today. It is often held up as the choicest piece of evidence against her – why would she marry the man who killed her husband? Surely, she must have been having an affair with him and colluded in the plot to get Darnley out of the way? This was the tale told by Mary's detractors at the time and it continues to hold sway today, though there have also been attempts to romanticize the relationship between Mary and Bothwell. He has been given the persona of a dashing, lovestruck hero at times. Elizabeth was appalled at Mary's marriage to Bothwell, though she supported Mary's decision to meet the rebellious subjects who opposed Bothwell on the field at Carberry Hill in June of 1567.

By the time Mary fled across the Solway Firth on 16 May 1568, the die was cast. We have been conditioned ever since to think Elizabeth was everything Mary was not. Where Elizabeth was cautious, Mary was reckless. Elizabeth was scholarly, Mary was frivolous. Elizabeth suspicious, Mary gullible. The classic portrayal of the two has Mary ruled by her heart and Elizabeth by her head.

ONE OF THE best ways that we can counter these personas and give Mary space to embody the complexities of queenship, of womanhood, and of faith, is to turn to her letters. We benefit from the huge number of letters that survive from her during this period, many of which are written in Mary's own hand. She was not always allowed to have her secretaries with her while held captive in England, so she turned to penning more of her letters herself than she had previously been accustomed to, having clerks at her disposal during her personal reign to deal with business and official correspondence. Mary was an expert in the culture of early modern correspondence. She had been brought up at the French court, with access to some of the best academic and social learning. Her earliest surviving letters date from 1550 when she was only eight years old in France and show that she had quickly mastered the art of letter-writing. A letter from Mary to her mother, Marie de Guise, from 1550 offers us our first glimpse of the iconic signature and the accomplished italic script that would become prized by collectors over the centuries.[12] We can see Mary's self-fashioning in the signature – Marie R, with the 'R' indicating her royal status.

Letter-writing in the early modern period was more than simply a means of communicating information. Letters were embedded with social and interpersonal cues that we can easily miss today. It is also true that social rank was much more explicitly understood in the period and recipients would expect senders to address them appropriately according to their status, influence and power. The very layout of the letter could be read as courteous or insulting: letter-writers used blank space on the page to convey how they had understood the dynamic of their relationship with the person receiving the correspondence. Lengthy empty space could indicate respect or deference and was especially common between the end of the letter and the signature. Often, we see letter-writers leaving an enormous blank space with their signature placed in the bottom right corner of the page. This visual marker made it clear to the reader that the sender was being respectful. Though it is also true that people used this same technique to flatter (usually when they were asking for something) or if they were perhaps in trouble of some kind and seeking forgiveness. And the alternative was true – if a writer didn't leave a lot of empty space on the page, they might be stating their refusal to be deferential. Mary was well versed in these strategies. In her letters to Cecil, she preferred to position her signature right below the letter text, leaving little blank space. We can see this in an example from the early years of her captivity, dated 4 December 1569 when she had been moved to Coventry.[13] In this way she was telling him, no matter how courteous her language might be, she was still very much superior to him.

Other visual features could also reveal how you really thought about your relationship. Letters were often delivered in packets with multiple ones being sent together depending on who you could get to deliver them for you. There was no official postal system in the sixteenth century and so letter bearers were servants, friends, even strangers passing through on the way to the location you wanted the letter to reach. To keep prying eyes from reading the contents of a letter you needed to prepare it using different tools. Envelopes were not used to send letters until the nineteenth century and so letter-writers used different techniques to secure their correspondence in Mary's lifetime. Different processes of letter-locking were employed, with letters being sewn shut, or slices of paper taken from the page and used to pierce the folded letter, almost like a key in a lock.[14] Wax seals were then placed over the slits or holes to offer further security. Mary was known to use some of the most secure ways of folding and sealing her letters, reflecting her awareness of Walsingham's surveillance and interception. She often used a system called the spiral lock, where a slice of paper from the centre of the page was threaded through multiple slits[15]. If the letter was opened by someone before it reached the intended recipient, then it would be impossible to close it again without the damage showing. These features of the letters are easily overlooked by modern readers because once the letter was opened, the piece of paper that made up the lock was often discarded. We know that Mary used the spiral lock on one of her final letters prepared the night before her execution.[16]

Letters are often also preserved flat, meaning we can lose sight of other important features that can tell us about the relationship between sender and recipient. How you folded your letter was also important. Letters that were folded into tiny packets could be passed surreptitiously, or hidden in the pages of a book, or even in the sleeves of a gown. These miniature letters could be used for clandestine correspondence, either secret information or perhaps as a love letter.[17] You could take the time to carefully fold the completed letter in an intricate way, changing the direction of the folds each time, known as plaiting. This was often understood as a sign of intimacy or closeness. We find it in letters between spouses for example, and Mary herself may have used it when writing to relatives such as her mother Marie de Guise.[18]

How you addressed the person you were writing to was also critically important. Today we understand the term 'friend' to mean a 'close acquaintance',[19] or someone with whom we have a positive relationship at least. Some of the oldest uses of the term connote a sense of alliance and letter-writers would often use it when they were trying to convince someone to support them. It could also imply a sense of Christian piety. Yet, the term friend was also used by early modern letter-writers to emphasize a distinction in social status. Because 'friend' suggests a degree of familiarity or similarity at least, it would be unusual for someone of a lower rank to address a recipient in this way. Mary used the term friend across her correspondence, almost as a mark of her favour, but also to show her magnanimous and noble conduct.

By calling someone a friend, she was also reminding you of her own royal status. Writing to Cecil as a friend then, as she did in an example from November 1569[20] could also be a way of keeping him in his place. Even during the most difficult times of her captivity, she always signed off to Cecil with her customary subscription 'your good friend'.[21]

Modern readers can sometimes find the formulaic style of early modern letters off-putting. We are used to reading letters as private documents, as texts that can give us insight into the writer's inner thoughts and their feelings. When Mary wrote her letters, however, the culture of letters was slightly different. Letters were not always expected to be a private exchange between two individuals. In fact, letters had been read aloud for centuries, and this continued during her lifetime. It is likely that Mary's secretaries and ladies-in-waiting would have read letters out loud to her that had been sent by various correspondents, especially during the frequent periods of illness she suffered. Letters, even when sent between close and intimate relations, tended to follow conventional patterns. This is especially clear in the opening and closing phrases used in letters. Mary almost always ended her letters with a benediction, commending the person to God's safekeeping, even when she was unhappy with them. In a letter from Mary to her sister-in-law Annas Keith, Countess of Moray in 1571 she threatens Annas with her vengeance, yet still ends 'commending you to the protection of God'.[22] We might try to read a lack of sincerity to this, but in fact it was a standard formula of letter-writing.

Mary has suffered especially from our modern desire to reconstruct her emotions. Her letters have been scoured for examples of her passionate nature and her generous outlook. There is emotion in Mary's letters, and we will see it throughout this book, but it is important to be cautious. Mary could also use emotive language for very canny purposes. Emotion was a strategy. It could be used to elicit sympathy, or to persuade. In fact, Mary's emotive language in her letters was one of her successful tactics during her English imprisonment and allows us to move away from the cliché of the queen who was foolish enough to wear her heart on her sleeve.

THIS BOOK THEN will tread a well-worn path, travelling through Mary's years in captivity in England. We, too, will seek to walk beside Mary, as so many have done before. But this time, we will look afresh at the circumstances of her imprisonment years. We will use her extensive correspondence to guide us through the nuances and the complexities of her lived experience. We'll interrogate the plots and schemes. The newly decoded letters will be at the heart of our journey reminding us to ask ourselves what can we really know about Mary? Like her, we need to be both cunning and open-minded. We need to unravel the layers of her letters to let the full picture become clear. Mary was a strategist, and it is time we gave her the credit she deserves.

Captive Queen will move from Mary's earliest days in England following her flight from Scotland until her execution on 8 February 1587. Each chapter places her letters at the heart of the story. On 16 May 1568 Mary crossed the Solway Forth from Scotland. She had left behind a son and a kingdom. England, she believed, held freedom and a sister queen. Instead, she came to realize too late the trap she had thrown herself in. Her relationship with Elizabeth, so central to her years in captivity, opens this book. The politics and the plots to secure her freedom, from local rescues such as the Northern Rebellion of 1569 to the international invasions that were part of the Throckmorton Plot of 1584, are investigated. Negotiations for marriage, including to the Duke of Norfolk, or for violent action, as encapsulated by the Babington Plot of 1586, are explored. The struggle for Mary's restoration and freedom is at the heart of this book. But the drama of Mary's years as a captive cannot be understood in isolation from her everyday life. We will consider the realities of her experience during these tumultuous years. What was her life like? Who kept her company? How did she maintain her royal status in a prison? And most importantly, how did she reach out beyond the walls of her jail to stir loyalty and support right until the very end?

CHAPTER ONE

Sister Queens

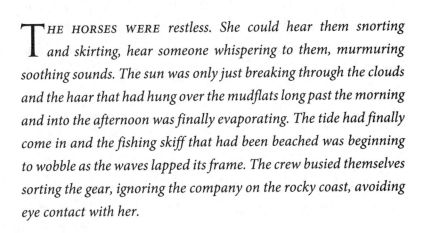

Whereas you wrote to us that we in former letters blamed them that keeps not promises but thinks one thing and does another: we would that you should remember the same.[2]

T HE HORSES WERE restless. She could hear them snorting and skirting, hear someone whispering to them, murmuring soothing sounds. The sun was only just breaking through the clouds and the haar that had hung over the mudflats long past the morning and into the afternoon was finally evaporating. The tide had finally come in and the fishing skiff that had been beached was beginning to wobble as the waves lapped its frame. The crew busied themselves sorting the gear, ignoring the company on the rocky coast, avoiding eye contact with her.

One of her companions made to speak, but she cut him off – 'the decision is made'.

This small group had journeyed with her from that grim battlefield. They had ridden through the night, wrapping themselves in their cloaks as they snatched fitful bursts of rest. After three days, they reached the abbey at Dundrennan. A brief respite, a momentary sanctuary. It was there that she had informed them of her plan to cross the water. To a man, they had missed no opportunity to try to persuade her otherwise, to plead with her to change her mind. But Mary had decided.

She watched as the captain stood up, looked hard at her, and nodded. It was time to go. She had already said her farewells to the men left at the top of the sandbank, but she accepted a final bow from them, gifted them an encouraging smile, and turned away to scramble down the hillock towards the water. She stepped confidently into the small vessel, batting away an outstretched hand, landing steady and still. She was wearing the riding clothes she had managed to scrabble together from the servants at Dundrennan; there were no bustling skirts to navigate. Good thing too, she mused. There would have been no room for the voluminous fabrics – she would have had to strip to her shift to squeeze into the boat and think of the gossip that would have caused! She laughed, imagining the scandalized look on the faces of those dour preachers back in Edinburgh.

Settling herself in the vessel, the fishermen pushed off from the coast. The wind had picked up while they waited and now it gathered them up, bustling them quickly away from the land. Mary watched as the men faded from view. Gazed for a moment as Scotland receded. She had left her kingdom once before, never knowing when she would return. This time she would not be gone long. She would return to claim her throne. She just had to convince Elizabeth to help her. Shaking away any doubts, she drew herself up and turned her eyes away. Looking ... looking ... always towards England.

MARY, QUEEN OF Scots left her kingdom and her people for the second time in her life on 16 May 1568. It would be her final journey: Mary would never see Scotland again. When she had first left Scotland back in 1548, she had been a child. She was an honoured guest, eagerly anticipated in her destination of France. This time, on a bright but blustery day in spring 1568, she had no procession of ships accompanying her, just a small group of tired but devoted companions. They sailed in a small fishing boat from the Dumfriesshire coast. Four hours later, they arrived in England, docking at the port of Workington in Cumberland in the early evening. Her supporters had tried to persuade her not to make the journey, reminding her of the fate of her ancestor James I who 'on venturing into that realm in time of peace, had been treacherously constituted prisoner'[3]. Would she not be better travelling to France to seek aid, some of them asked. Mary though understood that she could not go to France at this moment. That country was consumed by civil strife and religious wars which had broken out into open hostilities only the year before. France was too wrapped up in her own troubles to aid Mary. She also recognized that her former mother-in-law, Catherine de' Medici, had no desire to see Mary return to France, having her own dynastic plans for her surviving sons. Catherine would be likely to frustrate Mary's aim to gather men and finances. There was also a part of her that chafed against the suggestion of returning to France, where she had been crowned queen, as a fugitive in all but name.

Could she stay on in Scotland instead? Her companions cautioned her that by going to England she was leaving her supporters in Scotland without a leader. She had lost the Battle of Langside a few days previously, on 13 May 1568, when her forces had been overcome by those led by her half-brother James Stewart, Earl of Moray and his ally Kirkcaldy of Grange. Yet she still had backing among the Scottish nobility and could retreat to the territories of her supporters to regroup. Perhaps the thought of weeks, or even months, hiding away and travelling only at night between fortresses and safe houses was too much. Maybe she couldn't face the idea of being contained and restrained, a queen in name only. And so, Mary chose a third option: she would go to England and seek the support of her fellow queen, Elizabeth. Little did she know that she was walking into a worse sort of captivity. Into a prison from which she would never be free again.

How had Mary ended up here? How had she come to be travelling on an everyday working boat, with a small party of supporters and attendants, fleeing her kingdom? We can trace the course of these momentous events back to 1565 when Mary married her second husband, Henry Stuart, Lord Darnley. Darnley was a handsome and athletic young nobleman. The Scottish diplomat James Melville of Halhill described him as 'the lustiest and best proportioned man', noticing how quickly he caught the eye of the queen.[4] His height was attractive to Mary, herself said to be unusually tall for a woman of the time. He was energetic and an accomplished dancer, literally sweeping the queen off her feet when he joined her to perform several galliards at the Palace of Holyroodhouse on 25 February 1565. The English ambassador Thomas Randolph reported that Mary had been distracted from the cold and stormy weather of her recent journey through Fife by dancing several times with Darnley, quipping that the queen was 'come home lustier than she went forth'.[5]

Darnley had spent his childhood in England after his father, Matthew Stewart, Earl of Lennox, had been exiled from Scotland in 1545. His mother, Margaret Douglas, was the niece of Henry VIII and as such Darnley had a distant claim to the English crown. His royal blood made him an intriguing match for Mary, bringing her one step closer to her goal of inheriting the English throne should Elizabeth die childless. That he had spent such considerable time in England also meant that the English nobility might see him as a suitable consort should Mary ever gain the throne in that kingdom. And in fact, several English nobles briefly supported this campaign to secure a marriage between Darnley and Mary, feeling that it would avoid an external threat from France or Spain. But at the same time, this English upbringing alienated him from his Scottish peers. His father's traitorous behaviour during the years of English violence known as the Rough Wooing throughout the 1540s was also held against him. Several of the Scottish nobles feared that Darnley would undermine the Protestant cause in Scotland. His own religious persuasion was unclear, especially because Darnley's mother, Margaret Douglas, was a committed

Catholic. These nobles feared that a Catholic consort would encourage Mary to renege on the policy of accommodation and conciliation that she had pursued since her return from France in 1561.

It was widely accepted that Darnley's parents had been scheming for this marriage since Mary had first returned to Scotland in August 1561, if not even earlier. There were rumours that he had travelled to France following the death of Mary's first husband, Francis II of France in December 1560, under the guise of offering condolences on behalf of his parents, but with the true aim of placing himself at the centre of Mary's attention. The Earl and Countess of Lennox were arrested for such intrigues by the English in 1561 and not released until 1563. But then, seemingly from nowhere, Elizabeth began to show favour to Darnley, encouraging Mary to restore the Earl of Lennox's estates in Scotland and inviting Darnley to her court. She even granted Lennox permission to return to Scotland in late 1564, with Darnley following early in the new year.

Elizabeth's motivations for returning Darnley to Scotland remain unclear, considering that his marriage to Mary would enhance the latter's claim to the English throne. Over the centuries, biographers have theorized that William Cecil, Elizabeth's most devoted principal secretary, had intentionally set up Darnley as bait for Mary, somehow foreseeing how disastrous the marriage would be. Others have claimed the matter of Darnley as one of Elizabeth's few errors in judgment. It is more likely that Elizabeth was playing her usual strategy of keeping everyone around her guessing – by 1563 she was under pressure to name a successor and by changing the fortunes of Darnley's family she was able to keep equivocating, able to address the question while never really giving a proper answer. It was also true that she feared Mary would make a powerful international match in her search for a second husband, bringing French or Spanish influence right to the back door of England.

At first then, a marriage to a grateful nobleman might seem the lesser of two evils. She had even gone so far as to suggest that Mary marry her own favourite, Robert Dudley, Earl of Leicester – though in reality Elizabeth was well aware that even to suggest such a betrothal was a snub to Mary. Dudley was the son of an executed traitor, who had only recently been raised to the earldom of Leicester. The rumours swirling at court and abroad that he and Elizabeth were more than simply close friends made it even less likely that he could be in the running to secure Mary's hand. To some of the Scots nobles though, Leicester would have been their first choice – he was a Protestant, aligned completely to Elizabeth, who could secure the Anglo-Scottish diplomacy which they had established during the final years of the regency of Mary's mother Marie de Guise. Leicester's lack of Scottish title or property also meant that he was not allied to any faction or family in Scotland. As Elizabeth anticipated, Mary refused Dudley as a suitor.

What Elizabeth did not expect though was for Mary to then take control of the situation herself and leap into action. Mary called Elizabeth's bluff, and dismissed the fears of the nobles in Scotland, by appointing Darnley to the title of Earl of Ross in May 1565, followed a few months later by making him Duke of Albany. Both titles gave him status enough to be recognized as King of Scotland. On 18 June 1565 Elizabeth belatedly tried to stop Mary from going ahead with the marriage by sending a messenger demanding Darnley's return to England, and she sent a more explicitly hostile second letter a week later about 'such cause offered to us of offence and mislike'.[6] Elizabeth was too late – Mary had made her mind up. It was to be Darnley. On 29 July 1565, Mary married Henry Stuart, Lord Darnley, in her private chapel at the Palace of Holyroodhouse, in a Catholic ceremony.

4

THE MARRIAGE THOUGH quickly proved troublesome. Mary's half-brother, James Stewart, 1st Earl of Moray, and one of the most powerful nobles in Scotland, Archibald Campbell, 5th Earl of Argyll, were so opposed to Darnley and to the simultaneous rising fortunes of his Douglas faction that they rose in open rebellion almost immediately after the marriage was solemnized. Mary was initially dumbstruck by the betrayal of her sibling and one of her closest nobles and friends. Eventually though, she rallied and was determined to hunt down the traitors. For a few weeks in August and September 1565, Mary led her forces across the country seeking a confrontation. Moray was forced to escape to England, leaving his capable wife, Annas Keith, in charge of his estates. Though Elizabeth was outraged in principle at the thought of subjects rebelling against their lawful monarch, funds nevertheless made their way through the English ambassador Thomas Randolph to Annas, intended for her husband. In her fury, Mary turned to Spain for support, with King Philip II of Spain agreeing to send several thousand crowns via Antwerp. The funds never reached her – they were lost at sea off the coast of Northumberland. But by October 1565, many of the rebellious lords had nevertheless submitted to the queen, leaving Moray isolated. Even his dear friend, Argyll, returned to the queen's side.

While outwardly Mary ruthlessly put down resistance to her marriage and any challenge to Darnley's authority, privately she was beginning to have doubts of her own. It quickly became clear that Darnley's youthful exuberance, though charming while hunting or dancing, was unattractive in a king. He had little understanding of the duties required of a monarch and he claimed Mary's attention at all times, throwing tantrums when he did not get it. He had been doted on by his mother and raised to believe unrelentingly in his own status and influence. He was impetuous and rash, prone to drinking heavily and lashing out aggressively. His own father even left court a few weeks after the wedding, tired of his son's behaviour. Darnley was determined that he be granted the crown matrimonial which would allow him to reign in his own right should Mary die before him. Mary, heeding the concerns of her nobles, and recognizing Darnley's political immaturity, refused to agree. By the end of the year, she had taken to having Darnley referred to only as the 'queen's husband' rather than as King of Scots. Nevertheless, by October 1565 Mary was rumoured to be pregnant, though this was not confirmed until the new year. The pregnancy is perhaps more a reflection of Mary's commitment to her duty as a reigning queen than a mark of any real reignited passion and love towards her husband.

Mary's pregnancy did little to ease the strain in her marriage. Darnley was becoming increasingly jealous of the friendship she bestowed upon her French secretary, David Rizzio. Other disaffected lords, who disliked the reliance that Mary placed upon a Catholic foreigner, manipulated the childish Darnley into signing a bond agreeing to remove the troublesome secretary. Mary likely heard rumours of the plot in advance, since Randolph wrote a letter to Cecil in early March 1566 giving details of a possible coup, yet she seemed not to suspect her husband's involvement, nor did she know the specifics of any planned actions. Thus around 8 o'clock on the evening of Saturday 9 March, Mary was enjoying supper in her private chamber at Holyroodhouse. The room was sumptuously decorated, with rich fabrics cloaking the low reclining bed and exquisite tapestries lining the walls, yet it was not a large space. This was a place for close gatherings, for the queen's informal company. Chatting casually around the table were David Rizzio and Lady Jean Stewart, Countess of Argyll and Mary's illegitimate half-sister, and Elizabeth Keith, Countess of Huntly. While the intimate party ate and drank, downstairs the palace guards were being overpowered. A group of armed men burst through the unprotected chamber door and forced their way into the small space. In the chaos, the Countess of Argyll caught a falling candle which was perilously close to setting the curtains alight. The rebel leader, Patrick Ruthven, 3rd Lord Ruthven, demanded that Mary hand over Rizzio. Mary refused. The secretary sprung behind the queen, clinging to her skirts. One of the men pointed a firearm at her and another threatened to stab her. Mary was six months pregnant: it made shockingly little difference to her attackers.

Dragging David Rizzio out of the chamber into the hallway, the intruders set upon him with their weapons. He was stabbed more than fifty times. Darnley's weapon was left in Rizzio's body to make it clear who had sanctioned this action. When the deed was complete, the rebels threw his body down the stairs and stripped him of his jewels and clothing. Mary was held under guard in

ABOVE: Mary, Queen of Scots as a young woman.

LEFT: James Stewart, Earl of Moray, son of James V and his mistress Margaret Erskine, and half-brother of Mary, Queen of Scots. He became Regent of Scotland on behalf of Mary's infant son James in 1567 after her forced abdication from the throne.

RIGHT: William Cecil, Lord Burghley, chief advisor of Queen Elizabeth I of England, who was convinced that Mary, Queen of Scots presented a threat to England's security and was determined to keep her from the English throne.

LEFT: Henry Stuart, Lord Darnley, Mary's second husband. Gossip flourished about Mary's involvement in his murder at Kirk o'Field in Edinburgh in February 1567.

RIGHT: James Hepburn, Earl of Bothwell, Mary's third husband. His capture of Mary led to their marriage and, after fleeing from the defeat at Carberry Hill in 1567, he died in a Danish prison.

BELOW: The murder of Mary's secretary David Rizzio when she was pregnant and dining with close companions was designed to terrify her into acquiescing to the demands of disaffected lords.

LOCHLEVEN CASTLE, IN WHICH MARY QUEEN OF SCOTS
WAS IMPRISONED.

ABOVE: Lochleven Castle where Mary was held captive for almost a year and forced to abdicate from the Scottish throne. She escaped in May 1568 and quickly raised supporters before being defeated at the Battle of Langside.

BELOW: Dundrennan Abbey where Mary rested before leaving Scotland for the last time and crossing the Solway Firth to England. She would spend the rest of her life in captivity.

ABOVE: Workington Hall, home of Sir Henry Curwen, who was the first to greet Mary after she landed in England. This was one of the finest manor homes in Cumberland.

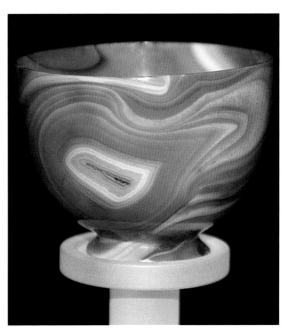

RIGHT: The Luck of Workington. This luxury agate cup was gifted to the Dowager Lady Curwen as thanks for her care of Mary and her companion Agnes Fleming, Lady Livingston, during their stay at Workington Hall.

LEFT: Henri, Duke of Guise, Mary's cousin and keen supporter of several schemes for her release from English captivity including the Throckmorton Plot.

RIGHT: Michel de Castelnau, Sieur de la Mauvissière, French ambassador to England from 1575–1585. He established a secret channel of communication through the French embassy for Mary to send and receive letters without English agents reading the contents.

RIGHT: Elizabeth Talbot, Countess of Shrewsbury, known as Bess of Hardwick. She was the wife of Mary's longest serving jailor, George Talbot, Earl of Shrewsbury and for a short time a close companion of the captive queen before they had a spectacular falling-out.

BELOW: Margaret Douglas, Countess of Lennox, mother of Henry Stuart, Lord Darnley and grandmother of James VI. Though she and Mary were estranged following Darnley's murder, the two reconciled over their shared devotion to the young James.

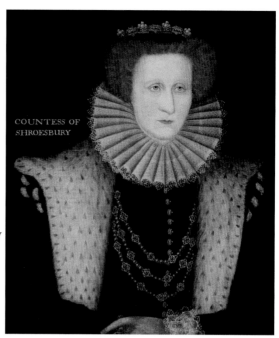

COUNTESS OF SHROESBURY

LEFT: Thomas Percy, Earl of Northumberland. He tried to bring Mary into his personal protection following her arrival in England and later rose against Elizabeth, leading the Northern Rebellion of 1569 during which Mary was kept under closer supervision in Coventry.

BELOW: This romantic imagining of Mary and John Knox recalls his persistent hectoring of her during her personal reign in Scotland.

the palace but managed to speak with her husband. Either she was unaware at this stage that Darnley had been involved in the murder of her secretary, or more likely she was savvy enough to realize that her only way out of this dangerous situation was to bring him back to her side. In any case, she persuaded him that the men who had committed this act were likely to turn upon him too. The following night she was able to escape, with help from the Countess of Huntly, who convinced the guards that the queen was taken ill from shock and smuggled a letter to her son George Gordon, 5th Earl of Huntly. He was able to gather a party of supporters at Seton Palace, less than ten miles south-east of Edinburgh. Mary, and Darnley, rode out at midnight the day after the murder under the guidance of her master of the horse, Arthur Erskine. Meeting their supporters at Seton, they then continued to the security of Dunbar Castle: a fortress owned by one James Hepburn, 4th Earl of Bothwell.

♃

IF THE MURDER of Rizzio was intended to wrest the queen's support back towards her husband and his sometime allies, it failed completely. The rebels involved were forced to flee into England, while her half-brother the Earl of Moray, future Regent of Scotland, was able to return, conveniently claiming no knowledge of the events. A letter from Mary to Elizabeth at this time offers her own thoughts about the 'wicked and mischievous enterprise' raised against her by men who had shown themselves for what they truly were:

At first has taken our house, slain our most special
servant in our own presence and thereafter held our
proper person captive treasonably whereby we were
constrained to escape straightly about midnight out of
our palace of Holyroodhouse to the place we are for the
present [Dunbar] in the greatest danger, fear of our life
and evil estate that ever princes on earth stood in.[7]

She raged at the injustice of these men claiming sanctuary in England, condemning Elizabeth for not apprehending them and sending them immediately back to Scotland to face punishment. Mary cleverly played upon Elizabeth's fears of French or Spanish interference in Scotland by reminding her that:

We are assured, and not so disproved, but other princes
that will hear of our estate, considering the same will
favor us so much as to help and support us (if need
be) to defend us and our realm [and] the Word of God
which commands that all princes should favor and
defend the just actions of other princes as well as their
own.[8]

That Mary had a secretary write this lengthy letter to Elizabeth shows her anger and hurt – it was more usual for her to write to Elizabeth in her own hand as a mark of affection and kinship, emphasizing the close bond Mary wanted to establish between them. Here, Mary was cold and distant. That she had the letter penned in Scots and made no effort to write in French as she normally did with Elizabeth, is a further marker of her wrath. The relationship between the two queens remained frosty until the birth of Mary's son, James VI on 19 June.

Some effort was made to bring Darnley publicly back into Mary's inner circle. She joined him on a hunting trip in the Ettrick Forest in the Scottish Borders in August. But Mary was disgusted by his actions, and it quickly became clear that the couple were not to be reconciled. He returned to his old tricks, throwing tantrums, and drinking more and more. When Mary refused to respond to his antics, he decided to cause maximum drama by leaving the country. Though he did write to France and Spain to discover whether he could travel there, nothing came of his scheme. Instead, he was left to sulk. He refused to attend his son's baptism on 17 December 1566, locking himself in his rooms at Stirling Castle before quietly slinking off to his father's property in Glasgow as soon as possible. Ambassadors avoided him at the exuberant celebrations guessing, correctly, that he was still out of favour with the queen. A few weeks prior to James's baptism, Mary had met with some of her noblemen at Craigmillar Castle, just outside Edinburgh, to discuss the 'Darnley problem'. It was put to her that she could seek to divorce her second husband, but Mary was unwilling to do anything that might disinherit her son or question his legitimacy in the future. The nobles almost certainly then suggested to her the possibility of removing Darnley by more permanent methods. Whether Mary herself ultimately consented to this murderous proposal we will never know for sure, but she clearly was aware that the option to 'put him off one way or another' was being seriously discussed.[9] She may have decided to turn a conveniently blind eye, but she was most likely not aware of the specific plans drawn up to assassinate Darnley. As such, when Darnley returned to Edinburgh in late January 1567, she visited him regularly. He was lodged in a townhouse at the former church property of Kirk o' Field, but this was because he had been ill for some time, possibly suffering from smallpox. He was not staying at the Palace of Holyroodhouse then to avoid spreading contagion throughout the royal household, not because, as some have claimed, that Mary knew some terrible event was about to befall him.

On 9 February, Mary visited Darnley once more. The couple chatted happily for an hour or two and then she left the property to attend the wedding celebrations of Bastian Paget, a musician and attendant in her household. In the depth of the night, around 2 o'clock, a tremendous explosion ripped through the building, the sound being heard across the city. Darnley's body was found in the garden, with a length of rope and a chair nearby. It looked like he had tried to make an escape from the house by being lowered from a window but had met some other threat before he could cross the grounds. There were no obvious injuries: no marks of strangulation or violence. Barbara Martin, who lived in an adjacent house, testified that she heard a tumult shortly before the explosion, and striding to her window, saw thirteen men approach Darnley's lodging through the alley. After the explosion, she said she saw the group leave the same way they had come and that she called out to them, asking what evil act they had done. A second woman, May Crockett, who lived in the vicinity told a similar story. On hearing a loud noise, she had jumped from her bed, where she slept with her twin children, and rushed to her door in nothing but her shift. She saw men, some dressed in fine silks, running through the alley and asked them what the noise had been, but they ignored her and continued on their way.[10]

Darnley's murder was the central catastrophe of Mary's personal reign, tipping her into a calamitous fall from power that would ultimately lead her to seek refuge in England eighteen months later. Her behaviour immediately after her husband's death led to suspicion and gossip. Rather than go into official mourning, she continued to attend events. Crucially she did not set up an inquiry into the murder until forced to do so when Darnley's father, the Earl of Lennox, issued a public proclamation claiming to know who was responsible. He named the Earl of Bothwell as his son's killer. Mary, though, had turned to Bothwell for support in the chaos of the days and weeks following Darnley's death. Her reliance on the man accused of her husband's murder led to salacious rumours that Mary was in love with Bothwell. Like wildfire, the gossip took flight. First, that Mary had been having an affair with Bothwell even before the murder. Then, inevitably, if they were lovers, surely she must have known about Bothwell's plot? But wait – not only did she know of the scheme but she had also contrived it and begged her lover to rid her of her troublesome husband. Crude drawings of a mermaid or siren and a hare began appearing across Edinburgh: the siren being Mary and the hare the emblem of Bothwell's house. The stories spread beyond Scotland, reaching Elizabeth's ears. Elizabeth warned Mary that she must not 'look through her fingers' when it comes to one 'who had done her such pleasure'.[11] She clearly meant Bothwell.

Bothwell was undoubtedly a useful ally to Mary at this critical point. But were they having an affair? Almost certainly not. Mary admitted that he was forceful in his pursuit of her following Darnley's death but there is no evidence that they were in a physical relationship before then. Letters produced against Mary later, those infamous documents known as the Casket Letters, to which we will return, have woven a tale of lust and passion between them. But the Casket Letters were forgeries: they were excerpts of letters addressed to Bothwell by other women, merged into innocuous correspondence from Mary to him. It is nevertheless true that Mary did go on to marry Bothwell. While she was riding back to Edinburgh from a visit to her baby son at Stirling Castle, Bothwell intercepted Mary on 24 April. He convinced her that she was in danger, that there were rebels pursuing her. With his characteristically bombastic force he compelled her to journey with him instead to his fortress of Dunbar.

At Dunbar, Mary was forced into a sexual relationship with Bothwell. He took advantage of her vulnerable state and coerced her emotionally. He physically dominated the space, constraining her in his property. Bothwell had planned this: he had already sought a divorce from his wife, Jean Gordon, and he had secured support from several nobles for his intention to marry Mary in an agreement known as the Ainslie Bond.[12] Mary, having been forced to share her body with Bothwell, agreed to marry him. We cannot underestimate the emotional trauma she had been experiencing or downplay Bothwell's coercion. We might share Elizabeth's disbelief that Mary married 'a subject, who besides other notorious acts, public fame charged with the murder of her late husband, besides the touching of herself in some part'.[13] But we can empathize with Mary; though a queen, she was human after all. People don't always make the right decisions in difficult circumstances. Mary possibly felt she had few allies left to her, and Bothwell offered strength at a time of potential chaos (though this support was certainly offered with his own plan for power in mind rather than altruistically). She also would have felt compelled to fashion an outcome which might overcome the gossip surrounding their physical relationship, coercive though it had been.

4

WITHIN A YEAR of marrying Bothwell, Mary would be stepping into that small fishing vessel, never to return to Scotland. Immediately after they were wed, Scottish nobles rose once more in rebellion. Mary and Bothwell led their forces to meet the rebels at Carberry Hill near Musselburgh on 15 June. To avoid a battle, Mary negotiated Bothwell's safe passage and agreed to return to Edinburgh. She was escorted back and to her anguish was forced to endure the townspeople's humiliating jeers and insults: 'Whore!' 'Murderer!' 'Witch!' Within days she was moved to Lochleven Castle, a tower house in the middle of a loch in Perthshire. At the end of July, she sadly suffered a miscarriage. She may have lost twins, but the pregnancy was at such an early stage this cannot be confirmed. Recovering from a fever, she was naturally consumed by melancholy and despondency. In this traumatized state she was forced to sign her name to an official document of abdication. Through her tears, she proclaimed that the text would never be binding, because she was forced to sign under duress.

Mary remained imprisoned at Lochleven for almost ten months. Though the house was on an island, it was not a wilderness. Lochleven was easily accessible from Stirling and Edinburgh and Mary was not left to suffer alone. She had the company of formidable ladies, who recognized a fellow woman's suffering, despite their personal grievances or political differences. Margaret Erskine, Lady Lochleven, ran the household on behalf of her son William Douglas, Laird of Lochleven. She was also the mother of Mary's half-brother James Stuart, Earl of Moray, now Regent of Scotland. Both she and James's wife, Annas, ensured that Mary received the care and attention she needed after the loss of her pregnancy. Her closest attendant, Mary Seton soon joined her, and Mary was permitted to go wherever she liked within the property and the grounds of the island.

After almost a year, though, it was time to make her escape. On 2 May 1568, a young attendant in the household, Willie Douglas, made sure that all the boats were beached or wrecked except for one. Mary, cloaked in dull fabrics and covering her face, slipped out of the house, and followed Willie through the gates, which he locked behind him to hold up any pursuers. They jumped into the one boat still available and sped across the lake in the darkening light of the evening. Waiting to meet her on the mainland was George Douglas, brother to her jailer, William Douglas. He had stolen some of his brother's best horses, which were luckily enough stabled on the mainland, not on the island itself. Joining him was George, 7th Lord Seton, one of Mary's most constant and devoted men and Mary Seton's half-brother. Lord Seton and Douglas led a small force of armed men, and they quickly took off at a gallop. Mary was ecstatic: riding through the open country, towards a new start. They escorted her to Seton's fortified tower at Niddrie, around midway between Edinburgh and Linlithgow, where the queen was finally able to enjoy an evening of friendship and a night of restful sleep cocooned in her new liberty. The

Earl of Huntly quickly came to her, along with John Maxwell, 4th Lord Herries of Terregles and John, 5th Lord Fleming. The Hamilton family didn't waste a second: Claude Hamilton, son of James, Earl of Arran and Duke of Châtellerault, brought large numbers of their tenants and supporters to her cause. Although the Duke of Châtellerault had flirted with Protestantism while acting as Regent of Scotland for Mary during her minority and had bounced between a pro-French and pro-English policy, largely favouring whichever helped his own cause, his sons were more constant in their Catholic faith and open support for Mary. Within a week, she had gathered more than six thousand men to her cause, an army considerably larger than that hastily pulled together by Regent Moray. The two forces met at Langside, just outside Glasgow, on 13 May 1568.

Though Mary had the greater numbers, and the fierce joy and enthusiasm created by her escape, she was forced to watch in despair and horror from a nearby hillside as her forces were slowly, but with grim efficiency defeated. The Earl of Argyll had chosen Mary over his old friend Moray, but on the morning of the battle he was struck by a sudden illness. Whether an attack of a long-standing intestinal disorder, or an epileptic fit, he was unable to lead her forces as he had promised. At the same time, the vanguard of her force, led by Claude Hamilton, was cooly taken out by Kirkcaldy of Grange, who ambushed them as they filtered through the alleyways of the village. After less than an hour, it was clear there was to be no victory this day. Mary, terrified that she would be captured and returned to a prison from which there would be no escape this time, fled. She was now on her way to England, though no one but she knew it yet.

4

MARY TRAVELLED FROM the battle at Langside to Dundrennan Abbey, in Dumfriesshire with sixteen companions. It took them three days, travelling only 'with the owls'[14] forced to seek shelter in remote spots during the day. One lady stayed by Mary's side: fleeing in terror from the battle at Langside, riding hard over the treacherous moors, lurching from place to place under cover of darkness. Agnes Fleming, Lady Livingston, shared the sour milk and oatmeal and bedded down on the mossy ground beside the queen when they paused for rest. Lady Livingston was the sister of Mary Fleming, one of Mary's closest attendants and one of the 'four Marys' who travelled with her as a child to France and remained at her side until her marriage in 1566. Lady Livingston's husband, William also travelled with the party from the battlefield to Dundrennan. The Flemings were devoted to Mary. Lady Livingston's younger brother, John, 5th Lord Fleming also joined the small group of supporters who journeyed with Mary into England. Both Lord Fleming and Lady Livingston were Mary's cousins, their mother being the illegitimate sister of Mary's father, King James V, and Mary's governess in France until 1552. At the Battle of Langside, Lord Fleming had watched the fighting alongside Mary from a neighbouring hill.

The party were led by Lord Herries. Herries was one of the most powerful border lords in Scotland and was described as 'the wisest' of the nobles, though he wasn't always an ally of Mary's. When Mary married Bothwell, he joined the rebels, and it was not until Mary was forced to abdicate that he allied himself firmly to her cause. He went on to lead her forces at the Battle of Langside following Argyll's collapse, and he travelled with her to the shelter of Dundrennan Abbey, where one of his sons was the commendator.[15]

As Mary stepped onto English soil, climbing from the boat onto the pier at Workington she was greeted by Sir Henry Curwen, a landowner, and Member of Parliament for Cumberland. He received her with the respect and honour befitting a queen, despite his discomposure at being forced to accommodate her royal person. He escorted her to his home, Workington Hall, one of the finest manor homes in the region. The house had grown around a central tower dating from the fourteenth century, expanding to become a comfortable family home. Curwen's mother the Dowager Lady Curwen organized fresh linen and clothing for Mary and Lady Livingston. To thank them for this kindness, Mary gifted them a small drinking vessel, a *quaich* from the Scots Gaelic. Known as the 'Luck of Workington Hall', it was carved from agate and had been made either in Paris or Milan.[16] The cup had been brought by Lord Herries, possibly taken when he left Dundrennan Abbey.

Enjoying a brief moment of rest at Workington Hall, Mary wrote to Elizabeth. She implored her to take pity on her poor state, which no gentlewoman should have to endure. She outlined the events of that had forced her to seek refuge in England, starting with the murder of her secretary Rizzio back in 1565. She entreated Elizabeth to let her come in person to explain her miserable misfortune, emphasizing that she had nothing to offer but her own person.[17] The very next day Richard Lowther, deputy governor of Cumberland arrived at Workington Hall with a few hundred armed men provided by Thomas Percy, the 7th Earl of

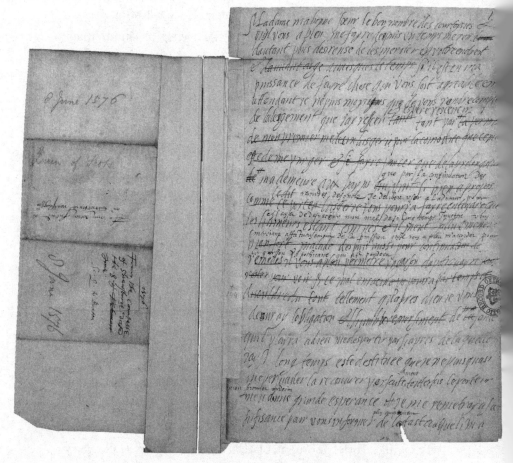

This letter from Mary to Elizabeth gives us unusual insight into the real-life process of composing correspondence. Rather than having a secretary write a tidy copy, Mary has sent this letter in her own hand and opening with her usual address, 'Madame my good sister' to emphasize the intimate relationship she wants to have with Elizabeth.

Northumberland. Both Lowther and Northumberland assured Elizabeth that they would entertain the queen of Scots as was fit and proper but that they would allow no one from her party to escape their presence, nor would they permit any visitor until Elizabeth informed them of her will in this matter. With no choice but to go with these men, Mary and her party left Workington and travelled to Carlisle Castle. Northumberland visited her personally on 21 May and they spoke for several hours. He may have been trying to persuade Mary to come into his own keeping, with offers of help and support, either to reach Elizabeth or be more safely secured in the English north. He would certainly attempt such things later as we will see. Afterward at this point, he demanded that Lowther pass Mary over into his personal care, but the deputy refused, saying he could not do so until he had permission from Elizabeth. Northumberland flew into a rage, swearing and screaming at Lowther, with 'great threatenings with very evil words and language'.[18]

Elizabeth quickly sent one of her most trusted courtiers to take charge of the situation in Carlisle. Sir Francis Knollys would be Mary's first, proper, English jailor. Knollys was a respected and well-liked gentleman. He first met Mary at Carlisle on 28 May when he arrived with Lord Henry Scrope of Bolton. It has been said that Knollys was charmed by Mary, that he was seduced by her wit and conversation. It is more likely that he was responding to the complexities of his predicament. At this very early stage, no one knew what would happen to Mary. Would she return to Scotland, supported by Elizabeth, to reclaim her throne? Would she be moved on to France? Could it even be that in the future Mary would inherit the English crown as she so heartily desired? It was not in Knollys' interest to antagonize her, and he made an effort to recognize her royal estate as best he could. He was conscious though that he was treading a thin line, negotiating always to keep both Mary and Elizabeth on side. Knollys remained at Carlisle until July, when he was permitted to move Mary to Bolton Castle, Lord Scrope's seat. Mary was hysterical at the move, fearing it was a public statement that she was indeed a prisoner, but she was canny enough to realize that she needed to keep Knollys on her side. She knew that he was reporting daily to Cecil, giving details of their conversations and so she agreed to listen to his readings from the English prayer book.

Almost immediately after Mary arrived in England, William Cecil set in motion his long game. He made a list at the end of May, titled 'Things to be considered upon the Scottish queen's coming into England'.[19] He broke down in great detail what he saw as the 'dangers' of three situations that he felt might realistically come to pass at this stage. First, if Mary were allowed to travel to France, he feared that there might ultimately be an invasion of England. He was brutally honest about the loss of Calais and the fact that England was no longer an ally of Burgundy, while Mary's presence in France would restore the auld alliance between Scotland and France, undoing all the effort put into establishing a policy of Anglo-Scots amity. In his own words: 'We stand alone.'

This was to be Cecil's mantra when dealing with Mary for the next two decades. England could not afford to allow any potential threat to solidify around Mary. His second consideration was the consequences of Mary returning to Scotland to reclaim her throne. He feared that Scotland would become so riven by civil war, that Mary herself would not be allowed to live. More importantly from his own perspective, neither would the infant King James. Such a scenario could not be allowed to happen, for once again it would mean violence and international intervention right on the border of England. The final option, to keep Mary in England, was also not without its threats. Cecil was utterly convinced that Mary's presence would draw rebels and traitors from all corners of England regardless of faith or status, 'for no man can think but such a sweet bait would make concord between them all'.[20]

While Cecil debated the best action to take, Mary remained at Bolton Castle. Bolton was very secure: it had only one entrance and high walls. Mary was given Scrope's own apartments and furnishings, including tapestries and rugs that were brought from other nearby properties to make the rooms more comfortable for her. Several attendants and servants had also joined her, either while she was at Carlisle or after she arrived at Bolton. Mary Seton had managed to rejoin her, and the women were rarely apart. Mary was allowed to take exercise in the grounds and the nearby parklands and to her delight, she was allowed to ride regularly. She wrote a steady stream of letters to supporters back in Scotland, as well as to those in France and Spain.

As the summer turned to a damp autumn though, Mary realized that Elizabeth was genuinely considering putting her on trial at the instigation of the Regent of Scotland and his allies. They claimed they had discovered incriminating letters between Mary and Bothwell, which proved that she was responsible for Darnley's murder. Elizabeth was indeed persuaded to go ahead with the trial, though she only ever referred to it as a commission. She assured Mary that this was only to set out the truth of the matter and afterward a decision could finally be made regarding her liberty. From October until December 1568, the commission was to investigate Mary's 'guilt'. Mary could do little to prevent them from going ahead. The revelations made would shape her memorialization for centuries to come.

CHAPTER TWO

Caskets and Commissions

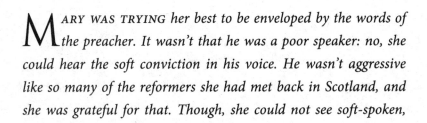

*Our rebels, for what offers they can make,
will not get the support from this country
that they pretend; and of our part we will
assure you that [...] we hope to get such
sufficient succors of friends to impede the
unfortunate intention of our rebels and cause
them to know their duty to our honor.*[2]

M ARY WAS TRYING *her best to be enveloped by the words of
the preacher. It wasn't that he was a poor speaker: no, she
could hear the soft conviction in his voice. He wasn't aggressive
like so many of the reformers she had met back in Scotland, and
she was grateful for that. Though, she could not see soft-spoken,*

mild-mannered Sir Francis Knollys employing a blustering zealot in his household anyway. The preacher had chosen the parable of the good Samaritan and the audience had been swept along with his reading. And yet she could feel her mind drifting, leaving this room and returning to the private chapel at Holyrood.

Leaving the Latin murmurings of the priest with his vestments glittering in the candlelight, in her mind she stalked panelled corridors that blurred to rough stone passages. A heavy oak door appeared before her. Ignoring the guards on either side, she shoved it open and found herself looking down into a cradle. Her infant son wriggled and mewed. Before her mind allowed her to pick him up, she was in another room, in another castle. Looking out over a glistening loch, she could see the sun slowly set, burning the space around her with orange light that darkened slowly to red. And on travelled her mind, on a journey bringing her right to this room, with the preacher still extolling the virtues of that good Samaritan.

Perhaps her face had begun to show her wandering mind, for Lady Livingston, seated on a lower chair to her left gently nudged her. Returning to the here and now, she leaned closer to the fire and shook herself from her reverie. As Knollys turned to look upon her, she gave him a small smile, and turned her eyes back to the preacher. She did her best to look enraptured. It could be worse, she thought...

WHILE MARY, QUEEN of Scots spent the summer of 1568 becoming increasingly anxious and frustrated despite the care of Sir Francis Knollys at Bolton Castle, her enemies were not idle. Back in Scotland, the Confederate Lords, those men who had come together to force her abdication, realized that if they were ever going to make Mary's exile permanent, they needed to ensure English support. An Act of the Scottish Parliament was passed which proclaimed that Mary had been legitimately held and forced to abdicate because the Confederate Lords had discovered irrefutable proof of her guilt in a series of crimes. Mary, this official act declared, was an adulteress who had begun a sexual affair with Bothwell months prior to the death of her husband, the King of Scotland, Henry Stuart, Lord Darnley. More shocking still, she had been the one to persuade Bothwell to murder Darnley.

The lords were explicit in condemning Mary, clarifying in this act of parliament that 'it is most certain that she was privy, art and part of the actual devising and deed of the forenamed murder of the king, her lawful husband and father to our sovereign lord'.[3] The lords were not holding back: Mary 'justly deserve[d] whatsoever has been done to her in any time past, or that shall be used towards her for the said cause in time coming'.[4] The nobles who had risen against Mary had of course – they declared – only been moved to act due to the heinous nature of Mary's crimes, each of these men being 'in their hearts fully persuaded of the authors and devisers of that mischievous and unworthy fact'.[5] Moreover, they claimed, they feared that Mary, being 'so enthralled and so blindly affectionate to the private appetite of the tyrant' would then start bumping off the nobles themselves.[6] What else could these men do but keep Mary closely held and ensure she was removed from the throne?

The Act also set out that the Confederate Lords were assured of Mary's guilt because they had discovered 'divers privy letters' written entirely in her own hand. These 'privy letters' had been found during a search of Bothwell's apartments at the Palace of Holyroodhouse, concealed in a locked silver casket. They were at pains to emphasize that these 'privy letters' had been found before Mary was forced to surrender at the battle of Carberry Hill on 15 June 1567, pre-empting any insinuation that these were rather conveniently 'discovered' after the abdication, as several of Mary's supporters would suggest. These letters have become infamous as the 'Casket Letters'. They fit into a wider propaganda campaign to discredit Mary, jointly encouraged by the Regent Moray and Cecil.

One of the key architects of this smear campaign was George Buchanan, the pre-eminent Scottish scholar and historian. Buchanan had been close to Mary in the early years of her personal reign after her return to Scotland from France in 1561. He had designed theatrical performances for her court, including at the spectacular celebrations for James VI's baptism. Buchanan regularly had private audiences with Mary where they discussed Latin texts, especially the works of Livy. Nonetheless, he held quite radical views on monarchy, being against autocratic royal rule. Instead, he believed that the people should hold the keys of power with their monarch ruling for them as they saw best. The people could, and should then, rightfully be able to remove a ruler that they felt was unjust or acting against their interests. He also had close ties to the Lennox family, who had supported his academic career. Thus, when Darnley, the son and heir to the Lennox titles, was murdered, Buchanan was particularly rattled. In the aftermath of the events at Kirk o' Field on 9 February 1567 he turned resolutely against Mary.

THE CONFEDERATE LORDS might claim that they had evidence of Mary's guilt as an adulteress and murderer, but they still needed to convince Elizabeth that she should side with them. Cecil had tried to persuade her that it was in her own interests to have a Protestant Regent in Scotland. He continually reminded Elizabeth that should Mary return to her throne there would inevitably be a war in Scotland between the two factions, those who called themselves the Queen's Men and those who stood firm behind the young King James, led by the Regent Moray. This war would inevitably threaten England as European nations intervened and fought on both sides. Yet Elizabeth, for her own part, was instinctively unsympathetic to their cause. She chafed against any suggestion that subjects should be empowered to rebel against their rightful ruler. If she were to publicly give support to the Scots lords, then she was leaving herself at risk of legitimizing rebellion. This was especially hazardous when her own reign was disputed both at home and across Europe.

The Confederate Lords understood that it was critical they convince Elizabeth that they were justified in their actions against Mary. Moray had assured Cecil that the evidence they had uncovered was strong. He sent a dossier that included eight letters sent to Bothwell by Mary, two marriage contracts which showed that the couple had agreed to marry before he had divorced his first wife, and twelve love poems. The letters and poems, Moray claimed, referred to the adulterous affair between Mary and Bothwell, but most importantly, they related to Darnley's murder. Despite holding this damning evidence, Moray was strangely reluctant to let Cecil examine the original documents which were penned in French. Instead, he sent Scots translations. The originals have since been lost, possibly destroyed after James VI reached his majority.

Under Cecil's guidance, Elizabeth ultimately decided that there would be a series of official investigations into the events leading up to Mary's flight into England in May 1568. She would not countenance any suggestion that this was to be a 'trial' of Mary. Instead, this was to be only a commission, a quasi-legal conference. Elizabeth claimed that the commission was intended to bring an end to the discord between Mary and her subjects. Cecil, on the other hand, had more blatant aims. He intended that the commission would prove Mary's involvement in the murder of Darnley, ensuring that she could never then return to the Scottish throne. What would need to be done with her after this pronouncement, he was still himself undecided, as his earlier note shows. He carefully edited a letter from Elizabeth to Moray emphasizing 'so surely if she [Mary] should be found justly to be guilty thereof [Darnley's murder], as hath been reported of her, whereof we would be very sorry, than indeed it should behove us to consider otherwise of her cause'.[7] The Scots lords would be able to present their evidence, these 'diverse privy letters', to explain why they had deposed Mary and, more importantly, why Mary should not be supported by England in her efforts to reclaim her throne.

Outraged, Mary immediately refused to acknowledge any such commission. She demanded to see the documents that were being produced as evidence against her, but she was denied this. And in fact, she never would be permitted to view the texts. Nor would anyone else appointed to act on her behalf. She then turned to her royal status to challenge the commission. As a queen, she could not be brought to trial by her subjects. And as a queen of Scotland, she most certainly could not be tried by an English court. Cecil, recognizing the flimsy legal case, claimed that Elizabeth could lawfully investigate because Scotland was a 'satellite state' of England[8]. Though this terminology ruffled the feathers of the Scottish Confederate Lords, if they wanted to keep Mary out of Scotland, they needed to go along with Cecil's scheme.

In July 1568, Mary was informed that the commission would go ahead despite her protests. Scheduled to begin in late September of that year, Moray and a few key supporters including James Douglas, 4th Earl of Morton, were given passports of safe conduct to come to York to present their arguments to a panel of nobles appointed by Elizabeth. Mary was ordered to appoint commissioners to act as her representatives in the case. She was not allowed to attend in person. Incensed, she wrote to Elizabeth rebuking her for doing 'this dishonour at the request of my rebels, as to send commissioners to hear them against me, as you would do a mean subject, and not hear me by mouth.'[9] Elizabeth insisted that it was in Mary's interest to submit to the commission, because once the truth was openly established, she could return to Scotland or move on to France.

In a further effort to appease Mary, Elizabeth appointed several conservative noblemen to the panel of English commissioners directed to oversee the events. These men were as reluctant as she was to condone the rebellion of subjects against their monarch. The judges included the prominent nobleman Thomas Howard, 4th Duke of Norfolk, who was suspected of having Catholic sympathies. More importantly, Norfolk was not a close member of Cecil's circle, and was less likely to be swayed by his persuasive influence. He was joined on the panel by Thomas Radcliffe, 3rd Earl of Sussex, a respected courtier, and Sir Ralph Sadler, a veteran diplomat who had extensive experience as an envoy to Scotland. Both men, though sharing Cecil's Protestant faith and understanding of the political advantages of a regime led by the Confederate Lords in Scotland, were practical men who were not easily led by the evidence being put forward against Mary, who they recognized still as a legitimate monarch.

Reluctantly then, Mary was forced to agree. She appointed John Leslie, Bishop of Ross, as her main representative. Ross had been a close confidant of Mary's since he travelled to France in 1561 to join her on her journey back to Scotland. He was one of the few Roman Catholic men appointed as one of her privy councillors and was promoted to a succession of titles. When Mary appointed him as her chief commissioner, she also tasked him to act as her ambassador to the English court. Appointed alongside him was Lord Herries, who had remained with her since the flight from Scotland, and Robert, 5th Lord Boyd. Boyd had been an ally of Bothwell, but then switched to the Confederate Lords after the Queen's defeat at Carberry in 1567. He returned to Mary's cause when she escaped from Lochleven and remained her close advisor, staying in England as her representative until early January 1570. Mary was not content to simply assume that Elizabeth's goodwill would override the machinations of Cecil and his allies. She sent a letter in cipher to Ross shortly before the commission opened reporting that her jailer, Sir Francis Knollys, seemed put out that he had not been asked to attend as a judge. She told Ross that there was some jealousy between Knollys and Norfolk in this regard and that he should foster this discontent among the English judges to see what advantage might come from it.[10]

Though Mary acquiesced to the investigation in the end, she nevertheless offered a damning challenge to Elizabeth: 'Do with my body at your will, the honour or blame shall be yours.'[11] As Mary accepted that she was indeed a prisoner in England, she realized that she had to develop a more proactive strategy. If Elizabeth would agree to treat her as a prisoner, as a common subject, then Mary would seek help from others. Others not necessarily motivated by Elizabeth's best interests. She signed off this letter to Elizabeth with the ominous parting shot: 'There may be things that move me to fear that I shall have to do in this country with other than you.'[12]

MOST HISTORIANS AND biographers agree that the Casket Letters were not genuine. They were, to varying degrees, forged by the Confederate Lords to present a version of events that suited them. Because the originals were lost or destroyed, we must rely on contemporary transcriptions and translations and on a series of notes made by Cecil. The marriage contracts are the least controversial. They showed that Mary had agreed to marry Bothwell before he was divorced, and we can corroborate this because she admitted herself that she had sinned by having sex with a married man and wished to repent of this act through matrimony.[13] Though as we have seen, this sexual relationship was one based upon coercion rather than the passion that her enemies tried to claim. Mary had felt compelled to then marry Bothwell to mitigate these circumstances.

The love poems were included by the Confederate Lords because they supposedly exposed Mary's lust for Bothwell. They needed to emphasize the passionate affair between the two because this was the primary motivation for her to then have Darnley murdered. These poems are not sparkling examples of the genre. Mary had been trained in courtly poetry by the French poet Pierre de Ronsard as a young woman. Ronsard was known as the 'prince of poets' by his compatriots. Mary then was no amateur composer. The phraseology of the examples sent as evidence against her on the other hand, were clumsy and stunted. It is unlikely that they were even composed by someone whose first language was French.

The eight letters were the most damning – if they were genuine. The two most incriminating letters are known as the 'Glasgow letters' because they were reputedly sent from Darnley's father the Earl of Lennox's property while Mary visited Darnley during his sickness. This was the smallpox which eventually led to his stay at Kirk o' Field and distance from the royal household. The shorter of the two Glasgow letters was written by a woman who was reprimanding her lover for his attitude to their romance. The man had promised to write to her while he was away from her company, but he had not done so, much to the woman's despair and anger.

The Confederate Lords argued that this letter proved that Mary was planning to move Darnley from Glasgow with the intention of harming him. They based their case on the fact the writer of this letter noted that she was planning to 'bring the man' with her when she returned to Edinburgh where she was 'to be let blood'.[14] Regent Moray assured Cecil that this meant that she was planning to spill blood. In other words, Mary was admitting to Bothwell that she knew Darnley was about to be harmed. To accept this line of reasoning requires a considerable leap of faith. Especially when the letter in fact refers to the matter of letting the blood of the writer herself. This was a common medical treatment for a range of illnesses in the early modern period. Physicians would open a vein and draw a considerable volume of blood from the patient to restore the balance of the humours – the four bodily fluids believed to dictate a person's physical and mental wellbeing. These bodily humours were at the heart of medical practice in the premodern period. If any of the four humours – blood, phlegm, yellow bile (known as choler) and black bile (called melancholy) – were out of balance then letting blood from different places on the body could help return them to a state of equilibrium.

This medical context is even more convincing because the writer also mentioned that she had been suffering from a pain in her side. Mary regularly suffered from a condition which caused severe pain and gastrointestinal distress. At Jedburgh in the Scottish Borders in October 1566, she had been so unwell with this recurring illness, which began with the usual pain in the left side of her abdomen, that she feared she would die and had set out her will and testament. Her doctors, turning to their humoral theory, diagnosed a disorder of the spleen. Though this was the worst bout she suffered, Mary would continue to relapse with the same symptoms throughout her life. Modern attempts to retrospectively diagnose the Scots Queen have included the debilitating blood disorder porphyria and a gastric ulcer, which had presumably ruptured while she was in Jedburgh and caused her near-death experience. Whatever the cause, this letter is much less incriminating when read in this context.

The Confederate Lords nevertheless persisted with their position. They argued that there was a third piece of evidence hidden in this letter that proved Mary's knowledge of Darnley's forthcoming murder. The writer mentioned that she had asked someone called 'Paris' to bring her something that would 'much amend' her. Clearly, the lords argued, this cure was to be her lover, Bothwell, who would mend her lovesickness, rather than the more straightforward explanation of medicine for a physical illness. And damningly in their eyes, she had asked this 'Paris' to attend her. Paris was the nickname of Nicholas Hubert, a Frenchman who had been Bothwell's valet for almost twenty years. By 1566, Hubert or Paris had been employed by Mary. The lords maintained that Paris was still in Bothwell's pay and had acted as their go-between to facilitate their affair. After Mary was imprisoned in Lochleven Castle, Paris fled to Denmark, but he had been forced back to Scotland in June 1569. The Confederate Lords interrogated him, but he refused to corroborate their story. On 10 August he was tortured and, unsurprisingly, he confessed. He suddenly told the lords everything they wanted to hear; he had indeed been asked to bring Bothwell to Mary for a liaison and he agreed that she had known Darnley was to be killed. He was quickly hanged without trial.

The second Glasgow letter was much longer. The Confederate Lords argued that it gave insight into Mary's love for Bothwell and proved that she planned the murder of Darnley. There are several specific details which ring true. She referred to a conversation with Darnley telling him that he would be brought from Glasgow so that her own physicians could treat his illness. She admitted that she wanted him closer to her in Edinburgh so that she could see him get well, but also remain closer to her son, who was usually at Stirling Castle under the guardianship of the Earl and Countess of Mar. Mary noted that Darnley would only agree to this journey if she would return to him 'as heretofore at bed and board'.[15] It was widely known by contemporaries that Darnley wanted to renew a sexual relationship with his wife, so this is a realistic inclusion.

The Confederate Lords had originally claimed that Mary had planned to poison Darnley by having him brought to one of her favourite properties, Craigmillar Castle, outside Edinburgh. Yet this letter actually showed that the timelines for this murderous plan were not realistic. Instead, the lords then changed tack and argued that these letters proved the plan had in fact always been to bring Darnley to be killed at Kirk o' Field. But here again, the schedule of events outlined in the letter itself simply does not add up, accepting the vague date of 'this Saturday from Glasgow', which had been squeezed onto the page. When Mary was in Glasgow, Bothwell had been in the Scottish Borders, and when she turned toward Edinburgh, Bothwell had gone first to Glasgow. The timeline offered in the letter was too tight for them to have passed letters between one another and then bring Darnley to Kirk o' Field by the date of his murder on 9 February 1567.

These two letters, and indeed all the Casket Letters, were not addressed to a specific person. They were also undated, except for a variation on the addition 'from Glasgow this Saturday morning'. For a while it was believed that these letters were written to Bothwell from a former lover, Anna Tronds. Anna and Bothwell had begun a relationship while he was in Copenhagen in 1559. Anna later argued that she and Bothwell had been married and sued him for compensation. Theirs was not an especially happy relationship. He had brought her to Scotland for a short period, during which she may have given birth to his son, William. Though the complaints of a disappointed lover fit Anna's experience, it is more likely that the first Glasgow letter was indeed genuinely drafted by Mary, but to an unknown recipient and not in the weeks leading up to the death of Darnley. It was then altered to suit the Confederate Lords' purposes. The second, longer letter, is almost certainly an amalgamation of genuine excerpts from Mary's correspondence to an unknown recipient and forged sections embedded into the text. Whether these additions were penned by a previous lover of Bothwell's or not, we can be sure that these two letters do not prove that Mary and Bothwell were having an affair, and they certainly don't tell us that she planned to kill Darnley.

Three other letters were more effusive in their sentiments of love and desire. The Confederate Lords included them because they hoped that they showed how desperately in love Mary was with Bothwell. All three are very different in style and it has been long recognized that they are unlikely to have been written by one person. The love letters also complain that the couple had been forced apart, yet from the moment of their marriage Mary and Bothwell had barely spent a few hours away from one another.[16] The final letters were used to suggest that Mary had been complicit in her own abdication by Bothwell. Not only does this utterly ignore the horrific coercion she was subject to by Bothwell at Dunbar but it forgets that contemporaries, including some of the men who were now arguing that Mary was guilty, were determined to rescue her from his imprisonment at the moment of her kidnapping.[17]

The Confederate Lords needed these letters to be convincingly accepted as having been written in Mary's own hand. Mary herself always maintained that she had never written such texts. By bringing together a mix of letters that might have been genuine and slipping forged bits and pieces in among them the lords were more likely to overcome the problem of the handwriting. Cecil was intimately familiar with Mary's hand: not only from her own letters to him but because he had read almost all the letters sent to Elizabeth. He would not be easily fooled in this regard. His own suspicions are evident in some of the comments he made on the transcriptions of the letters that he was sent. He added notes and questions in the margin, clearly trying to follow the confusing train of events that were being presented by these documents. Crucially, he also noticed that the translations sent over by Moray were not rigorous or even realistic.

The Scottish lords had tried to set events in the present tense when translated into Scots. Cecil scored this out, returning the phrases to the past tense, as they were in the French. This suggests that the letters had indeed been earlier compositions that were altered to fit the narrative being woven by the Confederate Lords against Mary. We know that Cecil was having doubts about this evidence because he tried to prevent Paris from being executed, asking Moray to bring him to be interrogated in person by the English commissioners. He was not impressed, but probably not surprised, when Paris was killed before this could happen. And yet, by now Cecil was so invested in his plan to have Elizabeth turn against Mary and openly support the Confederate Lords, that he had to make the best of the situation. The commission would go ahead.

THE ENGLISH JUDGES, the group of Confederate Lords led by Regent Moray, and the men appointed to represent Mary, met at York on 4 October 1568. Mary's commissioners opened the proceedings. They set out their case by reminding those present that Mary had been unjustly forced to suffer greatly at the hands of these men, who they referred to consistently as rebels. They reiterated Mary's conviction that these documents that were being produced against her were not genuine. Finally, her commissioners asked to see these texts in person so that all might see them for themselves.

Moray refused to present the original texts. The Confederate Lords were still not certain that this commission would rule in their favour, despite Cecil's personal support for their cause. They realized that Elizabeth was not yet convinced and was undoubtedly still unwilling to proclaim Mary a murderer. It was, however, risky to withhold these key texts. If they offered irrefutable evidence of Mary's crimes, why on earth would you not show them to the world? This was the line of thinking that the English judges quickly followed. Norfolk, the most likely of the three judges to be sympathetic to Mary, was scathing of the Confederate Lords' approach. He complained directly to Cecil that this was the 'doubtfullest and dangerous that I ever dealt in: if you saw and heard the constant affirming of both sides not without great stoutness, you would wonder!'[18] Norfolk was brave enough to speak aloud the one thing everyone was thinking: the Confederate Lords 'seek wholly to serve their own particular turns' and 'they care not what becomes neither of queen nor king'. He went on to emphasize that the Confederate Lords 'play at no small game, they stand for their lives, lands and goods'.[19] Norfolk told Cecil that this risk to their safety made them cautious to explicitly accuse Mary of murder with the Casket Letters. He came right to the point and told Cecil that there would be no suitable decision because these men wanted to know for sure that they could rely on Elizabeth's support and yet this support could not actually be offered. He also warned Cecil that if the original letters were finally brought to the commission then Mary would without doubt demand to attend in person. Cecil could not allow that to happen.

Even the Earl of Sussex struggled to see how the commission could reasonably find in the Confederate Lords' favour based on the poor case they were presenting. After a fortnight of stalemate, he informed Cecil that if the original documents were produced then Mary would be able to deny them. Worse, she would simply turn the charges back upon her accusers and, using their own evidence against them, show that they were in fact guilty themselves of the murder of Darnley.[20] Cecil realized that the commission was not going the way he had hoped and planned. The proceedings were adjourned for almost a month while he tried to bring things back on track. In the meantime, Moray was accommodated by Sussex and allowed to travel around the Yorkshire countryside to enjoy the outdoor pursuits. Mary, of course, remained held at Bolton Castle. When it restarted, the commission was moved closer to the English Court, reopening at Westminster on 26 November 1568. Cecil had also added extra judges to the panel. His brother-in-law Sir Nicholas Bacon was appointed. Cecil also added himself as a judge. It was clear to the Confederate Lords that things were looking up.

In this, the second act of the commission, Moray openly declared that Mary had killed her husband, the King of Scotland. Mary ordered her own representatives to leave, refusing now to acknowledge any possibility of a fair hearing. Waiting until her commissioners had left, Moray then brought out the original Casket Letters and allowed the English judges to carefully examine them. Cecil, leading the panel, judged that the documents were indeed in Mary's own hand, despite his earlier misgivings. And yet, Elizabeth scuppered his scheme just as he got close to achieving his aim. She intervened directly, adjourning the commission for a second time. When it began for the third and final time on 14 December at Hampton Court, Elizabeth attended herself to supervise. She also added yet more judges, this time a plethora of conservative nobles including the Earl of Northumberland who had already tried to support Mary.

Mary once again asked to defend herself in person but was yet again refused. She issued a statement via her chief representative, the Bishop of Ross, on 19 December. Here, she did exactly as

Sussex had warned Cecil: she declared that it was in fact those men who were accusing her who had conspired to the murder of Darnley. She angrily refuted the veracity of the documents being used against her, ending her proclamation:

> *And with God's grace we shall first make such answer*
> *thereto that our innocence shall be known to our good*
> *sister and all other princes, and suchlike shall charge*
> *them as authors, inventors and doers of the said crime*
> *they would impute to us.*[21]

Because Mary was not to be permitted to speak to Elizabeth directly or to challenge the evidence against her, Elizabeth agreed that the commission could not come to a fair judgment. She adjourned the trial indefinitely. As 1568 came to a close, Mary was not declared innocent, yet the Confederate Lords had not achieved their desire to see her proclaimed guilty either. Things, it seemed, were no further forward than they had been in May earlier that year when Mary first sought refuge in Elizabeth's kingdom.

AND YET THERE was a change in the air. Mary's new approach would be more combative. She was no longer willing to wait patiently, hoping that her status and her sufferings would be recognized by Elizabeth and her council. She needed to seek outside help. Before the first round of the commission had begun in York in October 1568, Mary had made her intentions clear. Some of her supporters abroad had heard that she was enjoying listening to Sir Francis Knollys' readings from the English Bible and indeed had been seen joining the audience at sermons preached by local Protestants brought to Bolton Castle. Fearing that this would jeopardize her standing with her Catholic allies across Europe and with local English traditionalists who looked to her for leadership, she took care to stage a public rebuttal. Declaring herself a devout Catholic in her apartments at Bolton, she ensured that there were Catholic servants, attendants, and gentry in attendance who would be sure to pass on the message that the Scots Queen remained committed to the faith. Knollys questioned Mary in private afterwards, somewhat disgruntled by her performance because he had taken her interest in the reformed religion to be genuine. Revealingly, she responded: 'Why would you have me lose France and Spain and all my friends in other places by seeming to change my religion?'[22]

From then on, religion was to become more explicitly part of Mary's strategy to free herself from this English captivity. During her personal reign she had been content to follow a path of accommodation and reconciliation, successfully balancing – at least until the Darnley marriage – the Catholic and Protestant causes in Scotland. She had been forced on several occasions to offer reassurances to the Pope that she remained a dutiful daughter of the Catholic Church because she had done so little to restore the faith in her own kingdom. Her Guise relatives also challenged her on this part, questioning why she had not allied herself more with the Catholic nobility. Her faith during these years was, for the most part, a personal matter. She regularly heard mass in her private chapels but did little to support those of her subjects who wished to celebrate their faith publicly.[23] And during the early months of her time at Carlisle and Bolton it was in her own interests to seek the approval of her Protestant jailors by acquiescing to sermons and readings.

Now, though, as it was becoming clear to her that she could not rely on Elizabeth to intervene on her behalf, Mary would carefully recraft a performance of Catholic piety which would, she hoped, encourage support from France and Spain, as well as the affection of English Catholics. She wrote a series of letters to King Philip II of Spain in November 1568 as the second act of the commission was being adjourned, assuring him that she was 'a dutiful, submissive and devoted daughter of the holy Roman Catholic Church, in whose faith I wish to live and to die'.[24] After the inconclusive ending of the commission, she went even further. She wrote to John Hamilton, Archbishop of St Andrews, early in January 1569 explaining that she was actively seeking the support of both Spain and France. Writing in cipher, she went so far as to state that she hoped to receive several thousand men to aid her.[25] What the purpose of these soldiers would be remains unknown, but it is clear that Mary was making much more aggressive plans for her freedom.

Throughout the autumn and winter of 1568, Mary had also been directing her supporters back in Scotland. The Earl of Argyll, recovered from his collapse at the Battle of Langside in May 1568, had become the de facto leader of her party. He, and several other noblemen, wrote letters on Mary's behalf seeking Spanish and French support for her cause.[26] They had also begun gathering men and weapons in expectation of open warfare between the two sides, the Queen's Party, and the King's Party. Argyll, who was the most influential nobleman in Gaelic-speaking Scotland, used his networks in Ireland to secure further support for Mary. Cecil genuinely feared that Argyll would raise his Gaelic subjects in Ireland and encourage Catholic Ireland as a landing site for French or Spanish soldiers who would then seek to rescue Mary.[27] During her captivity, Ireland would become a site of Mary's transnational strategy, with faith at the centre of the diplomatic intrigues. During her personal reign she had tried to appease Elizabeth by preventing Scots mercenaries from travelling to Ireland, but the stakes had changed with the instigation of the commission. Elizabeth was furious that Mary was meddling in Scotland and Ireland – though as Mary had already made clear, she could not realistically be expected to accept her situation without seeking help from allies.

While Mary was experimenting with her new strategy, her jailor was trying to extricate himself from the job. Knollys begged Elizabeth to let him leave Bolton and return south. His wife, Catherine Carey, first cousin and chief Lady of the Bedchamber to Elizabeth, had fallen ill in the summer of 1568. By the end of the year, it was clear that she would be unlikely to recover. Selfishly, Elizabeth refused to let Knollys leave his post and return to his wife. Catherine died on 15 January 1569 at Hampton Court Palace. With her death, Knollys was finally allowed to leave Bolton. Mary was also leaving. She was being moved to Tutbury Castle in Staffordshire where she would be placed under the care of a new jailor, George Talbot, 6th Earl of Shrewsbury. Little could she have imagined that she would spend the next seventeen years in his company.

CHAPTER THREE

By Sword or by Marriage

*I will be about to use myself so that, so far
as God shall give me grace, you shall never
have cause to diminish your good conceit and
favor of me, while I shall esteem and respect
you in all my doings so long as I live, as you
would wish your own to do [...] I write to
the Bishop of Ross what I hear from the Duke
of Alva, governor of the Netherlands. Let
me know your pleasure at length in writing
what I shall answer now, my Norfolk.*[2]

JOHN BEATON WAS cold. The sun had been determinedly making its way through the gloom of the early morning, but out here on the moor, with no trees or shrubs to cushion the blows of the wind, he felt the chill settle under the folds of his cloak. He started to pace out a broad circle just to keep up the circulation in his toes. After a few minutes of this mindless wandering, he heard someone approaching. Stilling himself, he prepared his excuse for being out so early – he had climbed up the moor to gather the early tormentil the physician had recommended for the queen's most recent bout of colic. This was not normally a job he would take on as master of the household, but with the ladies suffering similar pains, he had volunteered to gather the little yellow flowers. It was a convenient cover for this unusual morning outing.

Coming towards him were two men, heavily cloaked like himself, against the icy air. The brightening sunlight was behind them as they reached him, so that he couldn't make out their faces. The shorter of the two offered a polite greeting. How to be sure these were the men he had planned to meet out on the moor? A sharp bolt of exasperation was directed at Mary for accepting the men's request, but he stifled his frustration. John Beaton was a devoted servant of his exiled queen. He would do whatever she asked of him. Even meet with conspirators within a short distance of the guards at Chatsworth House. Anything to secure her freedom...

MARY HEARD THAT she was being moved on from Bolton Castle in late January 1569. She was pleased to leave but was dismayed to hear that Sir Francis Knollys would no longer be her primary custodian. Knollys had strived to maintain Mary's dignity and seemed genuinely moved by her sufferings. Despite their religious differences, and the awkward predicament they found themselves thrust into, they had gotten on well with one another. Her new custodian, George Talbot, 6th Earl of Shrewsbury, was an unknown entity. He was another Protestant, though not an overly zealous one. He was, though, one of Elizabeth's greatest noblemen, with a keen sense of his own position and status. Mary would have to start from scratch, once again, to gain the trust of this keeper and bring him around, at least as far as possible given that Elizabeth was never going to place her in the household of a man likely to turn against the English queen herself. On 20 January, Elizabeth wrote to Mary, seemingly in a generous mood, explaining that she knew Mary had grown to dislike Bolton. So, she had arranged for the Scottish queen to be sent somewhere more honourable and agreeable to her status.[3] This gesture would prove to have a considerable sting in the tail: Mary quickly came to detest her new lodgings at Tutbury Castle.

Tutbury was a medieval stronghold that had been rebuilt and renovated countless times over the centuries. It was well suited to its new role as a prison: the main building was isolated, surrounded by an extensive enclosure. It sat upon a slight hill, with views across the open countryside so that any approaching visitors – expected or unexpected – would quickly be spotted by those on guard. By the time Mary arrived, it had been left to stumble into a severe state of shabbiness because Shrewsbury preferred his other properties at Sheffield and Wingfield. The buildings desperately needed substantial repairs in some quarters, with things being only patched up to combat the worst of the gaps in the woodwork and holes in the roof. Damp was invasive, with even the grandest rooms suffering from its chilly effects. Efforts were made to brighten up the castle in anticipation of Mary's arrival – or at least to disguise the severity of the problems. Tapestries from the royal collection at the Tower of London were sent to adorn Mary's public and private chambers. Classical and religious imagery was preferred, with the labours of Hercules and the Passion of Christ included in the examples sent.[4] Shrewsbury's wife, Elizabeth, known as Bess of Hardwick, also sent some of her furnishings from the couple's property at Sheffield to dress the castle for the queen.[5]

Mary enjoyed the journey from Bolton Castle to Tutbury in Staffordshire. Recognizing that a move farther south was only further proof of her imprisonment, Mary initially fought against the move. But the chance to ride out, even in the icy winter, filled her with that old sense of freedom and she rejoiced in the travel. Knollys accompanied her, and had secured horses for all her attendants, noting with some disgruntlement the cost of such an endeavour. This was no naïve act of kindness, however, because Knollys also employed more than twenty soldiers to keep close to the party at least until they reached the vicinity of Sheffield, when he made it clear that the Earl of Shrewsbury should be picking up the tab or otherwise bringing his own armed men to complete the journey.[6]

Each stage of her journey was never more than sixteen miles, which for an accomplished horsewoman made for a comfortable ride, even with the insistent icy gusts that dogged their steps. The party stopped at Ripon, Wetherby, Pontefract, Rotherham, Chesterfield and Wingfield, before finally reaching Tutbury on 4 February 1569. It had taken longer than expected for Mary to reach their destination because while resting at Rotherham her companion Lady Livingston fell ill, forcing her to stay behind while the rest of the party travelled on to Chesterfield. When Mary heard that Lady Livingston was sick, she was herself struck with an attack of the pain in her side and refused to move on to the next destination until her friend could catch up. Knollys admitted that there was a chance that Mary 'had feigned herself sick' but he bluntly excused the extra night's stay because 'we thought it best to yield so much to her fancy'. He went further, adding that 'also we were glad by this kind of curtesy to seek to make her the more tractable and to avoid the cumberous inconveniences that otherwise might have happened'.[7] Clearly, it just wasn't worth the effort of antagonizing Mary by this point in their journey. Knollys was tired and frustrated and knew when to pick his battles. He admitted that he was happy to take the hospitality on offer from the owner of the property in Chesterfield for a further night, especially as this was one of the most comfortable locations they had stayed in so far.

Mary was finally welcomed at Tutbury by the Earl of Shrewsbury who noted that she was polite and calm at their first introduction. His was an impossible task: maintain Mary as fitting for her royal status, but on a meagre budget from the crown. He was caught between living with a queen who might yet regain Scotland, and obeying his own monarch who insisted that Mary must never be allowed to 'gain rule over him'. It was never quite clear to Shrewsbury whether Mary had Elizabeth's favour or not – a confusion Mary herself shared! His priority was to make sure that Mary always was supervised and could never escape her captivity. And yet, he was ever conscious of her royal status.

His first attempt to bring these two opposing positions together was in the challenge of reducing the number of servants and companions in attendance upon Mary. She caught him off guard by agreeing to the change without any great fuss, though she did baulk a little at the suggestion that she let go at least thirty of the almost sixty people who had journeyed with her from Bolton to Tutbury. Her stableboys and horsemen were not permitted to remain, though Mary convinced Shrewsbury to let them take accommodation in the nearby village, taking her horses with them. She demanded that her women be exempt from the changes to her household, and this was also allowed. Remaining with her after the cull were Lord and Lady Livingston, a handful of valets, including Bastian Paget, whose wedding she had attended a couple of years earlier in Edinburgh, as well as her Scottish secretary Gilbert Curle, and her master of the household, John Beaton, brother of her ambassador to France, James Beaton, Archbishop of Glasgow. She also kept a surgeon in attendance, Arnold Collomius. One gentleman who had come to join the party at Tutbury, Sir John Morton, was watched on increasing suspicion of being a secret priest.[8] Mary Seton, Mary's closest companion, had been permitted to leave Lochleven shortly after Mary's own escape and had travelled to join her mistress at Bolton. She, too, was allowed to stay at Tutbury.

Knollys finally departed the following day. Mary felt his departure keenly. He had been one of the few constants during the last six months, never treating her with hostility despite the challenges both of them were forced to endure. As he left for London, her representatives, the Bishop of Ross and Lord Herries, were journeying towards her. She looked forward to their arrival, hoping that they would have news from court, or a comforting word from Elizabeth. When they arrived on 7 February, however, they were not allowed to stay within the confines of Tutbury and were forced to find accommodation in the small town of Burton, some three miles away. Ross and Herries were soon joined by Lord Boyd as well. The trio were forced to write to Cecil to ask for permission to see Mary, because Shrewsbury refused to let them have private meetings until it was signed off by Elizabeth. Boyd was insulted that he was not given access to Mary and angrily condemned any sinister reports against him, complaining that he and his compatriots were 'willing to remain and deal uprightly in all their doings'.[9] Elizabeth did eventually relent and commanded Shrewsbury to allow Mary and her advisors to meet privately, though she still wanted them watched carefully just in case they might decide to 'practice in the country'.[10]

ELIZABETH WAS RIGHT to be suspicious. As February 1569 came to a close, whispers were fluttering on the winds. Noises, faint and indistinct at first, were beginning to be heard in London, of support for Mary from all directions. Plans, ripe only with possibility and potential in the spring of 1569, were taking shape to rescue her. Cecil's greatest fears it seemed were coming true. Foreign aid for

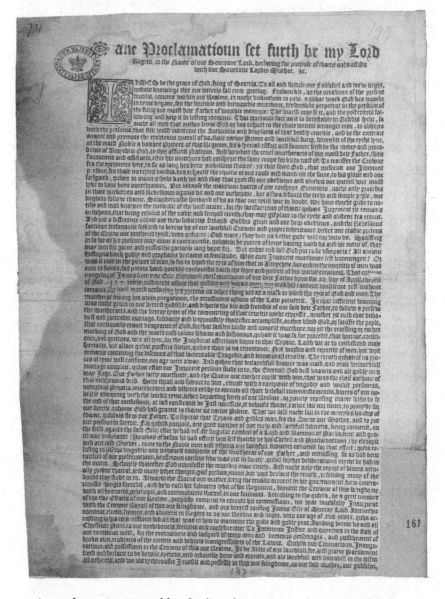

A proclamation issued by the 'Lord Regent, in the name of our Sovereign Lord, declaring the purpose of them who assisted with our Sovereign Lord's Mother'. This was released following growing support among the Scottish nobility for the captive Mary, to caution them that the legitimate ruler of Scotland was the infant James VI, and those who ruled on his behalf.

the captive queen was the subject of more and more covert reports from the continent. Even worse, there were concerns that support was available much closer to home. Shrewsbury had warned Cecil and Elizabeth that keeping Mary in his territories of Yorkshire and Staffordshire was a risky idea. If Mary were ever to slip his grasp and escape, then he had no doubt that the local people would enthusiastically help her to cross the moors and slip back into Scotland. Yorkshire, he narrow-mindedly reminded them, was 'corrupted with Popery'.[11]

The first threat appeared to come from Scotland where Mary's supporters had been rallying since the inconclusive commissions of late 1568. Regent Moray was so concerned by these efforts on Mary's behalf that he issued a proclamation on 13 March 1569 declaring that 'Satan and his ministers not contented to God's will' had corrupted Mary.[12] This evil influence had infected her and her supporters and caused her to seek to turn foreign princes, including Elizabeth, against the lawful King of Scotland, James VI. Writing to Cecil upon reading the declaration, Mary insisted that he 'guard one ear and think impartially'.[13] Her request was in vain: she heard a few days later that Elizabeth had agreed to send men to stand with the Regent Moray against Mary's own supporters. The Regent was slowly forcing the nobles and lairds of Scotland to submit to the new regime and declare themselves loyal to the infant king.[14] At the same time, her representative, the Bishop of Ross, was accused of using his time in England to rustle up support for Mary among the nobility there.[15] In a ciphered letter from early April 1569, we learn that Ross had also sent a messenger back to Scotland to seek out intelligence and gather support, especially in the north of the country.[16] Once again, Mary was prevented from seeing Ross or her other advisors, Lord Herries and Lord Boyd. She was also to be moved for 'safe keeping' to another of Shrewsbury's houses at Wingfield in Derbyshire.

Wingfield was in many ways a more comfortable property than Tutbury. It had been built in the 1440s as a luxurious manor house. Planned for pleasure and comfort, rather than as a military fortification, the buildings were more accommodating for the queen, though there did remain a fortified tower from which guards could watch the approach of visitors. The house benefited from large double courtyards and a palatial Great Hall, as well as an enclosed garden. Wingfield was considerably larger than Tutbury and was a bustling place in comparison, with space for many more servants and stabling for numerous horses. Mary remained at Wingfield throughout 1569, enjoying the gardens in the summer, but complaining of the smell from the medieval garderobes.

For a moment, it seemed that Cecil had managed to quench any sparks of support that might free Mary. Certainly, by the end of April things were quieter in Scotland. Most of Mary's supporters had been pressured into declaring for the young King and Regent Moray. Hearing of the plight of her supporters in Scotland torn between their titles and property, and their support for her, she wept and claimed that she 'made small account of her own life, but to see her friends so spoiled for her sake was as grievous as death could be'.[17]

This success might have influenced Elizabeth's decision to restart negotiations between Mary and Confederate Lords. She still hoped that it would be possible for Mary to return to Scotland in some fashion which did not dishonour her royal status but nevertheless would maintain the Anglophile government there. The Bishop of Ross was once again given the role of Mary's primary representative and travelled to London to take part more directly in the discussions. Amazingly, considering the bad blood between the Regent and Mary, it was suggested that there be a 'perfect reconciliation' between both parties, and that Mary should pardon all offences against her.[18] A council of twelve of the 'wisest' men in Scotland would adjudicate any disputes. Elizabeth was still adamant that Mary give up her claim to the succession of the English crown and this was added to the notes of the negotiations. Before this could go any further, however, Mary was forced to deny that she had ever had conference with the Duke of Anjou, King Henri II of France's youngest son. Cecil had discovered that there was a suggestion that Mary and Anjou marry, and that to secure this match, Mary had agreed to sign over her rights to the crown of Scotland and to England to the French prince.[19] For every step forward, it seemed, matters would take several back.

AT THE END of September 1569, things were looking even more dangerous. Shrewsbury wrote to the Council of the North, a group of nobles, gentry, and ministers, demanding to know more about the state of affairs in the area. Elizabeth had been informed that 'something hath been proposed touching' Mary and she was by no means content to wait and see what these secret plans might be.[20] Mary had found herself brusquely returned to the confines of Tutbury a few weeks earlier and by October she noticed that there was an unease in the air. 'Seeing the suspicion of me, the sudden change of my guards and treatment of my servants,' she complained to Elizabeth, meant she was 'forbidden to go out, and intruded on in my chamber with pistolets and arms in fear of my life!'[21] Henry Hastings, Earl of Huntingdon, was appointed as an additional jailer. Mary loathed Huntingdon: he was a committed Puritan and was much harsher when dealing with her. Huntingdon had a distant claim to the English throne through his Plantagenet ancestors, making him a novel threat to Mary. She feared that his arrival on the scene at Tutbury meant that she would suddenly find herself the victim of 'an accident' which would conveniently clear the way for his own pretensions to the English succession. Her belongings were searched, and her ladies interrogated. What had caused this sudden change in her treatment?

Rumour had reached the court in London that the northern nobility of England was unhappy. A faction had begun to gather led by Thomas Percy, 7th Earl of Northumberland and Charles Neville, 6th Earl of Westmorland. This group resented their declining influence in English politics, a result of the influence of Cecil's centralizing policies. The northern counties of England remained traditional Catholic strongholds and as Shrewsbury had warned, Mary offered an alternative ruler of similar religious persuasion, around whom they might coalesce. Mary's very presence in the north of England was potentially a prize for those who were disillusioned with Elizabeth and her advisors. As we have seen, Northumberland had already tried to remove Mary to his personal protection when she first arrived in Carlisle and though he didn't succeed then, he continued to harbour hopes of laying his hands on the captive queen. His wife, Lady Anne Percy, an openly devout Catholic, had met briefly with Mary when she arrived at Bolton Castle before Knollys was commanded to stop people visiting the Scottish queen. From then on though, Mary regularly sent gifts to Lady Anne, including a gold ring and some French perfume.[22]

In the summer of 1569, Northumberland and Lady Anne had joined the earl of Shrewsbury and his wife Bess, and the Earl and Countess of Westmorland in hunting with Thomas Radcliffe, Earl of Sussex. Outwardly things seemed normal. Secretly, however, while visiting his London property in Blackfriars, Northumberland had been meeting with the new Spanish ambassador to England, Don Guerau de Spes. Northumberland had reaffirmed his faith after his wife introduced him to Catholic devotional texts. His Catholic faith made this new relationship with the Spanish ambassador suspect in Cecil's eyes and their movements were subsequently watched. It was reported that Northumberland had made clandestine enquiries of some of Shrewsbury's servants to discover how easy it would be to carry Mary away from Tutbury after she was transferred there after Bolton.

Hearing that Mary was later to be held at Wingfield, Lady Anne was determined to visit the queen there. She was familiar with the layout of the property and knew some of the servants based there from several visits to the earl and countess over the previous few years. Bastian Paget, one of the few attendants permitted to stay with Mary by this point, was intricately involved in Lady Anne's scheme to win Mary's freedom. Disguising herself as a nurse, Anne was to come to Wingfield under the ruse of attending to Bastian's wife, who was at this time heavily pregnant. Once inside the house, Anne would gain access to Mary's chambers and the two women would swap clothes, letting Mary sneak away while Anne would wait behind in her place. Improbable though this sounds, Shrewsbury himself believed it could have worked had Anne managed to get into Wingfield. He admitted that his servants were friendly with the countess and even confessed that it would have been feasible for Anne to portray herself as Mary because the two women were of similar height and stature.[23]

Before these schemes could be put into action, however, the Earl of Northumberland, along with Westmorland, was summoned to court to publicly show their continued submission to Elizabeth. They decided not to go. Accepting their excuses, Elizabeth demanded their attendance for a second time a few weeks later. The earls still did not turn up. In November 1569, Sussex was sent by Elizabeth to visit Northumberland at his property of Topcliffe in Yorkshire with stern instructions that should they refuse to come to her for a third time, then they would be setting themselves against her. Northumberland made himself scarce. Lady Anne reassured Sussex in his absence that Northumberland had been unwell before and was now simply attending to estate business: of course, he meant to travel to London immediately to present himself to the queen. As Sussex rode out from Topcliffe, reaching the boundaries of the estate, he was dumbfounded to hear the bells being rung to call tenants to rise in open rebellion.[24] The first serious armed threat to Elizabeth's reign was being announced. The Northern Rebellion of 1569 had begun.

WHAT DID THIS uprising have to do with Mary? Back in February 1569, Nicholas White was on his way to Ireland to take up a position as Master of the Rolls of Ireland at Cecil's request. He stopped at Tutbury to visit Mary and report back his thoughts to Cecil. He warned Cecil that 'fame might move some to relieve her, and glory joined to gain might stir others to adventure much for her sake'.[25] White was ahead of the game. By the late summer of 1569, Northumberland had come to the same conclusion. Mary was to be the focal point of the northern earls' religious and social gripes. If they could whisk her away from her prison, they would be in a powerful position both at home and with foreign supporters. As one historian recently put it: 'Mary certainly served as a source of both inspiration and temptation for northern lords already given to conspiracy'.[26] Mary was the best bargaining chip on the table. As a result, she was moved even farther inland from Tutbury to Coventry on 25 November to keep her away from the rebels. She stayed at first in an inn before being moved to a townhouse because the castle was falling apart. Huntingdon, to Mary's dismay, attended her there. She was outraged to learn that he had gone to hear some 'lewd preachings' against her in the town.

Despite some initial successes, including claiming Durham Cathedral, ripping up the Book of Common Prayer, and reinstating the Catholic mass there, the rebellion was short-lived, fizzling out as quickly as it had burst into fiery action. Hearing of a substantial force being sent to meet them in December, Westmorland and Northumberland fled to Scotland. Lady Anne joined them. She had been the most committed participant in the uprising, leading a party of loyal tenants independent of her husband, and riding while in the early stages of pregnancy to intercept post between the Regent Moray and Cecil. Henry Carey, Baron Hunsdon, who led Elizabeth's forces had astutely recognized that she was the one driving the men to continue, describing her as 'the gray mare ys the better horse'.[27] Anne would remain a supporter of Mary during her years of exile, first in Scotland and later in the Spanish Netherlands, and we will come across her again later.

Mary denied that she had anything to do with the rebellion. In fact, when she was first informed of the plans, she claimed that she had urged the earls not to rise because it would lead to the loss of innocent lives. More selfishly, she was also unsure that violent action against Elizabeth would be helpful to her own cause, despite the earls' claims to be acting in her interests. And yet, Mary's coded letters give hints that she may have been more involved than she liked to admit.

She had her secretary design a new cipher so that she could communicate surreptitiously with the French ambassador to England, Bertrand de Salignac de la Mothe-Fénelon. In these ciphered letters, Mary asked for direct aid from the French king Charles IX. She also urged her cousin Henri, Duke of Guise, to give financial aid to the rebels who had fled into exile on the continent. When pressed about this, she didn't deny these requests for French support, reminding Cecil yet again that she was within her rights to gain her freedom using any means in her power. Her captivity was, as she told him once more, illegal. Cecil would have been reminded of Mary's earlier declaration to Elizabeth in July 1568, that if she were forced, she would gather help from any who were willing, both within England and beyond.[28]

While Lady Anne and the Earl of Westmorland managed to find sanctuary among supporters of Mary in Scotland, Northumberland was not as fortunate. He had tried to slip back into England but was captured. His run of bad luck increased when the border lairds who caught him decided to send him to Edinburgh where he was handed over to Regent Moray. Northumberland's arrival in the Scottish capital was a headache for Moray – he naturally wanted to keep Elizabeth happy and was keen to agree to her request that he send Northumberland right back to her. The Scottish lords though, even those who were no friend of Mary's, insisted that Northumberland should benefit from political asylum, as had been commonly accepted on both sides of the border for centuries. Moray was accused of being 'a quisling, unpatriotically abandoning Scottish interests and pandering to the old enemy'.[29] Stuck in a quandary, the Regent shipped Northumberland off to Mary's original jail, Lochleven Castle, in Perthshire. He remained there for more than two years while his wife and fellow rebels left for exile on the continent. Eventually, he was sold to the English in June 1572 and was executed at York on 22 August that year.

Just as the Northern Rebellion ended in December 1569, a new uprising flared from its smouldering ashes. Leonard Dacre, a Cumberland nobleman, raised his own tenants and gathered a substantial force. He, too, claimed that he would set Mary free from her captivity, despite having been initially reluctant to aid the northern earls in their own efforts a few months prior. In February 1570, Hunsdon was sent north once more, resoundingly crushing the rebels. Dacre also fled into Scotland before joining Lady Anne in the Spanish Netherlands. France and Spain had watched these northern uprisings with interest and some covert efforts were made to support the uprisings of 1569 and 1570. It was reported that Spanish ships were seen in the waters around

Montrose, while the Earl of Huntly had sounded out havens in Scotland where Spanish troops could land. But when Dacre was defeated and the English were able to comprehensively subdue the rebels, this foreign support diminished.

A few months later though, things had still not entirely settled down. In May, a small group of Catholic gentry and minor nobles decided that they were willing to take action to help set Mary free. Led by Sir Thomas Gerard, who was the father of the future Jesuit missionary John Gerard, the group planned to rescue Mary from Chatsworth House where she was enjoying a brief respite from the dour surroundings of Tutbury.[30] Sir Thomas Stanley and his son Sir Edward Stanley were at the heart of the scheme, planning to carry Mary off from Chatsworth to the relative safety of the Isle of Man from where she could either return to Scotland or seek safety in France.

There was a curious connection between the first rebellion of 1569 and this new plot: Lady Anne Percy's daughter Lucy would later marry Sir Edward Stanley. Lucy Stanley was a devoted Catholic like her mother, and had maintained links with Catholic families in Yorkshire since her mother's exile.[31] Mary was more interested by now in securing direct foreign support from either King Philip II of Spain or King Charles IX of France, but she was intrigued enough to send her master of the household, John Beaton, to meet the conspirators (on the moor above Chatsworth early in the morning to avoid detection) to discuss their plans and thank them for their actions.[32] Little eventually came of the plan by the Yorkshire men because Thomas Stanley was interrogated. These efforts, though seemingly insignificant to us, were viewed as highly threatening by Cecil because they coincided with the publication of a papal bull on 25 February 1570 which excommunicated Elizabeth. Pope Pius V's release of *Regnans in Excelsis* released English Catholics from any loyalty to their sovereign. Though it was not made openly public until May of that year, when it was pinned to the door of the Bishop of London's palace, Cecil was immediately informed by his spies and diplomats abroad. The papal bull had serious implications for the Catholics of England and for Mary. From this point on, English Catholics were painted as traitors.

MARY MIGHT MAINTAIN that she had not been an instigator of the rebellions of late 1569 and early 1570, but there was one charge she could not deny. While those around her had been designing various schemes for her release, Mary herself had been pursuing a different policy to reach the same end. She sought a marriage.

The nobleman and politician Thomas Howard, Duke of Norfolk, was first suggested as a potential husband for Mary before the commission at York in October 1568. He was a widower thrice over, with several surviving children, but was similar in age to Mary. Though he was not as physically striking as her second husband, nor as bolshy as her third, the match was nevertheless worth considering for a number of reasons, especially his status as the highest-ranking nobleman in England. He was in fact the only duke in England. He was also a grand territorial magnate with considerable wealth and influence. His family were largely Catholic, though he himself was ostensibly a Protestant. This faith meant that he would be an easier sell to the Scottish lords should Mary be permitted to return to Scotland. Mary was already quite close with his sisters: Margaret, Lady Scrope had attended her briefly at Carlisle and Bolton while her husband Lord Scrope was Mary's brief jailor alongside Knollys. Lady Scrope may have emphasized her brother's qualities; Cecil made sure to remove her from Mary's company, fearing her influence. Their sister Jane was married to the earl of Westmorland who would be one of the two leaders of the rebellion of 1569.

From Norfolk's perspective, Mary was also quite the catch despite her captive status. Not only was she still physically attractive and young enough to have more children, but she was also an anointed queen. She was of undisputed royal blood, there was still the possibility that she would be restored to her throne, and, crucially, Elizabeth might not be against the marriage because she had previously posited Norfolk as a potential suitor of Mary before her marriage to Henry Stuart, Lord Darnley. Many of the English nobles who disliked Cecil's power and dominance at court were also willing to support a marriage between Norfolk and Mary. Even Robert Dudley, Earl of Leicester, Elizabeth's favourite courtier, realized that not only would this match bring Cecil down a peg or two, but it would appease Catholic Spain and France should Mary be restored as a result.

Some have suggested that Mary played a 'negligible' role in the marriage negotiations with Norfolk, being led by her advisors, including the Bishop of Ross and the Scottish secretary of state, William Maitland of Lethington, who saw an opportunity to bring about some kind of reconciliation in Scotland and gain continental support.[33] Yet, Mary's letters show she grasped the opportunities offered by this marriage. Though the couple never met, they communicated via regular letters, with Mary calling him 'my Norfolk' and assuring him that she would 'esteem and respect [him] in all [her] doings so long as I live'.[34] She sent him gifts including a pillow embroidered with the motto *Virescit in vulnere vultus* (virtue grows strong by wounding) and he sent her a diamond. She also had a miniature of herself painted and sent to him. Mary convinced herself, probably influenced by the urgings of Ross and Maitland, that Elizabeth would approve the marriage.

Elizabeth most certainly did not approve. When Leicester informed her of it in August 1569, she flew into a rage. Elizabeth was always sensitive about matches involving her nobles, and the addition of Mary to the picture was sure to set her on edge. Norfolk was shunned at court and eventually withdrew without Elizabeth's permission on 15 September 1569. Fearing that Norfolk would join openly with the northern earls in their rebellion, Elizabeth ordered him to return to her side, but he panicked, having heard that he would likely be sent to the Tower of London, and so he fled to his property of Kenninghall. After feigning illness for as long as he could, he reached out to the northern earls urging them not to go through with their plans because it would lead only to their own and his death.

He was indeed sent to the Tower in early October 1569 and remained there until August 1570. Mary was distraught, not only that Norfolk had been sent to prison but that Elizabeth had not approved their planned marriage. It was at this point that Huntingdon was appointed her additional custodian and her rooms searched at gunpoint; Cecil had seized the opportunity to turn Elizabeth even further from Mary's side. He wrote to Elizabeth on 6 October 1569, just before Norfolk was escorted to the Tower. In this note he bluntly explained that 'the Queen of Scots is and shall always be a dangerous person to your estate'.[35] Mary responded in kind, writing to Elizabeth herself. In this forthright letter, she set out three possible options, beseeching Elizabeth to finally take some action in her favour. First, Elizabeth could let Mary come and speak to her in person, as she had been desiring since she first returned to Scotland from France in 1561. Alternatively, let Mary leave England either to return to Scotland to face her fate there or to travel to France. Finally, Mary begged that if Elizabeth was determined to keep her prisoner, then put her to ransom so that someone might secure her freedom and she would no longer need to waste away in tears and vain regrets.[36]

WHILE NORFOLK LANGUISHED in the Tower, Mary turned her attention back to Scotland. In early 1570, she issued new commissions of lieutenancy to the Earl of Argyll and the Earl of Huntly. They were to be her leading nobles back home and they were permitted by her to issue proclamations on her behalf. Huntly set up an alternative justiciary in the north and north-east of Scotland, using a royal signet to issue documents in Mary's name. At Edinburgh her men had coins minted. It was becoming clear to Cecil that the policy of supporting Regent Moray over Mary was not to be as straightforward as he would have liked. By 1570 there was a distinctive split between the King's Men and the Queen's Men. Moray himself was threatened within Scotland when one William Stewart planned to assassinate him.

Stewart was captured and tortured before being executed. Unusually, he was condemned to suffer death by burning, marking his crime as 'treason', proclaiming Moray's legitimacy as the Regent of Scotland. It was a sign of the heinous nature of Stewart's crime that he was killed in such a fashion, but also a reflection of the political turmoil in Scotland at this time. Cecil breathed a sigh of relief that Moray had survived this attempt on his life, but nonetheless it was obvious to all onlookers that Scotland was descending into chaos. The early years of James VI's minority have been summed up as a period of dysfunction where 'factionalism was rife, and the administration was never stable'.[37]

On 23 January 1570, Moray was attacked once more. This time, the assassin was successful. James Hamilton of Bothwellhaugh shot Moray as he passed through Linlithgow, one of the first political assassinations by firearm. This was a dreadful, potentially fatal, blow to Cecil's Anglo-Scots policy. Mary, on the other hand, rejoiced when she heard of her half-brother's death. She even offered to pay a pension to Hamilton's family. Such a vindictive reaction, though perhaps understandable considering her own personal tragedies, puts paid to any romanticized suggestion that Mary was a soft touch who was quick to forgive. Scotland was to be without a regent for six months, during which time a new bitterness seeped into politics there as national government completely broke down. Cecil convinced Elizabeth that they must intervene, and she reluctantly agreed to send 1,000 troops with the Earl of Lennox, Lord Darnley's father, to pacify the country. Lennox was elected the next Regent of Scotland on 12 July 1570.

Elizabeth hoped that negotiations to restore Mary in some way to Scotland, perhaps ruling jointly with her son James, might now be restarted once more. But as the father of the murdered Darnley, Lennox was not willing to compromise. He also set about eliminating those who had been implicated in his son's death and offered no mercy to those captured. As Scotland fell into civil war, there were a series of rival parliaments, with tit-for-tat forfeits of property and titles. For every parliament held by the King's party, the Queen's supporters would hold one of their own. Mary's men held Edinburgh Castle and large parts of the town, giving them access to the official regalia, the Honours of Scotland, whereas the King's men were forced to create replicas for their own parliaments. On the other hand, Lennox held one key piece: James VI. The young boy was paraded at the parliament held by the King's party in Stirling, wearing his royal robes and delivering a short but well-rehearsed speech.

Despite Lennox's heavy-handed rule, most of the nobles in Scotland were still willing to see Mary restored and they still expected her to be released from her English captivity. Norfolk was freed from the Tower in August 1570, and in October Cecil travelled to meet with Mary personally to discuss the negotiations for her return to Scotland, further encouraging the Scottish nobles that the restitution of Mary may yet come to fruition. But just as things looked likely to finally come to a positive conclusion, a new plot was discovered.

ROBERTO RIDOLFI WAS an Italian banker who had established himself as a go-between for Mary, her representative the Bishop of Ross, and the King of Spain. By 1571, Norfolk was creeping out of the cautious attitude he had maintained toward Mary since his release from prison in August 1570. He, too, became a part of this circle around Ridolfi. Back in the summer of 1569, Ridolfi had first proposed an audacious plan to free Mary via Spanish military aid, calling his design the 'Enterprise of England'. He was briefly imprisoned in the home of Queen Elizabeth's chief spymaster, Sir Francis Walsingham, leading some to speculate that he was turned into a double agent.[38] By 1571 he had doubled down on his plan. Mary would be freed from her prison by Spanish troops sent by the Duke of Alva with the full support of Philip II of Spain. Elizabeth would be seized, and a newly married Mary and Norfolk would assume the throne. Initially, Philip wasn't keen on this plan because he doubted whether the English Catholics would rise against Elizabeth as Ridolfi claimed. Alva was scathing of Ridolfi's abilities as a conspirator, judging that he was more bark than bite. He also pointed out that if this plan were to be discovered by the English, then Mary could very likely be executed. Yet, Ridolfi continued to meet with the Spanish ambassador de Spes and made sure that a new cipher was made available to all the participants.

Ridolfi's plot was unveiled when a young man was arrested trying to enter England at the port of Dover carrying suspicious books and large packets of letters. Charles Bailly was a servant of the Bishop of Ross, and he was returning from the Spanish Netherlands where he had passed correspondence on to Alva and Philip. He was taken to the Tower of London where he was threatened 'very severe' by Cecil who told him that if they did not cut off his head they would make sure to cut off his ears.[39] Bailly quickly admitted Ross's role, leading to him also being arrested. When he too was threatened with torture, he caved and revealed all. Ross confessed that Ridolfi had carried papal funds, which had been distributed partly to Mary's supporters in Scotland via Norfolk. Ridolfi had sent £3,000 to Ross from ambassador de Spes and, crucially, Mary it seemed was fully aware of the transaction, placing her at the heart of the plot. During his interrogation Ross also claimed that Philip II had agreed to send Spanish troops to invade England, partly because Mary had assured him that she would marry James VI to his daughter, thus joining their countries for generations.

Any original instructions from Mary to Ridolfi have disappeared but he claimed that she had written to him complaining of the cruelty of her treatment in England and the persecution of Catholics there. She did ultimately confess to corresponding with him, but she refused to accept that she had ever countenanced any threatening action against Elizabeth. She had only sought Ridolfi's experience as an intermediary for financial support for her cause. Cecil tried to trick her into admitting her role more fully, suggesting that Elizabeth did not care that Norfolk and Mary had re-established their intended marriage nor was she offended by Mary's attempts to secure foreign funds. Mary would not take the bait and added nothing else to her testimony. She dismissed Ross's evidence, pointing out that any man could be forced to falsely confess when faced with the rack. She described him as a 'flayed priest' who was only saying what Cecil wanted to hear. Undoubtedly, if he were set at liberty to leave England, she claimed, he would 'unsay what he has said'.[40]

The Ridolfi plot had serious, long-term repercussions for Mary. Most dramatically, Norfolk was returned to the Tower and tried for high treason in January 1572. He was executed on 2 June and his remains buried in the chapel of St Peter ad Vincula in the Tower. Parliament subsequently debated whether Mary should also be tried for treason, with growing calls for her own execution. Elizabeth intervened personally to ensure that a bill of attainder was not issued against Mary. Yet Cecil found other ways to punish Mary for her links to the plots of the past few years. Using the papal bull of excommunication as evidence of Catholic disloyalty, he made sure that a motion was passed to exclude Mary from the English succession. He also personally made sure that the dossier of slanderous claims that George Buchanan, a former friend turned enemy of Mary, had produced back in 1568 was suddenly published. Translating the text from Latin into a pidgin Scots to make it look like the English were not behind it, *Ane detectioun of the duinges of Marie Quene of Scottes* (*A Detection of the Doings of Mary, Queen of Scots*) was printed in late 1571. Her household was reduced several times, so that by the time of Norfolk's death she was allowed only sixteen attendants. Lady Livingston left for Scotland to return to her children, though she did continue to be an active supporter of Mary. She regularly passed secret messages between Mary and her Scottish friends. This led to her being briefly imprisoned in Dalkeith, but she refused to talk and was eventually released.

In Scotland too, Mary's cause suffered from the tumultuous events of 1570–1572. The outcome of the Ridolfi Plot led most of her remaining supporters to submit to the new Regent John

Erskine, Earl of Mar, brother of Arthur Erskine, master of the horse who had helped rescue her and Darnley after Rizzio's murder in 1566. Mar was more conciliatory than his predecessor Lennox, who had been assassinated by Queen's men at Stirling in September 1571. He was weary of war and convinced his fellow nobles on both sides that it was time for a neutral political policy. Yet a small band of Mary's supporters refused to surrender. Led by her sometime opponent turned ally, Kirkcaldy of Grange and William Maitland of Lethington, they held Edinburgh Castle, clinging to hope that Spanish support would materialize. They held out until May 1573, undermining the Pacification of Perth which was agreed in February of that year to end the civil wars. By this time the regency had passed to James Douglas, 4th Earl of Morton, who was directly commanded by Elizabeth to get rid of them. She sent troops to storm Edinburgh Castle. Kirkcaldy was summarily executed, and Maitland died in prison. Elizabeth did tell Morton that there was to be no disrespectful treatment of Maitland's body, but Morton chose to lock the corpse up in a room until rats crept under the door and feasted on the dead man's flesh.

By the end of 1572, Mary had seen at least four plots to free her fail. Her Scottish supporters had been forced to submit. Cecil had convinced Elizabeth to give up on her half-hearted concern for her royal captive. She had now been kept a prisoner for almost five years. It was time to take stock of the opportunities left to her.

CHAPTER FOUR

The Everyday Life of a Captive Queen

5 [1]

What reputation, think you, will remain to you for permitting me, without any compassion to languish so many years in a miserable state? And by the continuation of the bad treatment that I have received up to now I am going to end my days already too prolonged? In truth, I do not value, seeing the great illness that I have had these past years, and the state in which I am still at present, my health, which is only to support longer the treatment to which I am accustomed by the past, being too young and strong for death in a short time to deliver me from it.[2]

LIFTING HER ARMS *high above her head, Mary lets the cool pale linen shift fall over her skin. She takes a moment to breathe in the fresh scent of the fabric, a hint of the lavender preferred by her laundress in the warm summer months. She seats herself on her low dressing chair, sinking into the deep green damask cushions and lifting one leg, then the other, she lets her ladies slip on her silk stockings, tying them with a bright scarlet ribbon above her knees.*

Though she expects no visitors today, she still has the maids lace her into a fine-boned bodice, barely noticing the strain, so often has she experienced this dressing routine. The willow-bent farthingale is tied to the corset sides, but she waves away the girl as she brings over the rowle. She chooses the dark grey kirtle laced through with gold thread to catch the lingering summer light. The black taffeta sides and arms are added before her favourite white silk partlet with the embroidery worked high up the neck.

As the maids fuss around her, flattening out any lumps that have gathered under the many layers, she turns her mind to how she will prepare her hair. It is too warm for a full cap, perhaps she will simply have Mary pin a simple lace coif to her hair with gold beads to match the golden-threaded kirtle. Yes, then the breeze will at least whisper around her neck if she is allowed to take a walk in the gardens.

Turning back to the girls she lets them add the black velvet gown and, expertly balanced, has them put on her satin-lined day shoes. Straightening herself she glances in the gilded looking-glass – her hair is looking bright after she had the ladies wash it with the dandelion tonic the day before. Now to find Mary and put the finishing touches to the mask before she faces her jailor and his men once more.

WHEN THE DUKE of Norfolk was executed in June 1572, it suddenly struck Mary how implacable the reality of her captivity was proving to be. Open rebellion had failed to secure her freedom and now one of her greatest supporters in the English court was dead. She succumbed once more to the debilitating effects of physical illness and mental distress, a situation that was to become chronic as her captivity dragged on. Eventually she was permitted to keep a doctor, a surgeon, and an apothecary in her household to avoid incessant requests for medical attention. All three men were French: Burgoyne, the doctor, Gervase, the surgeon, and Nico de la Warre, the apothecary.[3] She was becoming ever more untrusting of English servants brought in to attend her and managed to persuade Shrewsbury to keep her preferred French physicians on-site.

Mary suffered from the old pain in her side throughout her captive years, but other ailments, both acute and chronic, developed. She complained of painful constipation and wind which she was adamant would be relieved if only she be permitted to exercise more outdoors. Lack of movement and the damp environment at Tutbury undoubtedly exacerbated early-onset rheumatoid arthritis, leaving her with such pains in her heel that at times she could barely walk. Shrewsbury provided thick matted carpets for her chambers, but even these were no match for the sharp pains which ricocheted up her leg and she was forced to use one of her expensive turkey rugs in the dining room just to ease the discomfort enough so that she could eat.[4] Perhaps as a result of the rheumatism in her feet, her leg also became painfully swollen, though this may have been due to an ulcer which struggled to heal.

She often caught colds and other viruses which she blamed on the draughts that blasted through every room at Tutbury because it was so 'flimsily built' of wood and plaster.[5] Migraines and sinus pains plagued her, forcing her to retreat to her bed for days at a time. In 1575, Mary was also struck by a 'tertian fever' which had reduced her to 'great weakness', most likely malaria caught from the swampy lands surrounding Tutbury.[6] The relapsing nature of the virus might explain why she seemed to suffer similar symptoms – fever, chills, headaches, joint pain and general malaise – at regular intervals throughout her imprisonment years.

Needless to say, her mental health also deteriorated under such physical distress. At times, Mary would fall into an almost catatonic state, usually when she had received some distressing news. In 1573, Shrewsbury admitted that she asked him to stop giving her any updates from Scotland because he only ever had bad news for her. She admonished him that if she were ever to be able to 'seek by all means to content my health' she must 'give no more ear to any advertisements from Scotland'.[7] She remained prone to bouts of melancholy, at times weeping for so long and with such vehemence that her face would swell until the 'colour and complexion of her face is presently much decayed'.[8] And though she made an effort to appear positive and cheerful for her ladies and attendants, her captivity 'nipped her very near'.[9] These distressing episodes continued even after she began wearing an amethyst ring, which she had been told would ward off melancholy and after seeking out powdered unicorn horn from her ambassador in France.[10] At the time, this was believed to be a miracle cure and was astonishingly expensive; it was produced from narwhal tusks or rhino horn.

To improve her health, Mary asked Elizabeth if she could be permitted to travel to visit the spa at Buxton. She prepared an impassioned plea, sending her physician himself to deliver the letter and declaring that she had been so long destitute of health that she could scarcely persuade herself that she would ever recover at all.[11] Elizabeth was, on this occasion, sympathetic and allowed Mary to journey to the hot springs there, which had been popular since Roman times, though she made it very clear that Shrewsbury was to closely guard his charge and keep her interactions with the other visitors to a minimum. Eventually he built a secluded lodge for Mary at Buxton – ostensibly so that she could enjoy the waters privately, but in reality, in response to Elizabeth's directions that the visits only go ahead 'without peril'.[12] These summer visits to Buxton became a brief period of pleasure for Mary and she looked forward to them, though she was always disappointed not be able to join in the socializing that took place among the visitors who would play games after taking the waters. She did on two occasions bump into Robert Dudley, Earl of Leicester, using the opportunity to renew their correspondence after her departure. At Buxton, she would bathe in the healing waters and drink from the springs, both of which were commonly believed to bring about cures for a host of maladies.

MARY'S EMOTIONAL DISTRESS was made worse by the loss of her close attendants. Although she had agreed to cutting the size of her household when she first joined Shrewsbury's keeping at Tutbury, saying goodbye to some of her favourite servants left her bereft. She pestered Cecil and Elizabeth to prepare passports so that her departing servants could travel abroad, return to Scotland, or journey elsewhere in England.[13] She was determined to find other employment for them, instructing her ambassador to France, James Beaton, Archbishop of Glasgow, to secure positions for Angello Marie (Angel Mary) and Gelis Le Royde when they arrived in Paris. She commanded the Bishop of Ross to find employment for Robert Mackeson, who had offered her such 'faithful service', but was forced to return to Scotland after his dismissal by Shrewsbury.[14] A further young Scot, Laurence Gordon, was supported by Mary by being sent to Cambridge to study. George Robinson was offered a continued salary from her if he remained in London where he could help secure clothing, books and medicines for her as and when she needed. Ross warned her that Robinson might not be allowed to act on her behalf in London, because Cecil would be suspicious of the boy's purpose, but Mary assured him that all would be well because the young man couldn't read or write so he was not likely to get involved in 'intelligence making'.[15] It seems Ross had the better measure of things because Robinson did not appear again in Mary's lists of servants or in her receipts and accounts.

As her captivity continued, Mary lost more and more of her confidants. Agnes Fleming, Lady Livingston, left for Scotland by 1572 as we have seen, leaving only Mary Seton as her noble lady-in-waiting. Seton's own maid, Janet Lindsay, asked to retire in April 1576 with Shrewsbury noting that the continued close living had made the women fall out. Janet was permitted to go back to Scotland because Shrewsbury assured Cecil that 'there is no danger of her practising'.[16] Mary also asked permission for some servants to retire in 1578, including one of her most devoted women, Mademoiselle Rallay. Now seventy years old, Rallay had been in bed since Easter because of a 'great catarrh', which Mary claimed was brought on by the poor living conditions that she and her servants had been forced to endure. She chastised Elizabeth for the 'bad treatment they receive in this prison'.[17] If Rallay were allowed to leave, then Mary wanted the daughter of Jean Scott, Lady Ferniehurst to join her household and sought a passport for the girl. She was only about fourteen and Mary claimed that she could not cause any suspicion because of her age and sex. In fact, the girl's mother was a devoted supporter of Mary and she had already been caught acting as an intermediary between the queen and her supporters in Scotland and the continent. Lady Ferniehurst and Mary also sent coded letters to one another throughout the 1580s.[18] It seems unlikely therefore that the young girl was to be just another servant and instead she would have been expected to help facilitate continued close communication between Mary and Lady Ferniehurst.

Unsurprisingly, Cecil refused this request, having already intercepted some of the coded letters between the women. So instead, Mary asked that Margaret Fleming, Countess of Atholl and her young daughter come and attend her. The countess was Mary's former lady-in-waiting from the years of her personal reign in Scotland and was the sister of Agnes, Lady Livingston. Elizabeth, though, also refused to allow the countess or her daughter to join Mary. She seemed suspicious that Mary wanted these ladies, especially because the countess was believed to dabble in witchcraft and was reputed to have the gift of prophecy. The Countess of Atholl had been implicated in a prophecy which said Mary would inherit the throne of England and had also used her so-called 'occult' powers to transfer Mary's labour pains onto another woman during the birth of James VI.[19] There was no way Elizabeth was letting Mary have her own resident sorceress.

In 1583, Mary suffered the greatest heartbreak when Mary Seton requested leave to retire to France. Mary had been one of the queen's closest companions since Mary had travelled to France as a child in 1548. She was the only one of the 'four Marys' not to marry and as such remained with Mary during the tumultuous years of her personal reign, and even joined her in prison at Lochleven. After fifteen years in English captivity, Mary Seton decided the time was right for a fresh start. She had lost two potential suitors during these years; Christopher Norton, son of Sir Richard Norton, fell in love with her while they were both at Wingfield but was executed for his role in the Northern Rebellion of 1569, and Andrew Beaton, brother of Mary's ambassador to France, James Beaton, Archbishop of Glasgow, also asked for her hand. In 1572, Andrew Beaton had succeeded their brother John in the position of master of Mary's household in captivity.

Mary Seton was reluctant to marry Beaton because she had previously taken a vow of chastity, and she admitted that she feared that he was of too low status, but after being cajoled by Mary, she agreed to the match. She demanded though that a dispensation from theological experts be granted before they wed and so Beaton promptly set off to the Sorbonne. To Seton's despair and guilt, he died of smallpox in Paris on 5 November 1577.[20] Devasted though Mary was to lose her closest friend, she agreed that Seton could go to France, recognizing her devoted companionship and personal sacrifices. She joined the

Convent of St Pierre at Rheims, which was headed at that time by Renée de Lorraine, Mary, Queen of Scot's aunt. Seaton would outlive Mary by almost thirty years, dying in 1615.

In the final years of English captivity, Mary had few female attendants, none of whom were noble ladies. Those that remained were all Scotswomen. Elizabeth Curle and Jane Kennedy were with her until her execution, joining her on the scaffold. Elizabeth was the sister of Mary's Scottish secretary, Gilbert Curle, while Jane was a distant relative of Gilbert Kennedy, 4th Earl of Cassillis, one of Mary's noble supporters in Scotland. Jane had joined Mary's household around 1569 and remained with her until the queen's death. Mary trusted the young woman with some of her jewels and silver plate and some of her most luxurious garments including gowns, a cloak and various caps and collars.[21]

Gilbert Curle's wife, Barbara Mowbray, was also one of Mary's few remaining ladies-in-waiting. She joined the household in 1584 and married Gilbert the following year, after Mary arranged the match. It was suspected that the wedding ceremony had been conducted by a Catholic priest that Mary had continued to secretly maintain in her household. Though Cecil and other Protestant courtiers were furious at this, Elizabeth seemed less perturbed; in fact, Mary had expressly asked if she could keep a priest for her personal services promising that he would 'bear himself as secretly as possible'.[22]

Barbara's sister Geillis also became part of the group of female servants who stood by Mary until the end. Geillis had joined the household just before Barbara and Gilbert's wedding and served Mary as a maid. The wife of another of her male servants also remained close to Mary until the very end; Christine Hogg had married Mary's secretary Bastian Paget in 1567 (theirs was the wedding Mary attended on the night that her husband, Henry Stuart, Lord Darnley, was murdered) and had journeyed with her husband to join the queen in her various English prisons.

THROUGHOUT THE LONG years in England, Mary's emotional torment was sharpened by her separation from her young son. Various proposals were suggested that might have brought the young boy out of Scotland to either join his mother or be cared for by his godmother Elizabeth, but the Scots ultimately rejected all such plans because James's physical person was often the only thing keeping power in the Regent's hands. There was also a secret plot instigated by some of Mary's noble supporters in Scotland to kidnap the young prince and send him to France. In 1573, Lady Livingston was implicated in this scheme; she was directed to encourage other noble wives to persuade their husbands to take part. In a coded letter, William Maitland urged her before his own death to 'cast a bone to nourish them more earnestly to persuade their husband hereof'.[23]

Though she was not able to see her own son, Mary did enjoy the company of other children during her imprisonment. In 1578, Arbella Stuart came to live with her grandmother, Elizabeth Talbot, known as Bess of Hardwick, wife of the Earl of Shrewsbury. Mary was enchanted with the little girl. She was the daughter of Darnley's younger brother, Charles, who had married Bess's daughter Elizabeth Cavendish in 1574 in a match most likely planned by Bess and Charles's mother, Margaret Douglas, Countess of Lennox. Her birth was one of the means of reconciliation between Mary and her former mother-in-law the Countess of Lennox. They wrote letters to one another about the infant, as well as about the plight of Mary's own child and Margaret's grandson, James VI, kept hostage by, as they saw it, unworthy men and raised away from the true Catholic faith. Margaret thanked Mary for her 'good remembrance and bounty to our little daughter, here who one day may serve your highness' in 1574.[24]

Arbella was a very clever little girl, learning several languages, and Bess described her in a letter to Mary as their 'little pore creature' who was wise beyond her years.[25] Mary went to great effort to secure jewels that had been left in trust for Arbella by the Countess of Lennox upon her death. Yet Mary's joy in Arbella was short-lived. The girl had a dynastic claim to the English throne through her grandmother the Countess of Lennox. As long as Arbella was a child this was not a particular threat to Mary, but as the girl grew up, her grandmother Bess pushed her claim above that of Mary's own child, James VI.

Another of Bess's granddaughters joined Mary's personal household. Elizabeth Pierrepont, commonly known as Bess, was the daughter of Frances Cavendish and Sir Henry Pierrepont. Mary was named godparent to the little girl, and she doted on her, letting her eat at her table and even share her bed. Young Bess was still with Mary in 1584, when her parents abruptly tried to have her removed her from Mary's care. They had learned that Mary's French secretary, Claude Nau, wanted to marry their daughter and they were scandalized because he was of a lower social rank.

Frances Cavendish was convinced that Mary was encouraging the romance between Nau and the teenage Bess, though Mary protested that she had in fact been trying to secure a position for Bess in Elizabeth's household.[26] Despite her parent's wishes, Bess remained with Mary until late 1586, becoming implicated in the final plot which ultimately would lead to the queen's death by acting as a go-between for the queen and conspirators.

Not all the children in Mary's life at this time brought worry or frustration. Bastian Paget and Christine Hogg's children were part of the household, with their eldest daughter, Marie, even performing some little tasks for Mary when she was only around five years old. Mary paid the girl a token salary of 200 sous, but by the time of her death little Marie was now entrusted with several jewels and clothing.[27] Mary asked that the Duchess of Guise take Marie into her service, but it appears she remained with her parents.[28]

Mary also took great pleasure in the company of animals. Though she was rarely allowed to ride out, she loved horses and continued to make requests for quality mounts for herself and her servants. She also gathered about herself a pack of dogs of all shapes and sizes. She regularly wrote to the Archbishop of Glasgow in Paris asking him to find 'pretty little dogs' for her, reminding him to send them over to her kept safe and warm in baskets.[29] Shrewsbury also gifted her some prize spaniels, and though she lamented the fact that she wasn't allowed to see them in action out hunting, she nevertheless loved these beautiful creatures. She had been allowed to take part in hare-hunting when she first arrived at Carlisle Castle in 1568 but this was curtailed as the plots around her began to swirl.

IN THE FIFTEEN years that Mary would spend in Shrewsbury's custody, she would live in many of his properties. Though she loathed Tutbury, and wasn't particularly impressed with Wingfield Manor, she came to appreciate his principal house, Sheffield Castle. She was first moved there for a short time in November 1570 while Tutbury and Wingfield were being cleaned. It was common for nobles to move between their properties because this allowed servants to remove the detritus that built up while large households were based in one place. Not only were rooms aired and fresh rushes strewn on floors, but the toilets were emptied, and food waste and animal products removed.

Sheffield was an extensive property, built of stone rather than the draughty wood frame that Mary so hated at Tutbury. It had extensive parklands surrounding it, which she loved to explore on foot or on horseback when she was given the rare chance. Shrewsbury had also built a handsome manor in the grounds on the site of a former hunting lodge and Mary would often move between the two. She grew fond of Sheffield because she was allowed to spend longer periods here, ultimately being kept there for almost two years, the most settled period of her imprisonment.

She also enjoyed short spells at Chatsworth House in Derbyshire. Chatsworth was Bess's house, not Shrewsbury's; she had purchased it with her second husband Sir William Cavendish in 1549 and continued to alter and renovate the property throughout the 1580s. This was a luxurious house, with the latest fashions in architecture and interior design. When Mary was held there her rooms were on the east side of the house and the rooms are still known as the Queen of Scots' Apartments today. She first experienced Chatsworth for only a fortnight in May 1569, but she did spend longer periods there, sometimes up to three months. Her final visit was in July 1581.

Regardless of the location of Mary's imprisonment, she was maintained by Shrewsbury in the dignity befitting of her royal status. When in public she was seated on a raised platform under a cloth of state featuring the arms of Scotland, while her ladies would sit on stools that were always kept lower.[30] In her private chamber she also had a smaller cloth of state raised permanently above her chair. Her bed was always covered in the most luxurious furnishings: she preferred rich green dornick for curtains (a damask fabric) and always demanded the highest-grade linens for her sheets, which were changed every day. Her bedding and cushions were stuffed with the best duck feathers while her pillows were filled with goose down and covered in bleached cotton.[31] She had several luxury items on display in her public rooms including gilded mirrors, globes and French clocks.[32] Her walls were hung with more green dornick to keep in the warmth (especially as her allowance of wood for fuel was continually reduced) and she filled her rooms with turkey carpets, luxury rugs that were so expensive they were normally only used as table coverings.[33] Only royalty and the very wealthy could afford to actually walk upon turkey carpets.

Her day would begin when the sentries were called from their posts at 6 o'clock in the morning by a drum. Geillis Mowbray, Barbara Curle, Elizabeth Curle and Jane Kennedy would help Mary wash, often drawing her hot baths scented with herbs and flower petals. If she was not in the mood for a bath, she would apply a facial tonic made from the finest white wine to freshen her complexion and dust sweet-scented powder on her neck.[34] Mary then had Mary Seton, the 'finest dresser of a woman's head and hair that is to be seen in any country' prepare her hair in a different style each day.[35] Seton was adept at creating realistic hairstyles using sixteenth-century extensions, adding volume while Mary's hair took its time to grow back after she had cut it during her journey south.[36] As her health deteriorated Mary began to lose her hair more permanently and was forced to wear full wigs, but Seton continued to use 'pretty devices' to disguise this. She would pin golden bodkins into the style or attach lace veils using jet beads and diamonds.[37]

Great care was taken of her appearance each day. This was one of the few things that Mary still had some degree of control over during her years of captivity, and the comfort that she took from her beauty routine and from fashion should not be dismissed. It was also an attempt to reconstruct her royal status while she remained imprisoned by displaying her wealth and her taste through fabrics and jewellery. Mary had convinced her half-brother the Regent of Scotland, James Stewart, Earl of Moray, to send her some of her clothes and accessories from Scotland shortly after her arrival in England, and she enhanced her wardrobe by having friends and family in France send her garments, textiles, and the latest patterns so that she could recreate these fashionable styles.[38]

She preferred to dress in dark-hued clothing: russet kirtles, tawny or dark violet doublets, black velvet gowns. It was more difficult to maintain dark coloured dyes, which tended to fade quickly, and so these colours were a mark of wealth and status.

This was further emphasized by the fabrics she purchased: silks, satins, damasks and even cloth of gold. Additionally, her cloaks were furred with ermine and wolf-pelts and her petticoats with the softest lamb and rabbit fur.[39] Elizabeth had deigned to send some clothing to her when she first arrived in England but these were so embarrassingly tattered and out-of-date that Sir Francis Knollys had been forced to pretend they were actually meant for Mary's servants.[40] Nevertheless, Mary wrote to Elizabeth asking for fashionable patterns and sending hand-embroidered coifs as gifts, hoping that their shared love of clothing would help build a connection between them.[41]

She regularly instructed ambassador Beaton to purchase the latest ribbons, lace, hair coverings and veils and send them from Paris.[42] Each day she wore the finest silk stockings beneath her gowns, adding black velvet mufflers when she was feeling the chill, and alternating between her favoured lace veils and velvet caps topped with feathers.[43] She would wear one of two stoles, the first made from a pine marten with gold gilding on the head and feet and the neck set with diamonds and rubies, and the other made from a stoat which was similarly decorated.[44]

She emphasized her royal magnificence through jewellery: golden crosses, collars of pearls, chains of jet and coral, agate bracelets, gilded girdle chains, sapphire rings, enamelled brooches, necklaces hung with rubies, diamonds, and emeralds.[45] Yet she was also playful and somewhat magpie-like in her approach to accessories. At her death she gifted several curious brooches and pins of various designs including a little bow and arrow, a scorpion garnished with rubies, a golden tree with a lady sitting in the branches while a young boy pulls them down, cupid, and a scene from one of Aesop's fables. Her jewels also demonstrate her genuine love of animals: they included a little white enamel bear, a green enamelled bird, an amber hart, a red enamelled ox, and a golden horse.

After her ladies had helped her wash and dress, she would hear mass or go to confession if her priest was able to perform his roles without undue attention. Otherwise, she would spend some time in private prayer. Mornings were often spent on her correspondence, writing letters in her own hand when she was able to, or quickly drawing up notes and drafts, which her secretaries Curle and Nau would polish and translate and as necessary encipher. Writing letters was a time-consuming affair. If preparing a letter of request or one designed to persuade (as almost all of Mary's letters were at this stage) the paper would be pricked to produce faint guidelines so that the lines of text were evenly spaced and to keep letterforms even. After adding the content, the pages would be folded, often in intricate ways as we have seen, depending on the relationship between sender and recipient. For lengthy letters that ran to several pages of paper, this could be tricky and even slightly uncomfortable on the hands. A lock might be cut from the page and threaded through this final packet for security, or alternatively the packet could be sewn shut. Wax would then be melted over an open flame and sealed by pressing a device with arms or monograms to indicate the identity of the person sending the letter.

Letter-writing was also a messy business. Inevitably melted wax would drip onto desks and even sometimes splash onto clothing or skin. Her secretaries would have kept a ready supply of sharpened feather quills available for her and supervised the making of iron gall ink by her kitchen servants. Ink took considerable time to prepare and there would have been a servant consistently stirring away at a pot. Iron salts and powdered oak galls – swollen growths on trees caused by the larvae of certain wasps – were put in their own separate pots with equal parts wine and vinegar and left to ferment. The fermentation process created a darker ink, so it could not be rushed. After three or four days the gall mix was heated and then stirred into the pot of iron salts, with some gum Arabic added to thicken the blend. This final mixture was then left for another four days before it was finally ready to use. Recipes urged the maker to keep some dregs back and mix these with 'rain water (that hath stood long in a tub or vessel) … for the older the water is, the better it is and keep that until you make more ink'.[46]

Shrewsbury's accounts show that Mary had huge quantities of wine and vinegar delivered and while the higher-quality blends would have been for consuming, she was also using these products for her epistolary production.[47] After she had finished writing, she would have often found her fingers and hands ink-stained and so a quick freshen up with water and scented oils using her silver gilt ewer was needed before sitting down to eat.[48]

The main meal of the day was dinner which was usually served between 11 o'clock and noon. Mary was served from the finest silver plate and crystal glassware and washed her hands between each dish in a silver gilt dish.[49] At each meal, she had the choice of thirty-two different dishes, while her ladies would have nine and her secretaries seven. Leftovers, of which there were always lots, were provided to the other servants, but also to her dogs. The second meal was supper, usually served between 5 and 6 o'clock in winter and later around 7 o'clock in summer.[50]

On days when she would fast from meat, she would have her

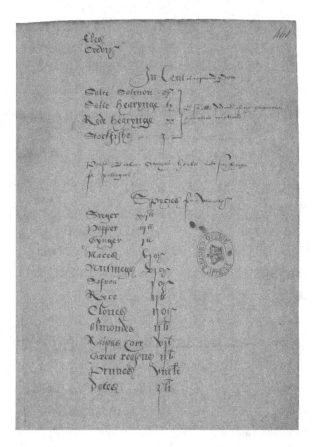

A note of the spices needed for preparing a month's worth of meals for Mary's household. The list of luxury flavourings includes: sugar, pepper, ginger, mace, nutmeg, saffron, rice, cloves, almonds, currants, great raisins, prunes and dates.

choice of a plethora of fish and seafood items, at least thirteen options per meal, including sole, skate, plaice and haddock, as well as crab and lobster. When they were in season and thus easily available, Mary preferred to have mussels and oysters on 'fish days' but she also enjoyed freshwater fish, such as salmon and bream, and regularly dined on eels. On the 'flesh' days – when she was not refraining from meat – at each meal she would be served a variation of recipes based on beef, veal, mutton, lamb, rabbit and pork. She preferred wild fowl to chicken but would accept capons if no wild fowl could be produced. All these dishes were flavoured with a variety of expensive spices from across the globe including capers, cloves, dates, figs, ginger, mace, nutmeg, olives, pepper, prunes, raisins and saffron. Meals were accompanied by manchet bread – the highest quality bread made from wheat – and pottage made from barley, onions and peas and seasoned with seasonal herbs. She would enjoy fine wines with her meals and in the evenings, but she also drank ale and small beer throughout the day. Up to twenty gallons of beer a day were needed for her personal use and to quench the thirst of her servants.[51]

To prepare these meals, Mary had her own kitchen staff, including a French master cook and a Scottish butler.[52] The dishes were served in silver dishes or little covered pots. Mary had her own trencher where her chosen bites would be placed and a set of silver spoons to eat with. She drank from crystal goblets, though she also had a mazer, a drinking cup without a stem made from a knot of maple wood and mounted with a silver-gilt band at the lip.[53] Throughout her captivity she was fearful that she would be poisoned, believing that her death would be covered up as part of her chronic illnesses; she had her servants taste her food and even sought out mithridate, a mythical concoction of ingredients that was believed to be an antidote to all known poisons.[54]

In the middle of the day, between dinner and supper, Mary would try to enjoy some physical activity. She would take long walks whenever she was able, even on one occasion joyously gambolling in the snow having been offered the opportunity to walk in the grounds during a snow-storm. Shrewsbury had hoped this would be so off-putting that Mary would stop asking him to be allowed outdoors for a bit.[55] If she was not permitted to exercise outdoors, she would walk in the great hall of whichever property she was held in.[56] Outdoors or inside, guards escorted her wherever she went, even following her to the rooftops when she sought solitude on the ramparts. Over time, even her ladies and her servants were shadowed by these armed sentries. By 1585, instructions were given that if any of her household were spotted out of bed during the night they were to be escorted back to their chambers and watched over or else sent to the porter's gate and held there until morning.[57]

Though she was no longer allowed to enjoy hunting, she still longed to be able to ride. Just a few years before her death, she finally accepted that she was not going to enjoy riding again and that such a privilege was never to be extended to her. Instead, she requested a coach pulled by two mares that could carry her while she took the air accompanied by her female servants. Though she would not be permitted, nor by this late stage was she physically able, to ride, she still wanted six geldings for her ladies to ride alongside her.[58] She also argued that if she were only able to use a carriage then she should be given more freedom to explore beyond the immediate grounds of her prisons because she was less likely to be able to escape, but once again this request was turned down.[59] Instead she was given an English coachman, one of the few servants who were not Scots or French and not directly appointed by Mary. Roger Sharp was clearly considered more trustworthy by her jailers, though he did stay in Mary's service until her execution.[60]

5

WHEN NOT ATTENDING to her correspondence or taking exercise, Mary spent much of her time embroidering. She had first learned the skills of fine needlework in France as a young girl and she continued to enjoy sewing during her personal reign. John Knox, leader of the Scottish Reformation and a vocal critic of Mary's, even complained that she preferred to sit at her embroidery during privy council meetings than engage with the business of state. Embroidery became a further solace for her during her imprisonment at Lochleven Castle where she would often sew in the company of her jailer's mother, Lady Margaret Erskine, and her sister-in-law Annas Keith, Countess of Moray. During her English captivity she once again enjoyed a women's sewing circle. Shrewsbury reported that Mary regularly joined his wife Bess at embroidery, writing to Cecil that; 'she sit working with the needle in which she much delighteth and in devising of works'.[61] He was at pains to point out that this was a perfectly innocent activity, adding that Queen Mary, his wife, Mary Seton and Lady Livingston (while she was still there) would chatter as they sewed but that 'their talk is altogether of indifferent and trifling matters without mentioning any sign of secret dealing or practice'. Needlework was one of the accepted, if stereotyped, pursuits of noblewomen, and though he assured Cecil that he was sure there could 'ensue no danger' from the communal embroidery, he would nevertheless 'make such straight restraint therein as shall please her highness to command'.[62] Shrewsbury was at such pains to emphasize the mundane nature of the women's interactions because he had been expressly told that he was to keep interactions between them to a minimum.[63]

Mary and the Countess of Shrewsbury struck up something of a friendship over their shared love of needlework. They produced several remarkable tapestries together which survive at Hardwick Hall and Oxburgh Hall, with the most famous showing a small mouse being tormented by a large ginger cat – an emblem for the relationship between Elizabeth and Mary. Mary signed her pieces 'MR' for Mary Regina or Mary the Queen, or with a monogram based on the Greek letter 'M'. At the same time, she sent gifts embroidered by herself to Elizabeth and to her French relatives. By the time of her death there were several unfinished pieces in her possession, as well as completed items such as embroidered pillows and canopies for her bedchamber. She had several small chests filled with samples, sewing threads and rolls of fabrics, ready to be used at her pleasure.[64] She also employed a French embroiderer, Charles Plonnart, in her household who would draw up the designs that she could then complete in thread.[65]

THE FRIENDLY RELATIONSHIP between Mary and her jailor's wife was short-lived. After months of simmering tensions grown from the everyday frustrations of living on top of one another, their friendship spectacularly blew apart, with tit-for-tat swipes at one another until Mary's death in 1587. When Bess and Shrewsbury married, she had been married three times before and had gained status with each. Her marriages had proved successful, with her second husband referring to her as his 'Good Besse' and her third as his 'own sweet Bess', and she ensured influential marriages for her sons and her daughters.[66]

Bess and Shrewsbury themselves also had a happy marriage at first, and he found her assertiveness and ambition attractive qualities, genuinely looking forward to being in her company.[67] But sadly their marriage disintegrated, in large part because of the continual stress of guarding Mary. Living on top of one another for so long, resentments inevitably built. The cost of housing Mary plagued Shrewsbury; he was forever writing to London seeking bills to be paid and his allowance for the costs to be sent to him. Though he was supposed to receive a regular payment to cover the costs of hosting a queen in royal estate, in reality he bore this burden himself. Mary, too, refused to contribute more than the bare minimum from her French dower funds because she would not countenance paying for her own imprisonment.

In 1581, he begged Elizabeth to release him from his role as Mary's keeper, lamenting that he had not been able to attend court and advance his own interests for far too long.[68] He was demented when his allowance was cut without explanation. Bess in the meantime alienated Mary by pursuing Arbella's claim to the throne at the expense of James VI. She also grew bitter about the costs of hosting the queen without any real benefit to themselves because Elizabeth was willing only to offer general thanks and commendations to Shrewsbury rather than any financial and or influential rewards. Both resentment towards her husband and towards Mary coalesced in Bess gossiping that Mary had seduced Shrewsbury. This was completely untrue, and Mary reasonably reacted with outrage. Her response was to compose a vitriolic letter listing all the disrespectful things that Bess had told her about Elizabeth, notably that the queen was sleeping with Leicester. Elizabeth seems never to have read this document, but she did force Bess to publicly apologize to Mary and admit that she had fabricated the story of an affair between the Scottish queen and her jailer. When Bess made an effort to rekindle their friendship in 1586, Mary was suspicious that she was only trying to gather information about various schemes in motion for Mary's liberty. She was unwilling to mend bridges, preferring to hold tight to the grudge she bore against Bess for her scandalous mutterings; in a coded letter to the new French ambassador, Guillaume de L'Aubespine, she explained:

> *I tell you plainly that her extreme ingratitude and the terms she has employed against me do not permit me with my honour (which I have more sought than all the greatness in the world) ever to have anything to do with so wicked a woman.*[69]

Biographers have tended to present Shrewsbury's failure to keep his wife and his charge apart as part of a broader weak-willed personality.[70] At the same time, Bess suffers from that tired gender trope of the domineering wife. She is also cast rather haughtily and certainly unfairly in the role of social climber whose desire for material wealth and status drove her poor, noble husband to despair. Her property and land acquisitions, and her forceful negotiations on behalf of her children and grandchildren, have been framed disdainfully as the absorptions of a 'woman of lofty pride, quick jealousy, and an almost insatiable ambition for herself and her children'.[71] No matter that these were in fact markers of personal success in the sixteenth century.

To enhance your own position and to preserve your dynasty were the key aims of gentry and nobility, and Bess was an expert at both. Bess, like many of her contemporaries, has suffered from gendered ideals of femininity, where ambition is seen to be something distasteful in a woman. Traditionally biographers have tried to place Mary in opposition to Bess, to emphasize the 'acceptable' qualities that Mary embodied as opposed to the less 'attractive' ones Bess displayed. One went so far as to claim that Bess was 'the exact opposite in nature to her new charge Mary Stuart, who was so feminine in both brain and intuition, and if proud, was also full of generosity and feeling towards others'.[72] Not only does this assessment unfairly slander Bess, who was close to her daughters throughout her life, inspired loyalty and devotion from her servants, and suffered an acrimonious separation from her husband, Shrewsbury, but it romanticizes Mary and insults her very human responses to the trials of her life. This was the woman, remember, who threatened her former sister-in-law, Annas Keith, with violence to her children if she did not give up royal jewels.[73] This was despite having rushed to comfort Annas after she lost a newborn son and Annas, in turn, sitting by Mary's bedside and nursing her through a miscarriage.

In the evenings, when it was harder to continue sewing by candlelight, even the white wax ones she had bought for her chambers, Mary would turn occasionally to music.[74] She had a pair of lutes and a book of music for the instruments in her possession, as well as a set of virginals.[75] She may have played herself, or she could direct her ladies to perform for her, accompanied by singing.

She would also recite poetry – including her own compositions – or read from books before retiring for bed. She would be stripped by the fireside by her ladies and dressed in a white linen nightshift, usually donning a furred night-cloak to keep off the chill while she said her prayers. One of her ladies would join her in bed where they would listen for the sentry drum announcing that the gates were to be locked at 11 p.m. As day after day slipped away, Mary roused herself once more and turned her sights this time to outside help. An English marriage hadn't worked out for her, but that didn't mean a foreign one wouldn't make a difference. English rebels hadn't managed to secure her freedom, but now it was time to bring in the big guns.

CHAPTER FIVE

Dons and Dukes

30.[1]

*If it should happen also that access to me
and news are restricted, you will be able
(under feint of sending me some book) to
write in white with interlines (alum seems
to be the best or nutgall). And although such
artifices be very hazardous and vulgar, they
will serve me in extreme necessity by way
and conduct of the carrier of this place.*[2]

D ON JUAN OF Austria watched the actors cavort across the floor.
Their costumes glittered and glimmered in the candlelight. He
had lost track of the story but the dark stained horns on the mask of
the man lurching out of the shadows suggested some kind of battle
between good and evil. Or was it the forces of chaos?

He had barely paid attention when they announced the title

of the drama that was to be performed that night. His attention had wandered, as it tended to, towards the young ladies seated together across the room. Most glanced at him and looked away, blushing, turning back to the masque, or else giggling and leaning into one another. One or two avoided his eye completely, silently communicating their resentment towards him.

He had no plans for seduction tonight. He was tired from riding out all day, first to inspect the troops, and then racing with his men across the flat open fields, revelling in the exhilaration of the rushing air and the pounding hooves. He stretched out his long legs, luxuriating in the slight discomfort in his muscles that came with a good day's riding. Besides, his thoughts had been returning again and again to another woman. A woman miles away from this court, a woman he had never even met. A woman of spirit they told him. One who shared his love of horses. She, too, took pleasure in quick remarks and witty conversations, relishing a night of good company. And yet, this unknown woman was a lady of faith, a lady of resilience and determination. She could bring him a crown of his own, letting him step out from the shadows of his brother.

Yes, he mused as the server filled his glass with more of the deep red wines he had brought over from Spain, this was a woman well suited to him. Mary Stewart, the Queen of Scots...

WHEN MARY DECIDED to look outside of England for help with her new plans for freedom, her thoughts naturally turned at first to France. She had after all been Queen of France and she was still a member of the powerful Guise family through her mother. Sadly, she was to suffer another disappointment: on Christmas Day in 1574, her uncle Charles, Cardinal of Lorraine died. Lorraine had been at the centre of the French court for decades and was committed to the enhancement of his family and the preservation of the Catholic faith in France, which he feared was under threat from the Huguenots. His death devasted Mary because he had been a figure of wise counsel throughout her life. He had written a coded letter to her earlier that year, reassuring her of his continued efforts on her behalf, but urging 'since you have so much patience, dissimulate still a little and do not embitter anything'.[3] She also realized that with his death she was now reliant upon Guise relatives whom she barely knew – some of whom she had never even seen in the flesh. Lorraine's brother, Francis, Duke of Guise had been assassinated in 1563 during confrontations with Huguenots in Orleans, bleeding to death over several days. Though her beloved grandmother Antoinette de Bourbon still lived, her influence had diminished, and Mary found that her letters were starting to drift gradually into silence.

The death of the duke and the cardinal had stuck severe wounds in the Guise network, but the duke's son and heir, Henri, had slowly been establishing his position at the heart of French politics after a few years fighting against the Ottomans and in the battles which plagued France during the wars of religion in the late 1560s and 1570s between Catholics and Protestants. He would become a dedicated supporter of Mary, monitoring the Duke of Norfolk marriage proposal and establishing contact with Ridolfi. In 1572, he helped persuade the French king to contribute several thousand francs to Mary's Scottish nobles.[4] While the young Guise would become one of Mary's most committed supporters at this point in her captivity, at the same time her captivity was useful propaganda for his campaign against Protestantism within France and beyond which had been growing ever more violent since he set up the Catholic League in 1576. He was a bombastic figure, steadfast in his hatred of the French Protestants who he felt had not been punished enough for the assassination of his father, Francis. His military career had left him with a scar on his face and the nickname Le Balafré – Scarface. But he was also charming and was unafraid to use his broad set of skills to get what he wanted, alternately playing the enchanter and the enforcer.

All the same, despite his wish to help Mary, Guise's ability to take any direct action on her behalf at this point was stymied by the wars of religion in France and by his need to re-establish the Guise dynasty as a powerful player at Court. He was also distracted by the charms of Margaret of Valois, daughter of Henri II of France and Catherine de' Medici. The two embarked on a brief but passionate affair, with some claiming that Guise genuinely thought to claim Margaret as his wife. Catherine de' Medici and her royal sons were unimpressed by Guise's attempts to woo Margaret, fearing that a revived Guise faction would be destabilizing for France. They had other plans for the marriage of the French princess; Margaret was instead wed to the Protestant Henri of Navarre as part of the peace treaty negotiated to end the religious troubles.

The year 1574 proved to be somewhat of an *annus horribilis* for Mary's French network, because in May of that year the King of France, Charles IX, also died. He had suffered for some time from what may have been tuberculosis and finally succumbed on 30 May. Catherine de' Medici claimed the regency while her son Henri III of France returned from Poland where he had only recently been elected king. He had not expected to succeed to the throne of France, being Catherine and Henri II's fourth son.[5] Despite being Mary's former mother-in-law, Catherine was not especially disposed to support her. She had been keen for Mary to leave the French court following the death of Mary's first husband Francis in 1560 and she was reluctant to antagonize Elizabeth by seeming to interfere with Mary's captivity as it dragged on into the 1570s. She would in fact become dedicated to securing a marriage between her youngest son, Francis, Duke of Anjou, and Elizabeth, so it was not in her interest to rock the boat for Mary's sake. Catherine always claimed that her first duty was to preserve the kingdom of France. Mary, as far as Catherine was concerned, was no longer France's responsibility.

Realizing that her French relations were not in a position to offer a great deal of practical support at this stage, Mary looked elsewhere. As she had done during periods of crisis before, including when she was still a reigning queen of Scotland, she reached out to King Philip II of Spain. If anyone would be able to secure her release in the mid-1570s, it was Philip. He was the most powerful Catholic king in Europe, reigning over territories that stretched from Spain to the Netherlands and into the lands that had been colonized and exploited in the Americas. Philip had the funds and the men necessary to undertake a successful military enterprise to free Mary. Unfortunately, if Mary was aware of Philip's potential, so were her English captors.

Cecil urged his spies to report the merest hint of any connections between Mary and Spain, noting that though the French threat was not dead, it was certainly dormant for the moment. His papers show how obsessed he became: formal intelligence reports, notes, gossip, rumours, surveillance reports, intercepted letters, all these documents were gathered and carefully analysed. He scribbled notes in the margins and underlined phrases and entire passages that he felt might offer some clue as to the extent of the communication between Mary and Philip. In 1573, the English ambassador to Scotland, Henry Killigrew was even sending Cecil updates on the 'bruits' or the chatter there on the growing conspiracy between Spain and the papacy on Mary's behalf.[6] The same plots were still being discussed in 1577 when Sir Francis Walsingham wrote to the Regent of Scotland, James Douglas, Earl of Morton.[7] This time around it seemed Mary was willing to play the long game; rather than rushing into schemes, she was content to take the time needed to allow plans for her liberty to develop.

The Spanish policy eventually coalesced into two avenues: a marriage and a military enterprise. Mary's marriage to the Duke of Norfolk might have failed, and the Northern Rebellion hadn't led to much success, but this time she had the might of Spain behind her. The planned marriage was to Don Juan of Austria, the younger, illegitimate half-brother of Philip II of Spain. He was born in Regensburg but was quickly moved to Spain where he was raised by a noble family before being formally recognized in his father, Charles V's, final will. He was an accomplished soldier, leading the papal and Spanish forces in their naval success against the Ottomans at the Battle of Lepanto in 1571. He was later sent by his brother, now King of Spain, to take up the position of Governor of the Spanish Netherlands. Don Juan was tall and athletic, with dark hair and a fashionable moustache. He was recognized as a capable military tactician but also an amiable man who made people feel at ease in his company. Dr Thomas Wilson, a diplomat, wrote to Leicester from the Spanish Netherlands that Don Juan 'who follows his own delight, rides his horses in the daytime and entertains in the night, gives audience easily to all'.[8]

A marriage between Mary and Don Juan had in fact first been mooted several years earlier. In 1571, following the victory at Lepanto, Philip began encouraging the match, believing that bringing the 'champion of Christendom' together with the Catholic Queen of Scotland – and potential heir to England – was a powerful move. But this was right in the middle of the negotiations with Norfolk and while Don Juan was an intriguing figure, Mary had committed, at least at that point, to her plan to seek her liberty through less violent means. Any match with a Spanish prince would be sure to stir up anger and retaliation among her English enemies. Norfolk, for the moment at least, was the better option in her eyes. Keeping the letter ciphered to avoid drawing attention to the link with Don Juan, she wrote to the Bishop of Ross explaining that even though the marriage was not something she wished to pursue, she hoped this would not cause Philip II of Spain to abandon her cause.[9]

Cecil got wind of Philip's offered match and examined Mary's agent and courier Robert Melville in great detail about it.[10] He was terrified that Mary would actually agree to the marriage to Don Juan and that there would be an invasion of Spanish forces via the Spanish Netherlands. This was not totally unfounded on his part, for while Mary was privately confessing to Ross that she was not interested in marrying Don Juan, she was encouraging her Scottish supporters to keep this avenue open so as to not alienate the Spanish king.

One of the most prominent of her Scottish supporters, George, Lord Seton, noted in his commonplace book at this time that there were great efforts being made on Mary's behalf by the English and Scottish exiles on the continent to encourage Philip to intercede directly on her behalf. Seton claimed that there would be huge numbers who would rush to join the Spanish if they invaded England, while many of the Scots nobles would also rejoin her cause.[11] Shrewsbury clearly felt there was some genuine threat behind these rumours when he wrote to Cecil noting that he was 'glad of Alva's troubles at home hoping thereby of more quietness elsewhere for this queen makes account that he will do much in her causes'.[12] The Duke of Alva, Fernando Álvarez de Toledo, was the Governor of the Spanish Netherlands from 1567 until 1573 and was at this point struggling to deal with a series of rebellions against Spanish rule there. But for these difficulties, Shrewsbury feared, then Philip might have been more determined to push through the marriage of Mary and Don Juan.

By 1575, with the Norfolk marriage fading into past failures, this new marriage was very much part of Mary's strategy to secure Spanish aid and military support for her freedom. Her old ally Lady Anne Percy, Countess of Northumberland began petitioning on Mary's behalf from her exile in the Spanish Netherlands. Mary noted in a coded letter from August 1576 that Anne had communicated with her about the possible marriage to Don Juan and the benefits this would bring to her cause.[13] Joining forces with Sir Francis Englefield, a fellow Catholic exile, she shared intelligence with Spanish agents on Shrewsbury's properties, suggesting the best means to approach the houses and how many men and horses might be needed if a force was sent to spirit Mary away from her prison. Lady Anne made an impassioned speech on Mary's behalf to the Duke of Alva, while Leonard Dacre was elected as a representative to travel to Spain to petition Philip II directly.[14] Mary had continued to offer financial support to the English exiles, but they also coalesced around her because of their shared faith and their desire to see the restoration of a Catholic monarch in Scotland and England.[15]

Philip responded quite enthusiastically but with his traditional strategic approach. He encouraged the Pope to rescind the bull of excommunication against Elizabeth, arguing that this had only hindered Mary's cause.[16] In many respects he was right, because this continued to fuel Cecil's fear that the English Catholics were willing to rise up against Elizabeth knowing they were resolved of any sin. But Cecil was not buying this apparently generous move and redoubled his efforts to find evidence of connections between Mary and Spain. He was sure that when Andrew Beaton travelled to the continent to seek Mary Seton's dispensation that the real reason for the trip was to meet with Spanish agents to discuss the final details for the marriage between Mary and Don Juan.[17] Shrewsbury agreed, writing that Beaton was 'too good a Spaniard' who had corrupted some of his own servants and tricked him into thinking he was a good man who was not involved in the plots.[18] There was no actual evidence that Beaton was intending to travel any farther afield than Paris, and when this became evident after his death there, Cecil looked instead at Andrew's relation James Beaton, Archbishop of Glasgow. Though Glasgow was Mary's ambassador to France, he was suspected of acting as a go-between for Mary and Spain. When he took a trip to the mineral springs at Spa in the Spanish Netherlands (modern-day Belgium), Mary warned him in another coded letter to be on his guard because the English thought he was actually going there to meet Don Juan to discuss the marriage and other 'practices and enterprises'.[19]

There was one slight problem which might curtail any Spanish match before it even began: technically Mary was still married. Bothwell had fled from Scotland after the Battle of Carberry Hill in June 1567 and had ended up in a Danish prison. Yet he still lived. Mary had refused to divorce him while imprisoned at Lochleven because she didn't want to make the baby she was carrying illegitimate. Mary sent the Bishop of Ross to Rome to seek a papal dispensation, claiming that their marriage must be annulled. First, she emphasized that she had been coerced into marrying Bothwell and therefore this could not be recognized in the eyes of the church or the law. But Mary also claimed that Bothwell had never had his previous marriage to Jean Gordon, by this time Countess of Sutherland, nullified and so her own marriage to him was void. This was a flimsy attempt to gain an annulment because both she and Bothwell had made much of the fact that his marriage to Jean had in fact been dissolved back in 1567. Jean Gordon also continued to possess a copy of the annulment and held on to it until her death in 1629 at the age of 83. In 1578, Ross instructed depositions to be drawn up setting out the case for Mary and Bothwell's marriage to be voided, but before these could be presented to the Pope, Bothwell died. He had suffered a horrific captivity chained to a post in his Danish prison and had been driven mad by his confinement.

30

MARY'S POTENTIAL MARRIAGE to Don Juan of Austria was intimately tied up with a secondary scheme that was supported by King Philip II of Spain. He had been persuaded by Pope Gregory XIII to support an 'expedition' against England. But this enterprise would be a proxy war; rather than directly attacking England, forces would land in Ireland and re-establish Catholic rule there. Ireland had long been seen as a threat by Cecil, Walsingham and others, and Mary's influence with the men of that country had been suspected ever since her early years of captivity when she had used her Gaelic connections to threaten foreign support against England. The Earl of Sussex expressed what many English nobles thought when he wrote that when it came to Ireland he 'often wished [it] to be sunk in the sea' because through that country they might 'endure such a ruin to England I am afeared to think on'.[20]

Throughout the 1560s, England had pursued an Anglo-Scottish policy that aimed to curb the travel between Ireland and the west coast of Scotland, which had long been a mercenary route, in an effort to finally subdue those who Elizabeth saw as rebels. Ireland was seen as a potential back door to England; in the past it had been the French who threatened to use it, but now Spain had begun investigating its potential. Lord Seton had claimed that the people of Ireland supported Mary's right to the English crown, largely because of her faith, and that they 'love and adore her as the rising sun'.[21]

Though he might have overexaggerated things a little, Philip, too, recognized that the Irish route might be an effective way to gain Mary's freedom. If Spain were to have a threatening presence so close to England's borders, perhaps Elizabeth might be more willing to agree to let Mary leave her captivity. Mary herself suggested that she could be transported to Ireland once Philip's men landed and from there make her way to the Spanish Netherlands to marry Don Juan. She later confessed that Spain was the most suited to her relief from captivity, so it was imperative that she and her agents and supporters encouraged Philip to continue to 'embrace her cause'.[22]

The Irish expedition was led by an English mercenary, Thomas Stukely. A Catholic exile, he had fought alongside Don Juan at the Battle of Lepanto in 1571 and had spent several years in Ireland. By 1575 he was in Rome mingling with English Jesuits and Irish malcontents. He was also in correspondence with Lady Anne Percy, who encouraged him in his pursuits.[23] Pope Gregory XIII provided Stukely with several thousand men and they set out for Ireland in March 1578. After a stop in Cadiz to refit their ships, Stukely abandoned the plan and sailed instead for Morocco to aid the Portuguese there. He had sent his Irish men home in advance and some did attempt a small-scale rebellion there, but this ultimately came to naught. Stukely, meanwhile, was struck by a cannonball in August 1578 and died of his wounds.

Mary might have been focused on how she could escape to Ireland in the first instance, but her intended husband planned a more direct route. He entreated his brother to let him use the cover of the Irish expedition to journey to England and rescue Mary. Though his plan was encouraged by Pope Gregory XIII, Mary seemed reluctant at this stage to countenance such an approach. In one of the newly decoded letters, we learn of her fears should Don Juan's plan be discovered. She was sure that Cecil would have her moved from Shrewsbury's keeping and placed in an even worse prison.[24] She also wrote to the Archbishop of Glasgow telling him of these same fears, explicitly stating that she would be in genuine danger if Don Juan were to land in England.[25] One of his couriers was intercepted in France carrying a letter about his proposed plan to free Mary and the news quickly made its way back to England. She complained that this meant her own letters were subject to even more surveillance by Cecil because he was determined to find letters between herself and Don Juan.[26]

In 1578, Cecil sent out a list of questions for the Spanish ambassador to England, Antonio de Guarás. Cecil specifically asked what letters the ambassador had carried for Don Juan and Mary and how far the marriage negotiations had reached.[27] No such letters have yet come to light, though it is likely that if Mary did manage to receive any letters directly from him these would have been destroyed to avoid falling into the wrong hands.

Cecil was taking no chances; he seems to have encouraged the English diplomat Dr Thomas Wilson to try to kidnap Don Juan so as to prevent the marriage from ever being realized. Guarás wrote a slightly hysterical letter on 20 September 1577 claiming that Wilson was trying to deprive Don Juan of his liberty and that the English meant to 'treat him as they do Mary'.[28] Mary, meanwhile, felt that Wilson could be kept quiet and suggested winning over his wife with gifts.[29] In the end, such measures were not necessary in any case. In January 1578, Cecil was alarmed to discover that the papal nuncio Philippe Sega had arrived in the Spanish Netherlands carrying the astronomical sum of 50,000 écus from Pope Gregory XIII. The funds were to be used by Don Juan to enter England on his quest to free Mary. Instead, he was forced to use this money in his campaign against the rebels in the Spanish Netherlands. Fortunately for the English, he suffered defeat at the Battle of Rijmenam on 31 July and he subsequently caught a fever. By October 1578, Don Juan of Austria was dead. Mary's hopes that a Spanish marriage would lead to her freedom were crushed.

30

SPAIN MIGHT HAVE been the focus of Mary's plans for freedom during the early to mid-1570s, but she had at the same time never really given up hope for Scotland. In fact, she tried to bring both countries together, encouraging Philip to marry one of his daughters to her son, James. Catherine de' Medici in turn offered a French princess to the young Scottish king, irritating Mary.[30] Though she longed to be restored to the Scottish throne, by the mid-1570s Mary was beginning to recognize that there might be another way that she could return home. It might be possible for her to rule Scotland jointly with her young son. Not only would this satisfy some of those nobles who had turned against her there, but it would also appease Elizabeth. While Mary was unhappy that James had been raised in the Protestant faith, she nevertheless continued to demonstrate 'zealous natural care' for her 'sweet and peerless jewel'.[31] In one of the newly decoded letters, Mary admitted that she would even agree to remain in captivity in England if Elizabeth would agree to her, and therefore also to James's, right to succeed to the English throne.[32]

In 1579, a new opportunity arose for Mary to reignite her Scottish plans. Esmé Stuart, 6th Seigneur d'Aubigny, arrived in Scotland from France and quickly captured the teenage James's attention. Aubigny was the first cousin of James's father, Henry Stuart, Lord Darnley and had become the heir to the Lennox title after Darnley's brother, Charles Stuart, 5th Earl of Lennox, died in 1576. Aubigny had returned to Scotland to claim this inheritance to the Earldom of Lennox. The English, and many of the Scots, suspected that Aubigny had really been sent to Scotland as a representative of Mary's cousin Henri, Duke of Guise. He was given several positions of prominence at the Scottish court and was awarded the title Earl of Lennox in March 1580. Elizabeth watched with increasing alarm as his influence grew; her anxiety reached a peak in December of that year when Aubigny led the accusations against the Regent Morton leading to his downfall, imprisonment and eventual execution. Cecil drew up a note of intelligence on 3 February 1581 discussing whether Aubigny had practiced with Mary and was acting as an intermediary between her and Guise.[33] The Privy Council also instructed Henry Carey, Lord Hunsdon to prepare up to 10,000 troops to be ready to enter Scotland because they expected Aubigny to have 'timely maintenance from foreign parts.'[34]

Mary was thrilled with Aubigny's ascent and overjoyed to see her son receptive to Guise's influence. Guise proposed an association whereby Mary and James would rule Scotland jointly, expecting Aubigny to convince James to agree. By this time though, Aubigny seems to have become genuinely fond of James, even converting from Catholicism to Protestantism. He suggested that James should only agree to the association if he were to retain his title, being King of Scotland, while Mary would be Queen Mother. To Guise's shock, Aubigny informed him that any plans for Mary's freedom would have to be organized by Guise, and that Scottish lords should not involve themselves directly in her release because this would prejudice their relationship with England.[35] Mary refused to accept the title of Queen Mother, though she was still receptive to the association and tried to get Elizabeth to see the benefits. She asked that her French secretary, Nau, be allowed to travel to Scotland to find out more and to act as her representative. This was never allowed, and she was forced to confess in a coded letter that she feared her letters regarding the association were being intercepted because the English were still undecided about its merits.[36]

In early 1582, the Spanish connection was once more linking up with Mary's Scottish plans. Two Jesuits, William Crichton and William Holt, made contact with Aubigny. They informed him that Philip II would be willing to raise an army to free Mary, but rather than returning her to Scotland to rule jointly with James, this force would set Mary on the English throne. The visit was quickly being discussed in the Edinburgh taverns and before long it was reported to Cecil. King James was forced to issue a proclamation denying that Aubigny had conspired against Elizabeth, even though Aubigny himself had written to Mary offering assurance: 'Courage then your majesty for you shall find servitors determined to offer their lives in your cause.'[37]

Though Mary was pleased that Aubigny was willing to help her, she was somewhat distrustful of him because he had previously turned his back on her, opting out of Guise's plans. She was also cautious about the involvement of the Jesuits. We might find this surprising given that she had by this late stage gone to such effort to portray herself as a Catholic princess who sought the support of the Pope. But as Mary astutely recognized, 'these people may blunder seriously unless they have wise counsel and advice', and it was important to check that their 'experience in matters of state corresponds to their zeal in religion'.[38] She suggested that the plans progress carefully to avoid bringing disaster to those involved and even protested that she did not wish for her own name and authority to be assumed unless it was absolutely necessary.

Her wariness of Aubigny was well placed. Some of James's Scottish nobles, already disenchanted with Aubigny's influence over the young king, worried that these relationships with Jesuits meant Aubigny might seduce James back to Catholicism. In August 1582, James was kidnapped and held for almost a year. Known as the Ruthven Raid because of its leader William Ruthven, 1st Earl of Gowrie, the imprisonment of the Scottish king stunned Mary. Aubigny was ordered to depart Scotland and by the time James was free once more, he had died back in France on 26 May 1583. Elizabeth still hoped to keep the option of joint rule in Scotland open, even going so far as to suggest a compromise with Mary whereby she would give up her claim to the English throne and Elizabeth would in turn issue a public proclamation stating that Mary was entirely innocent of the murder of her husband, Lord Darnley.[39] However, James was now determined never to be subject to a Regent or any other noble faction: he would rule in his own right. Unfortunately for Mary, this meant that he was no longer willing to concede to ruling Scotland jointly with her. The association, and Mary's Scottish hopes, were finished.

And yet. Just as things were looking desolate for Mary, once again a whisper of new possibilities made its way to her ear. Could it be that France and Spain would join together in her cause? Might there still be hope for her freedom from this lengthy captivity after all? Several ambitious and bold young Catholic gentlemen certainly thought so and they were willing to put themselves right at the heart of this pan-European scheme.

ABOVE: A page of ciphers that were used by Mary, Queen of Scots to disguise her letters during her captivity in England. These were found among a large number of papers during a search of her belongings at Chartley.

LEFT: Queen Elizabeth I of England. Mary tried to persuade Elizabeth to set her free so that she could return to Scotland and reclaim her crown or otherwise let her travel to France. Although Elizabeth disapproved of those who had rebelled against Mary, she could not risk foreign military support on England's doorstep.

RIGHT: King Philip II of Spain was leader of the most powerful Catholic nation in sixteenth-century Europe. Although he wanted to support Mary and was committed to restoring the Catholic faith in England, he remained cautious about invasion, at least until after her execution in 1587.

ABOVE: A coded letter from Mary to Thomas Howard, Duke of Norfolk, thanking him for his concern about her health and asking him to see whether Robert Dudley, Earl of Leicester, will give his support to their marriage plans. This letter was intercepted and decoded.

ABOVE: Tutbury Castle was a run-down property that suffered from terrible damp and freezing drafts. Luxury furnishings from the Earl of Shrewsbury's other properties and from the royal collections at the Tower of London were sent to improve its condition. Mary loathed it.

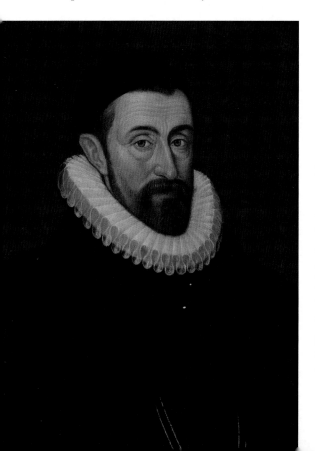

LEFT: Sir Francis Walsingham, Elizabeth's chief spymaster, who was determined to catch Mary in the act of conspiring against England. His expert team of cryptographers and intelligencers gathered the evidence needed to ultimately condemn Mary.

LEFT: Don Juan of Austria was the half-brother of King Philip II of Spain and Governor of the Spanish Netherlands from 1577. English agents were relieved when a planned marriage between Mary and Don Juan was curtailed by his untimely death in 1578.

BELOW: Anthony Babington and his accomplices meet to plot the assassination of Elizabeth, putting Mary on the English throne in her place. Although English agents were aware of this scheme, they allowed it to develop so that they could gather proof of Mary's involvement.

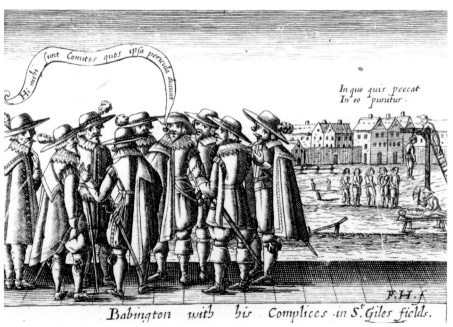

Babington with his Complices in S.t Giles fields.

layssant leurs gaiges lauctre faysant prier dieu
pour une royne qui a esté nommee tres chrestie
et meurt chatolique desnuee de toutz ses biens
quant a mon fylz ie le vous recommande au
quel le meritera car ie nen puis respondre
iay prins la hardiesse de vous enuoier deulx
pierres rares pour la sante vous la desirant
parfaicte annee heureuse et longue vie vous les
receuurez comme de vostre tres affectionnee
belle sœur mourante en vous rendant tes moyen
de son bon cueur enuers vous ie vous recomman
encore mes seruiteurs vous ordonnerez si il vous
plaict que pour mon ame ie soye payee de
party e de ce que me debuez et quen lhoneur
de Jhesus Christ lequel ie priray demayn a
ma mort pour vous me laysser de quoy fon
un obit et fayre les aumones requises
ce mercredy a deulx heures apres minu

Vostre tres affectionnee et bien
bonne sœur MARI R

RIGHT: Fotheringhay Castle, where Mary was taken to be tried for her involvement in plots which had intended to kill the Queen of England. She protested her innocence and dismissed the validity of the trial process, noting that she was never a subject of England, but a Scottish queen.

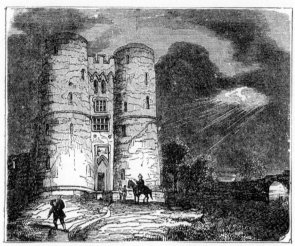

FOTHERINGHAY CASTLE.

LEFT: During the night before her execution on 8 February 1587, Mary wrote this letter to King Henri III of France, brother of her first husband Francis. She proclaims that she is to be executed like a criminal and that she 'dies a Catholic, stripped of all her possessions'.

BELOW: After almost twenty years in captivity in England, Mary was executed on 8 February 1587 at Fotheringhay. Her ladies helped her to the platform and Mary comforted them before her head was struck from her body.

ABOVE: Mary, Queen of Scots ensured that after death she would be memorialized as a persecuted Catholic Queen. Her letters reveal her convictions and her resilience throughout the tumultuous years of captivity in England.

CHAPTER SIX

The Throckmorton Plot

↑ [1]

*Monsieur de Mauvissière, I thank you
affectionately for your care and good diligence
in advertising me of this last agitation,
at which I am extremely grieved for the
cause and occasion that my enemies could
take on this, to persecute those of my party
in this kingdom, as they have already done
towards the Sieur de la Tour, towards whom,
and all his I pray God to give me grace
someday to acknowledge the wrongs that up
till now he has endured very unjustly.* [2]

W HEN THEY CAME, *they came suddenly. There was no time for the servants to shout a warning. Doors were flung open, frames shuddering with the force. She watched as her husband instinctively reached for a weapon – but the sword was across the room. Fool, she thought. Go for the papers first. By the time this same realization had come to him, it was too late. Two men had bundled him roughly out of his chair, while the others swiped everything off the desk into large sacks. Others were barging around the room opening drawers and wrenching at the chest beneath the window.*

Spinning quickly to the bookshelf behind her, she draped her embroidery over a small casket. Her needle stabbed the green velvet lid. She made no move to hide it, simply held it in front of her making sure that the needlework was facing out into the room. None of the men made any move to take it from her. After they had dragged her husband from the room, she waited for the stragglers to leave. She pushed the little box, still hidden beneath her sewing, into the hands of the young lad. 'To the Spaniard,' she whispered. He nodded and slipped away towards the kitchens and the back exit. She let out a long breath, feeling the delayed panic start to creep into her blood. Still, at least some of the Scottish Queen's letters would escape Walsingham's men.

A S THE CHRISTMAS festivities ended at Sheffield Castle and 1582 crept despairingly into the new year, Mary, Queen of Scots was despondent. She had little company, with only a few of her ladies remaining, her secretaries, and the guards who supervised her short walks on the flat roof of the castle's dining hall when she felt strong enough to venture outdoors. Visitors were scarce as the weather and the holidays slowed travel. It had therefore been several weeks since she had last received any letters. True, some notes had reached her over the holidays, those approved by Sir Francis Walsingham and permitted to arrive via the official channel. But beyond festive blessings and some mildly frustrating reports on the money raised from Mary's French properties, no news had reached her. More importantly, and more worryingly, no letters had been delivered along the second route, the secret route, the route through the French embassy in London that used coded disguises to help letters reach Mary from across England, Scotland and even farther away, and kept her connected well beyond her captivity.

The secret channel through the French embassy had been up and running for quite some time, at least since spring 1578. But it was not until this later stage, around about 1583, that Walsingham was made aware of it. He likely suspected such covert communication was happening in the embassy, but it was only when an inside man confirmed it, that he was able to take action. A figure calling himself 'Fagot' wrote to Walsingham explaining that one of the secretaries to the French ambassador to England, Michel de Castelnau, Sieur de la Mauvissière, was willing to betray his master. John Bossy has shown that 'Fagot' was probably Giordano Bruno, the Italian philosopher, who was staying in the French embassy at this time.[3]

Fagot, aka Bruno, informed Walsingham that the French embassy clerk Laurent Feron (though he never named him directly) was able to slip extra materials into the letter packets he delivered for the ambassador. Mauvissière himself admitted that the clerk was always at his side, though he did not suspect him of any underhand dealings. Feron was a naturalized Englishman of French descent. He lived in Mincing Lane, an area of desirable homes mostly owned by merchants. He was willing to act as a spy for Walsingham, as long as he was well paid for the job.

Mary and Mauvissière were initially both certain that this new route was secure. And for the first few years it seems to have been very successful, with most letters reaching their destination. So effective was it that the new Spanish ambassador, Don Bernardino de Mendoza, who had arrived in London in 1578 to replace Guarás, also used it to communicate with Mary and her supporters on the continent. The secret channel was especially useful for getting messages to Mary's agents in Paris including James Beaton, Archbishop of Glasgow, and a group of young Catholic gentlemen led by Thomas Morgan. Morgan was a Welshman who had trained as a clerk, becoming secretary to the Archbishop of York, Thomas Young until his death in June 1568. Morgan then moved into the Earl of Shrewsbury's household. It was here that he met Mary. He quickly joined her cause. He began carrying letters for her and when this was discovered Shrewsbury dismissed him, admitting to Elizabeth that Morgan's 'busy head might have had some lewd practices for the Scottish queen in offence of your majesty'.[4] He reported that Mary was furious with him when she realized he had sent Morgan away, giving him some 'very rough words' but he assured Elizabeth he would not stand by as Mary 'seeks to corrupt my men.' Morgan spent at least a year in the Tower of London but was eventually released.

Shrewsbury was kept busy trying to stop Mary from 'corrupting' his servants throughout the early 1570s. No sooner had he got rid of Morgan, than another of his men was denounced. In May 1574 the Scottish Regent, James Douglas, Earl of Morton wrote to the English ambassador, Henry Killigrew, giving intelligence about a young Scotsman, Alexander Hamilton.

Hamilton was a teacher based not far from Sheffield. He held his position thanks to Shrewsbury and had even been employed to teach the Earl's children, though it is unclear how Hamilton had come to be in Sheffield. It is possible he may have been one of the attendants who originally came with Mary when she was placed in Shrewsbury's custody and that she managed to negotiate a position for him. He was likely a kinsman of Claude Hamilton, who had been at the centre of Mary's circle before the Battle of Langside and during her flight into England. Morton had discovered that Hamilton was sending messages to George, Lord Seton, and suspected that these letters were from Mary. The correspondence seemed to be reaching Hamilton via a young servant boy in Shrewsbury's household. The boy had identified two other couriers of Mary's letters. The first was a well-made man with a black beard, who always wore a black hat pulled close over his face. The other was a woman named 'Janet' who he described as tall with yellow hair. Hamilton instructed the boy that he would be able to find him at the Red Bull pub in Doncaster or to send word via a glover in Sheffield when he had messages to pass on.[5]

Shrewsbury was thrown into a state of panic, terrified that Elizabeth would believe he was facilitating or outright encouraging

Mary's attempts to send secret letters. Nonetheless, to his credit he did try to protect Hamilton from these claims. He wrote to Walsingham relating that the Scot was simply a diligent teacher and that he had never given him any cause to think he might be a spy.[6] His efforts were in vain; Hamilton was taken in for questioning a few days later.

THOMAS MORGAN ENDED up in Paris where he secured a position with Mary's ambassador to France and the Archbishop of Glasgow, James Beaton, as a cipher clerk. This meant he had access to the codes used by Mary and her supporters to disguise their letters. He also took charge of Mary's French finances; by 1581, he had become receiver of Mary's dower revenues. Such prominent and responsible roles meant he quickly established himself at the centre of Mary's transnational European network. He associated with fellow Catholic exiles and though grateful to Beaton for the opportunity he had offered, soon became disillusioned with the ambassador's diplomatic approach to Mary's cause.

Walsingham, who had been English ambassador to France until April 1573, made sure that his replacement Valentine Dale continued to keep an eye on Morgan and sent reports on to Cecil revealing that Morgan had access to the French ambassador and continued to 'practice' in Mary's favour. Several letters in cipher survive between Mary and Morgan. Not only did they write to one another directly, if covertly, but Morgan often sent on letters to her from other supporters, including Lady Anne Percy. Many of these letters made their way through the secret channel at the French embassy.

However, by 1583 Mary had begun to suspect that this channel was compromised. In one of the newly decoded letters, we can see Mary's concerns start to build. She was especially worried that she had not yet received a response from Bertrand de Salignac de la Mothe-Fénelon, the French ambassador to Scotland. Mary was concerned enough to complain to Mauvissière that Mothe-Fénelon's sudden silence was out of character because he was a regular and supportive correspondent.[7] But Mary wasn't simply distressed about missing Mothe-Fénelon's usual devoted platitudes. Instead, she was anxious because she and Mothe-Fénelon had been discussing, via ciphered letters, the possibility of a new plan for her to escape her lengthy captivity. This plan would bring together French troops, Spanish funds, and Scottish supporters. It aimed to mount a triple attack on England: from Scotland where her supporters would convince her son to join her – despite his previous unwillingness – from Ireland where a rising would distract English troops, and from the continent where men would land and journey to set her free. If this plan was discovered, not only would Mary's secret communication channel be shut down completely and Mauvissière's support stymied, but several of her Catholic supporters would be executed. The scheme they had been discussing would come to be known to us as the Throckmorton Plot.

MARY WAS CONVINCED that the secret channel was discovered and that someone, a mole at the heart of the French embassy, had revealed all to Walsingham. And so, she had her French secretary, Claude Nau, draw up another letter disguised by cipher in which she urged Mauvissière to be more careful, informing him that she had heard from an unnamed visitor that the embassy was monitored 'day and night by spies all around your house who observe all who come and go there'.[8] She referred to the plot she had been corresponding about without giving any specific details but revealing that Mothe-Fénelon had assured her that the Scots, and by implication her son, would support it. Once again, she questioned why Mothe-Fénelon would suddenly stop writing to her, believing the letters could only be being intercepted somehow.

Mauvissière, though, remained dismissive and refused to countenance that the secret channel had been compromised. Mary's concerns were not new to him – she had regularly complained that she did not trust the letter bearers and clerks he employed, fearing to write even in cipher to her former mother-in-law Catherine de' Medici and asking Mauvissière to write on her behalf instead. Nau was also distrustful of the security of the secret route, protesting to Mauvissière that although he wanted to respond to a supporter who had reached out to Mary, he was too worried to write back, even using a cipher. Perhaps for Mauvissière these latest worries about the route were simply the grumbles of a woman too long denied freedom of conversation, a woman who was desperate to exercise some small degree of control over her circumstances? Or maybe he even felt slighted by her repeated complaints about the quality of his people. Could Mary not trust in his judgment? Had his discretion ever failed her before?

Mauvissière was an intelligent man as well as a competent and effective diplomat who was trusted as special envoy to England in 1572 after the St Bartholomew's Day Massacre. He was appointed as French ambassador to England in 1575 and remained in the post until 1585. He had been a soldier during his earlier life but was also a scholar, and the combination of his sharp intellect and worldly experience drew the attention of Mary's uncle the Cardinal of Lorraine, whose service he had joined by 1557. He quickly proved his diplomatic skills, acting with such tact and discretion that he was appointed as envoy to King Henri II of France, travelling to Scotland for the first time in 1559 where he became close to Mary's mother, Marie de Guise. His friendship with Mary's relatives spilled over into his relationship with Mary herself, and during his decade as ambassador in England they became so close that Mary was one of his daughter's godmothers.

Mary's stubbornness, at least as Mauvissière saw it, would cast a lingering cloud over their interactions with one another. Mauvissière was a man of moderate but steadfast beliefs: he was a committed Catholic, but he urged temperance in the negotiations between Scotland and England and indeed with the religiously divided groups in France. He was devoted to Mary's campaign for liberty, going so far as to implore Catherine de' Medici and her son King Charles IX of France to continue to support Mary after her imprisonment in England. He also beseeched Walsingham for permission to send Mary clothes and other gifts in 1576. And yet, he was not seduced by her charms to the same extent that many others were, being ever cautious of that stubborn streak that he had first noticed back in Scotland all those years earlier. In fact, Mauvissière confessed to the previous French ambassador to

England, Paul de Foix, that he found Mary's 'wilfulness' tiresome and complained that once she had decided on a course of action there was no persuading her otherwise, calling her 'intractable'.⁹ He was frequently frustrated by her refusal to heed what he felt was his own wise counsel. As her imprisonment dragged on, Mary for her part felt similarly exasperated by Mauvissière – she chafed at his trusting nature and his unwillingness to accept that his servants might betray him.

Mauvissière once again assured Mary that only three people besides himself knew about the secret route: Claude de Courcelles and Jean Arnault de Chérelles, who were both his secretaries, and Laurent Feron, the embassy clerk. All three men were trustworthy, beyond reproach. Or so he thought. Before turning Feron in 1583, Walsingham had attempted to embed undercover agents in the embassy. William Fowler, a Scottish poet who was happy to take a wage from the spymaster, had contacted Mary claiming a debt she owed to his late father. Though he initially convinced Mary that he was an ally, he actually denounced other people in her network including one Mosman, a goldsmith who had acted as a courier for her. He then managed to have Archibald Douglas brought into Mauvissière's confidence. Douglas had been tried for involvement in the murder of Henry Stuart, Lord Darnley but acquitted, much to the shock and consternation of the Scottish public.

By 1583, Fowler was back in Scotland and Walsingham debated bringing Douglas on board as an intelligencer. Fowler encouraged Walsingham to recruit Douglas, arguing he would be very useful and noting that he was a very accomplished cryptographer: 'Touching his knowledge in deciphering, which thing he denies, yet I assure your honour he is well practised in that art.'¹⁰ Mauvissière seemed to be convinced that Douglas was Mary's man, so this was an opportunity to have a double agent placed at the heart of the embassy. As the newly decoded letters show however, Mary doubted Douglas. As with Fowler, she had been taken in at the start, going so far as to recommend him to her son.[11] But she quickly changed her mind. It isn't clear what caused this sudden change of heart, but thanks to the newly decoded letters there is no doubt that she distrusted him: 'Beware of Archibald Douglas, for he has not been as sincere as he would like you to believe.'[12]

As the newly deciphered letters confirm for certain, Mary had been right to worry and Mauvissière's trust was misplaced: by this point Walsingham had secured his mole, the clerk Feron. His aims were threefold: discover the specifics of the secret correspondence channel so that he might draw out other figures involved, gather intelligence on Mary and her supporters, and find out to what extent King Henri III of France and Mauvissière were implicated in schemes in Mary's favour. Feron's efforts made sure the first was a success; Walsingham was now aware of exactly how Mary was communicating within England and beyond. There was less evidence of Mauvissière's own direction of any conspiracies, and indeed the newly decoded letters confirm this. But there was certainly enough to suggest that Mary was in contact with conspirators and was thus aware of schemes.

Mary's suggestion that Mothe-Fénelon's sudden silence was worrying was indeed cause for concern. As she thought, he had been writing to Mary, offering further thoughts on this new scheme. But his letters were somehow being prevented from making it to their intended recipient. Before Mothe-Fénelon's replies could reach Mary, they were being intercepted by Feron in the French embassy who passed these letters, along with several others from a variety of correspondents including Mary's own son, into the hands of Walsingham.

Mothe-Fénelon's intercepted letters included intelligence of Mary's involvement in a new plot that was music to Walsingham's ears – alarming at the outset perhaps, but quickly settling into familiar notes. The letters set out how this new plot would go so far as to send foreign troops into England to depose Queen Elizabeth. Troops led by the Duke of Guise, Mary's cousin. The letters also confirmed that the Spanish were aware, were even supportive, of this enterprise. Walsingham was dismissive only of Mothe-Fénelon's claims that the Scots were also in league with the French and Spanish plotters, knowing this was unlikely, though he did have to endure a rather frosty reception at James's court in September 1583 to just to make sure.

As Mary simmered with resentment and frustration, her relationship with Mauvissière was strained to breaking point. She called him a 'blunderer' and scolded him: 'After the discovery of all my intelligences that are sent from your house, I am myself in no doubt that one of your servants has been corrupted.'[13] Walsingham meanwhile had started turning this intelligence to his own advantage and stepped up his efforts to gather more evidence by having around-the-clock surveillance of the French embassy in Fleet Street. All he needed now was to find the go-between, the person ensuring the scheme could flourish. It didn't take him long. By April 1583, Walsingham had found this final link in the chain – a bold young gentleman, an eager Catholic who, despite his modest background, was connected to all the major players in this scheme. His name was Francis Throckmorton.

↑

THROCKMORTON WAS THE eldest son of Sir John Throckmorton of Feckenham, Worcestershire, and nephew to Sir Nicholas Throckmorton, English ambassador to France and later to Scotland. Sir John was not as successful as his brother Nicholas and had not enjoyed a court career. He was also deeply in debt, leaving his children a modest lifestyle. Despite these beginnings, Francis and his siblings benefitted from the care of their formidable mother, Dame Margery. It was she who made sure that her sons were raised in the Catholic faith. Dame Margery was accused on several occasions of hearing mass and, more significantly, of maintaining priests in her household who had taught her sons when they were still children.

Around 1572, Francis married Anne Sutton and they had a young son named John. In late 1579 or early 1580, Francis and his younger brother Thomas had travelled to the Low Countries, territories ruled by Spain. While there, the young men had become involved in the exile community of English Catholics, represented by Sir Francis Englefield, a former privy councillor under Mary Tudor who had fled England after Elizabeth's ascension in 1558. Francis at least was taken into Englefield's service during this time but returned to England by 1581, determined to aid the captive queen of Scots. He entangled himself in a 'growing band of idealistic young Catholic laymen eager to serve the cause of Rome'.[14] His time on the continent had established contact with the Spanish ambassador to England, Don Bernardino de Mendoza, for whom he carried letters. The French embassy in London, with its apparently secure means of transmission, became useful even to the rival Spanish, meaning that Throckmorton began to regularly frequent the embassy at Salisbury Court. There he showed himself to be a willing and successful courier and was slowly integrated into the network surrounding Mary. Around this time too, Mary started including a new code name in her letters, deciphered as 'Sieur de la Tour'. De la Tour was Francis Throckmorton. He was now intimately involved in the new plot.

On 28 April 1583, Francis Throckmorton was feeling confident. That spring evening, he had enjoyed a sumptuous meal with Mauvissière at the French embassy. Throckmorton had recently returned from Sheffield where he had delivered money to the captive Mary, Queen of Scots along with a packet of letters from various correspondents. His journey between London and Staffordshire was a regular one, for he had been acting as a courier for the captive queen for almost eighteen months. He had no reason to suspect that his actions were being watched by Walsingham's agents. He was secure in his belief that the secret communication channel was safe, and more importantly that his actions were righteous, certainly not treasonous. Walsingham, meanwhile, was content to wait and watch for 'diverse months' in the hope that 'there might some proof more apparent be had to charge him therewith directly'.[15]

At the French embassy, Throckmorton also met a fellow disaffected Catholic gentleman who went by several names. Charles Paget was a younger son of William Paget, 1st Baron Paget of Beaudesert, Staffordshire. In 1581, he travelled without licence to Paris and met with Walsingham, who was in the city negotiating the potential marriage of Queen Elizabeth and the

Duke of Anjou. Paget went so far as to propose that he become an intelligencer for Queen Elizabeth's spymaster and principal secretary. Walsingham, however, was not impressed by Paget's suggestion: he was well aware that Charles Paget was a Catholic who supported Mary's restoration. Sir Henry Cobham, the English ambassador to France from 1579 until 1583, had informed Walsingham that Paget was known to be a duplicitous and dangerous figure. In May 1582, Walsingham responded to Paget with the cutting message that he had 'of late got some knowledge of your cunning dealing, and that you meant to have used me for a stalking horse'.[16] Despite this setback, Paget continued to protest his desire to help the English state, going so far as to write to Elizabeth claiming 'if your eyes could penetrate my heart, you would see my great grief at your displeasure towards me'.[17]

However, at the same time, in Paris Paget associated with cipher clerk Thomas Morgan. Through Morgan, Paget also gained a position in Mary's ambassador to France, James Beaton's, household in Paris. Though the two younger men worked for Beaton, they were not afraid to strike out on their own in ways that they felt were more conducive to Mary's cause. They felt that Beaton was not as proactive as he should be and was content instead to rely upon the slow-moving channels of diplomatic negotiations. Money was also a source of tension, with Morgan being accused of mismanaging Mary's finances.

Ambassador Cobham reported to Walsingham that there was a divide among Mary's supporters in Paris, with Paget and Morgan viewed suspiciously by Beaton and his allies. This tension extended beyond Paris and was evident in the French embassy in London. Though Mauvissière was a committed supporter of Mary's cause, he also had an official role to perform. He was the representative of the French King Henri III and, as such, was required to act in the king's interests. Henri and his mother, Catherine de' Medici, were pushing the match between the Duke of Anjou and Elizabeth at this time and Mauvissière was intricately bound up in these negotiations. For him, directed as he was by his masters, the best way forward for Mary was for the marriage discussions to be a success because then Elizabeth might be more receptive to French demands for the Scottish queen's release. At the same time, within the embassy was a more militant faction, undoubtedly encouraged by the Duke of Guise. Servants and clerks acted from the safety of the embassy to publish and sell Catholic polemic texts. As early as 1576, Mary was aware of the problems created by these various factions within her French networks both in England and in Paris. Exasperatedly, she remarked that if one half were supporting her, the other would surely work against her simply to antagonize their rivals.[18]

Mauvissière fell under considerable pressure following the execution of the Jesuit priest Edmund Campion on 1 December 1581. Campion's excruciating torture and gruesome death shook the Catholic communities in England and abroad. Yet the French had done little to intercede and the embassy became a target for disaffection among English Catholics who felt they should have done more. In response, Claude de Courcelles, Mauvissière's secretary, began to restore the embassy's reputation. He was a more zealous Catholic and his sister had been a lady-in-waiting to Mary at Sheffield. He was also close to Morgan in Paris. He helped secure Throckmorton's involvement in the plot, finding him a position as a courier just before Christmas in 1581. He handed over all Mary's letters that arrived at the embassy, visiting Throckmorton's house in Paul's Wharf. Throckmorton then either carried the letters himself to Staffordshire or employed one George More to complete the journey.

IN 1582, HENRI, Duke of Guise, had set up a meeting to discuss possible means of freeing Mary and had not included Paget and Morgan, leading to further strife among the exiles. Despite initially being snubbed by Guise, Paget gained support from elsewhere. Mendoza was keen to utilize his services and skills, as Paget had become adept at travelling secretly out of France. Mendoza recruited him to carry correspondence to Spain. These skills would prove particularly useful in September 1583 when he travelled from Dieppe to Arundel on a secretive mission that would set firmly in motion the events we know as the Throckmorton Plot.

Paget's secret trip to England was fuelled by a second meeting organized by the Duke of Guise in June 1583. After throwing such a hissy fit at their exclusion the first time around, it seems Guise didn't want to risk further fuss and so Paget was brought into the fold. Arriving at Guise's private home in Paris, away from the spies of the royal court, Paget was led into a small room crowded with figures. Some of the men would have been familiar to him, such as his employer Archbishop Beaton. Others he may not have recognized, but by candlelight he would have made out the glimmer of the gold thread on the robes of the pope's representative Giovanni Battista Castelli. Guise was making a statement of his commitment to this potential enterprise by bringing as many interested parties together as possible. Over glasses of the best French wine, he set out his plans. This time, the scheme would go much further than simply setting Mary at liberty. Guise was planning an invasion of England.

Twelve thousand troops would sail from Spain to Flanders to avoid suspicion before turning back and landing in Lancashire. The plotters expected the persecuted Catholics of Northern England to happily rise to support the invasion force. They were probably deluding themselves – though there was a strong Catholic community in the northern counties, they did not necessarily support a French invasion, instead simply wanting freedom to worship openly. Nevertheless, Guise himself would lead a second, smaller force, landing in Sussex where they would be aided by disaffected Catholic noblemen including Henry Percy, 8th Earl of Northumberland, at his Petworth estate, and Philip Howard, 13th Earl of Arundel. So committed to this plan was Guise that he travelled to Normandy in July of that year to prepare troops. At the same time, he sent a spy into England to scout the coast and to make contact with the necessary English supporters. That spy was Charles Paget.

Travelling from Dieppe, Paget reached Arundel Harbour on 8 or 9 September 1583. He had paid the considerable sum of £7 – more than £1,000 in today's money – to evade attention and ensure the silence of the ship's master. Ordinarily, it would have taken the master of a small vessel an entire year to earn that amount. It is almost certain that the money was provided by Guise – Paget couldn't claim that much ready cash as an exiled secretary and while Mendoza appreciated Paget's skills, King Philip II of Spain was notoriously slow to pay out funds from his own pockets. Choosing from one of his many aliases, Paget settled for calling himself Mr Wattes. He revealed no details about his status or his reasons for travelling secretly, and in fact he barely spoke at all during the journey. He wore a good quality but dull-coloured cloak, practical clothing for the changeable autumn weather, avoiding ostentatious dress that might provoke questions about his true identity.

Three weeks later, the same shipmaster carried Paget, still known only as Wattes, back from Arundel to Dieppe. Landing on 27 September, Paget rested there after becoming seasick during the journey. Seeing him unwell, the shipmaster inquired if his passenger needed any further help, forcing Paget to admit that he would stay in the town for a few days to recuperate before heading back to his home in Rouen. This was a fabrication of course, but Rouen was a convenient cover location for Paget, meaning he could avoid association with Paris where many of the English Catholic exiles were based, and also because Rouen had an established community of English traders. Somewhat undermining his own attempts at distraction though, Paget had written to Walsingham in 1582 mentioning his journey to Rouen to partake of the English beer there. While in England, Paget had stayed with the Earl of Northumberland for at least a week, living in a lodge on the Petworth Estate. His other activities remain unknown though he may have met with Mendoza in person in London. Upon returning to Paris, Paget updated the Duke of Guise, and his findings must have been positive because the scheme was still scheduled to go ahead as planned.

Unfortunately for Paget, his visit to England did not remain secret for long. Monitoring the French embassy proved fruitful for Walsingham, and he expanded his surveillance to include Paget's elder brother, Thomas, Lord Paget. Shortly after Charles Paget returned to France, rumours of his recent intrigues reached England. Trying to distance himself from the plot, Lord Paget wrote a letter to Charles in October encouraging him to cease any activities that might be troublesome to the English authorities. He went so far as to claim that if Charles didn't stop his intrigues, then he would disown him. It is more likely, however, that Lord Paget was using this letter as a smokescreen, recognizing that his correspondence might be intercepted (which indeed it was) and aiming to hide his own suspicious contacts. He had, in fact, met with his brother while he was staying at Petworth and was likely informed of the invasion plans at this time.

In the first week of November 1583 the arrests began. Though Walsingham had managed to gather significant evidence of the plot, it is still unclear what sparked the decision to arrest those involved at this moment, for there was no great exposé. Perhaps it was the failed assassination attempt on Queen Elizabeth's life in autumn of that year when John Somerville had set out from his home in Warwickshire, proclaiming that he was going to London to shoot the queen. Mary denied having any knowledge of Somerville: 'The name of whom, or any other condemned for the same deed, I can wholly swear and protest before God never to have heard named, so wanting am I of ever having had any intelligence whatever with them.'[19] Somerville seems to have been suffering from a mental disturbance and was easily captured. Though his scheme was more of a bluff than any realistic danger to Elizabeth, he was held in the Tower of London where he allegedly killed himself in December of that year before being tried. Somerville was related to the Throckmorton family through marriage. His father-in-law, Edward Arden, was married to Mary Throckmorton, Francis Throckmorton's cousin. Warwickshire was a Catholic stronghold, and the Somerville and Arden families were known recusants. These connections, though apparently nebulous today, may have forced Walsingham's hand.

Francis Throckmorton was the first to be arrested. He was taken by surprise at his property near St Paul's Cathedral on 6 November 1583. Searchers burst into Throckmorton House while he was in the middle of composing a letter in cipher to Mary. They found several other incriminating documents including genealogies of royalty highlighting Mary's superior claim to the English throne. Even more problematic were maps of the English coast with notes of safe havens for landing large numbers of troops and a list of nobility and gentlemen who were considered supporters of the invasion. Problematic though these finds would prove for Throckmorton, his wife, Anne, made sure that the most crucial piece of evidence did not end up in the agents' hands. Unnoticed by the searchers, she passed a small casket covered in green velvet to a servant who delivered it to Mendoza. This casket contained the correspondence and other documents showing the extent of the plans, the backing of the Duke of Guise, and the network of those involved.

On 1 November, Thomas, Lord Paget had met with Throckmorton at the French embassy in Fleet Street. Hearing of Throckmorton's arrest a few days later, he decided it was time to leave England and turned to the Earl of Northumberland, who helped him to flee England with a small number of armed guards, on 23 November. Though Northumberland later maintained that he had no knowledge of the affairs of Lord Paget, Walsingham understood that Lord Paget had been the weak link. If interrogated, he could have confirmed that the earl had met with both himself and his exiled brother Charles and that the earl was aware of the invasion plans.

Thomas, Lord Paget attempted to excuse his sudden flight, writing to Cecil claiming that he had left only because he wished to travel, though he admitted that he did hope to receive the comfort of his faith now that he was in France. In a letter to his mother from the same date he was more open, remarking that all he had done was 'by God's appointment'.[20] He would spend the rest of his life as an impoverished exile in Paris, less committed to the cause to free Mary and restore Catholicism in England, yet never far removed from the network of plotters. He was one of the lucky ones.

Throckmorton was not so fortunate. At the same time that he was arrested, his mother, Dame Margery's, properties were searched, and she confessed that she had tried to get her younger sons out of England. After spending a few days at an obscure property on St Peter's Hill, Throckmorton was taken to the Tower. He was interrogated right away. At first, he claimed that the incriminating documents had not been his and he denied treason. He tried to sneak out notes on the back of a set of playing cards to his younger brother George, but these were discovered, leading to George's own arrest a few days later. One covert note did slip through the net, however. Mendoza informed Philip II of Spain that he had received a brief note, also written on the back of a playing card, that Throckmorton had thrown out of the window of his room at the Tower. Walsingham was unimpressed with Throckmorton's lack of co-operation, and on 16 November he was tortured by the rack. His joints were dislocated as he was stretched across a wooden beam, though he was considered to have been treated quite lightly, being 'somewhat pinched, although not much' by his interrogators.[21]

Walsingham felt that just the sight of the rack for a second time would be enough to make the young man break, and he was right. On 20 November, Throckmorton confessed in full. As Mauvissière bluntly but shrewdly explained to Mary:

> *He showed some resolution at the beginning and replied as a man of spirit but since then the agony of the torture to which he has been subjected four times, has made him tell them what he knows and also what he did not know so that by a single one of the least important offences he has confessed to will enough to hang him.*[22]

Throckmorton confirmed that he had been transporting letters for the Spanish ambassador for several years after being put in contact with him while in the Low Countries as a young man. He admitted that he had pressed Philip II of Spain to intercede on Mary's behalf and that he had knowledge of the Duke of Guise's plans to invade England. His own role was limited to carrying correspondence between Mary, Mendoza and Mauvissière, he maintained. When asked why he had become aligned with these treasonous factions, Throckmorton proclaimed that he wished only to see toleration of the Catholic faith in England but had been convinced by his fellow conspirators that should this be impossible, then force should be used to rescue Mary and set her in Elizabeth's place.

On 13 December 1583, Throckmorton managed to have a final letter smuggled out of the Tower to his wife, whom he addressed as his 'good sweetheart'.[23] Cicely Hopton, daughter of the Lieutenant of the Tower, Sir Owen Hopton, had become enamoured with Francis's younger brother George who was by this stage also imprisoned there. It is likely that she was the conveyor of this final letter. She was questioned the very next day, 14 December, and admitted that she had spoken with George in his room and that he had asked her to be a 'meanes' for his brother. Contemporary agents and modern historians have dismissed Cicely as a naïve girl who was flattered by the attention of the dashing younger Throckmorton. In fact, she was a brave young woman who was willingly involved in the underground Catholic networks of London. She was allegedly in love with a recusant named John Stonar, who had been imprisoned in the Tower for a few months in 1581 after a secret Catholic printing press was found on his family property in Oxfordshire.

Stonar's influence seems to have led to her decision to convert to the Catholic faith and she began carrying messages between those incarcerated and their contacts in London. Cicely was able to use her status as daughter of the Lieutenant of the Tower to move freely, and it was not unusual for her to deliver alms to prisoners. She was adamant that that father knew nothing of her activities. Despite being questioned, Cicely remained committed to her Catholic friends and would be implicated in further plots until her father resigned his post in 1589.

Whatever the means, together Francis, George and Cicely made sure that Francis was able to write to his wife one last time. In the letter, he admitted to his own role in the plot and confessed that he had named his fellow conspirators. He despaired that he had betrayed Mary, Queen of Scots and claimed that since he had failed her, he didn't care whether he lived or died. Throckmorton was tried at the Guildhall in London on 21 May 1584 and found guilty of treason. Brought to the execution platform at Tyburn on 10 July 1584, he refused to ask forgiveness from Queen Elizabeth.

As Throckmorton's wife was receiving his final letter, the Earl of Northumberland was confined under guard at his London property and was questioned repeatedly over the next few months, including during the Christmas festivities. He was later moved to the Tower where he continued to be interrogated but refused to confirm anything other than his meetings with Charles Paget in September 1583. Northumberland's sons had been in Paris before Paget's arrival, and he claimed that the men met only to discuss the prospects of these young men. Walsingham was unconvinced: Northumberland was always going to be suspect because his own brother Thomas Percy, Earl of Northumberland before him, had been executed in 1572 for his role in the rebellion of 1569. Thomas Percy's wife, Lady Anne Percy, was also still at large on the continent and was regularly involved in schemes and plots to restore Mary. Before a case could be built against him though, Northumberland was found dead in his Tower cell on 21 June 1585. He had died by a gunshot to the heart. There were several rumours that he had been quietly executed so that a public trial would be avoided. The official account said it was suicide.

A further casualty of the discovery of the plot was Mendoza, Spanish ambassador to England. After Throckmorton's confession in November 1583, Walsingham had increased the surveillance on the French embassy and several suspicious letters were intercepted before they could reach Charles Paget. They confirmed that Mendoza was still trying to facilitate Mary's release. Mendoza was expelled from England in January 1584, being taken from Dover to Calais. Though an official was sent to the court of Philip II of Spain to explain this action, the Spanish king refused to meet the messenger.

Thomas Morgan, too, suffered severe consequences for his role in the conspiracy. Elizabeth had demanded that he be sent back to England to face trial, but King Henri III of France consented only to imprison him in the Bastille. His papers were seized and though English ambassador to Paris Sir Edward Stafford tried to claim them, presuming that they contained compromising evidence against Mary, this was not successful. Instead, Mauvissière's former secretary Jean Arnault de Chérelles was appointed to go through them. As one scholar notes, he was probably picked to 'do Morgan and Mary a good turn on the quiet'[24] because he actually returned most of the ciphered correspondence to Charles Paget and gave over only a small sample to the English ambassador. These included nine ciphers that were never actually used by Morgan and Mary; he had simply made them up.

Nevertheless, the French king was nervous that the discovery of the Throckmorton Plot would have negative repercussions for Anglo-French relations. Though it had been directed by Guise rather than the crown, Elizabeth was still incensed. Henri III ordered Mauvissière to close down the secret channel immediately.

Walsingham made sure that the ambassador's reputation was tarnished, and he was instructed to show all letters from this point forth to Walsingham.

The men involved in the Throckmorton Plot all claimed that they were acting in Mary's interest and that they had her support for the actions planned. At the time though, Mary herself denied being consulted on their plans and distanced herself from incriminating reports. Having letters written in code gave her some plausible deniability because she was able to protest that the letters were not in her hand – and indeed it was usually her French secretary, Claude Nau, who penned the ciphered letters. She could argue that her intended words had been altered without her authority. This was a strategy Mary turned to again and again during her captivity, and the Throckmorton Plot wouldn't be the last time she employed such subterfuge.

Thanks to the newly decoded letters from this time, we are now able to prove that Mary certainly did know about the plot. She was in fact aware of it from the earliest stages. Two of these recently deciphered letters are especially illuminating. The first from 15 June 1583 features Mary's direct interest in the kindly Francis Throckmorton. She asked Mauvissière to apologize to Throckmorton because she had been unable to write to him in her own hand. More startlingly, she admitted that there would be 'great danger to herself' if Walsingham were to find out about her relationship with Throckmorton. The second of these recently decoded letters that help to verify her involvement in the plot is from a few months later when she suspected Walsingham had indeed discovered the plot. The deciphering project offers us this revelation: Mary offered to give £2,000 of her dowry money to her

Guise cousin to help keep the scheme afloat. Reading these new disclosures from the project alongside intercepted letters from her supporters makes it clear that Mary was simply keeping up a pretence. In the letter she had looked for from Mothe-Fénelon at the new year, he asked her outright what she felt about the Duke of Guise's 'deliberations' and even asked whether she wanted soldiers or simply funds sent to her. Charles Paget's intercepted letter to Mary from February 1584 lamented the sad state of affairs because 'the intelligence between your Majesty and your friends has been broken'.[25]

For Mary, the discovery of the plot proved difficult. The lack of security evidenced by the secret communication channel and her access to visitors led to the Earl of Shrewsbury being replaced as her keeper. In January 1585, Sir Amyas Paulet was appointed as her jailor. Paulet was a Puritan who was much stricter with Mary than Shrewsbury had been. With the secret communication channel openly known, Mary was forced to use the official postal route, knowing that all these letters would be monitored by Walsingham. Though she tried to avoid using this official channel, it was difficult to set up a reliable secret route after the Throckmorton Plot and she went several months without receiving letters. Letter packets piled up in the French embassy.

Queen Elizabeth was furious to learn of Mary's involvement in the plot and was especially incensed that Mary had schemed while Elizabeth had been negotiating for Mary's restoration to Scotland with James VI. Finally, in March 1585 the Act for the Safety of the Queen's Person was passed. The Act stated that anyone who plotted an attack against Queen Elizabeth would be sentenced to death, but so too would any claimant to the throne for whom the traitors acted. Mary herself was forced to endorse the act though she recognized that it placed her in genuine danger. The Act did specify that perpetrators would have a state trial, rather than a private execution, and it was this statute that would be used to try and execute Mary more than a year later.

Although the Throckmorton Plot was foiled by Walsingham's agents, risks remained. Mauvissière was replaced as French ambassador to England by Guillaume de l'Aubespine, baron de Châteauneuf in September 1585, but the Duke of Guise was not deterred by the discovery of the invasion plans. With Mendoza expelled to France, he was galvanized by the arrival of an important ally. It was not until the death of the Duke of Anjou in June 1584, when it became clear that the only heir to King Henri III of France was the Protestant Henri of Navarre, that he finally turned his attentions away from Mary. Throckmorton and Northumberland might be dead, but the Paget brothers remained at large in Paris. And indeed, Charles Paget at least continued to write to Mary. He would be implicated in another plot in 1586 with his letters to Mary used at her final trial. This final scheme to free Mary would become known as the Babington Plot and it to this that we now turn.

CHAPTER SEVEN

The Six Gentlemen

 ₁

Up till now, with all his artifice and
subtlety, he has not known how to seize
any opportunity sufficient to give faith and
proof to his turbulent imaginations, which
I am sure hold him well in play, and he will
not leave any stone unturned to surprise
me if I leave anything for him to bite at.[2]

MARY COULD HEAR knocking. It was coming from the Great
Hall below her rooms. The strikes ricocheted through the
walls and drummed themselves into her head. Though she was
able to turn them to a dull background noise, she could see it was

agitating the young women at her side. Jane's fingers were white, the brush she held unintentionally smacking the heavy damask fabric in time to the sinister drumming from downstairs. Elizabeth was rigid in her chair, the prayer book forgotten in her lap. Mary blinked as the candlelight caught the gold leaf of an ornate letter on the page. Her own fingers itched to pick up the pen that lay dripping ink onto the old desk and release the rage inside.

How she longed to screech and spin around this chamber, ripping the plain black hangings from the wall. How dare they strip her of her cloth of state. She would tear down their insult, shred the dishonour with her own hands. But then, really, what good would that do?

She drew in a deep breath. Held it. Releasing the air from her lungs she picked up the strip of paper. She threaded it through the folded letter in front of her, locking the letter tight. She would keep her frustrations – and her fears – to herself. Tomorrow they would see a queen.

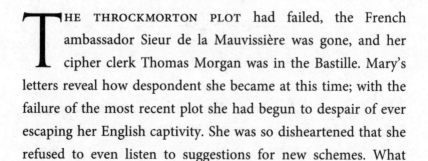

THE THROCKMORTON PLOT had failed, the French ambassador Sieur de la Mauvissière was gone, and her cipher clerk Thomas Morgan was in the Bastille. Mary's letters reveal how despondent she became at this time; with the failure of the most recent plot she had begun to despair of ever escaping her English captivity. She was so disheartened that she refused to even listen to suggestions for new schemes. What would be the point she asked? They were never going to succeed. She wrote in code to the Spanish ambassador, Don Bernardino de Mendoza, confessing that the period following the Throckmorton Plot was one of the most difficult she had faced in a long time. She admitted to him that she was:

> *So discouraged at the idea of entering into new*
> *attempts, seeing the failure that had attended previous*
> *ones, that I have turned a deaf ear to several proposals*
> *that had been made to me during the last six months*
> *by the Catholics, as I had no ground for giving them a*
> *decided answer.*[3]

Moreover, with the secret channel through the French embassy discovered and closed to her, Mary was without any useful intelligence. Official letters still arrived, ones Elizabeth's spymaster Sir Francis Walsingham had read over and deemed acceptable, but Mary's contact with those who agitated for her deliverance was cut off. The loss of these contacts stung; throughout late 1584 and on into 1585, her own attempts to write were undone with several letters ending up in Walsingham or Cecil's files. They all contained the same complaint: 'For these eighteen months I have been entirely without foreign news.'[4] With Walsingham's men watching for any sign that the secret channel was re-opening, letters stacked up in the French embassy. And then, as the summer of 1585 turned to autumn Morgan found a new courier who was willing to act his part in Mary's cause. This young man arrived back in England just before Christmas and was promptly arrested at Rye. He carried more than just letters with him. He was harbouring information about yet another plot. As Mary's ciphered letters show, this time her supporters were holding nothing back.

THE NEW COURIER was a young man named Gilbert Gifford. His family were from Staffordshire, with their main residence at Chillington Hall, about twenty miles from Chartley Castle where Mary was now being held. The Gifford family were Catholics. His father, John Gifford, had entertained Queen Elizabeth at Chillington in 1575 but was summoned a few days later to defend himself against reports that he had refused to attend church. He was eventually held under house arrest in London for his persistent recusancy. Gilbert Gifford had already left for the continent by the time of Elizabeth's visit to his family home, and in 1577 he entered the seminary led by William Allen at Douai. Gifford found it difficult to settle, getting into fights with fellow students and challenging superiors.

In 1579, he transferred to the English College at Rome but lasted only a year there, being expelled in 1580. After a few years wandering on the continent, he made it back to Allen's seminary in October 1583, now based in Rheims, where he was once more admitted, but under strict conditions of better behaviour. For a short while, he stuck to his word, even being admitted as a deacon in April 1585, but he continued to struggle with the seminary life and chose to depart for the last time later that year. As one biographer remarked, Gifford could be a 'difficult, truculent young man'.[5]

Despite deciding to leave the seminary, Gifford was still determined to remain involved in the counter-Reformation efforts. In October 1585, he was in Paris where he managed to contact the conspirators Thomas Morgan and Charles Paget to offer his services in Mary's cause. A good Catholic with local knowledge of Staffordshire, Gifford seemed an ideal courier of Mary's secret letters. Morgan gave him a letter of recommendation to show Mary so that she would know he could be trusted. When he arrived in Rye, this letter led to him being escorted to London to a house on Seething Lane, the city residence of one rather interested spymaster.

Walsingham held the young courier at his house for a short while, engaging him in private discussions. There is no doubt that it was during this time that Gifford became a double agent, acting for Walsingham in secret. They may have had intermittent contact with one another earlier while Gifford bounced from seminary to college on the continent, but this is not certain. What made him commit to Walsingham at this point is also not clear, and though it is possible he was threatened physically, it is more likely that Walsingham convinced him that Mary's chances were looking bleak despite what her supporters might proclaim.

And so, Gifford was persuaded to continue acting as courier, but to ensure that any letters to and from Mary were to make their way to Walsingham for perusal first. To make sure that Mary and her supporters believed Gifford was their man, a cover story was cooked up with a false report leaked by Walsingham that Gifford had been freed and was not suspected of involvement in any Catholic networks. At the same time, his father was allowed to return to their family home at Chillington in Staffordshire. This provided a convenient excuse for Gifford to be travelling to and from the county and London.

In the relief of finding what seemed to be a successful new secret channel, Walsingham hoped that Mary and her supporters would unwittingly give up their latest plans. Gifford began to hide letters sealed in waterproof tubes within barrels of ale that were then delivered to Chartley. Mary and her supporters believed that the brewer who dropped them off had been recruited to their side, but in fact Walsingham had paid him handsomely. Mary's new jailer Paulet was let in on the secret so that he wouldn't inadvertently discover them and put a stop to the route. Mary's replies were then sent out in the same fashion, with Gifford collecting them and carrying them to Walsingham.

Walsingham had very particular reasons for letting Gifford continue as a courier for Mary. In early 1585, the spymaster had foiled an outrageous scheme aiming to assassinate Queen Elizabeth as she travelled in her coach through London or, even more wildly, in her private gardens. William Parry, a former agent of Cecil's, who leapt erratically between loyalty to Elizabeth and allegiance to the Catholic continental powers, was executed on 2 March 1585 after confessing (and then retracting) that he had intended to shoot Elizabeth. Parry seemed to have undergone a genuine conversion to Catholicism during his travels in France and Italy during the early 1580s, but he was also seduced by visions of himself as an intelligencer. He had met Crichton in Lyons in 1583, when the Jesuit urged him not to assassinate Elizabeth because this would be a mortal sin. Morgan, however, had no such qualms and had encouraged the idea when they met in Paris that same year. Walsingham suspected that Morgan was continuing to urge young disaffected Catholic gentlemen that the only way forward was to kill the Queen of England. Gifford could now be used to shine a light on these most dangerous ideas and help Walsingham trace the latest recruits to Morgan's murderous schemes.

The man Walsingham then turned his spotlight on was nearly twenty-five years old and the heir to a considerable landed estate in Derbyshire. The family was suspected of Catholic sympathies and our young gentleman was also leaning towards that faith. He had inherited wealth and property upon his father's death in 1571 including houses in Lincoln's Inn, Barbican, and Temple Bar in London. He was married to Margery Draycott, daughter of a minor Staffordshire noble, and the couple had an infant daughter. He followed in the footsteps of Thomas Morgan, spending some time employed in the household of the Earl of Shrewsbury – as a page – before travelling to Paris. In 1580, he met with Morgan and Mary's ambassador James Beaton, Archbishop of Glasgow, in the city, spending at least six months in their company. Walsingham knew that this gentleman had acted as a courier for Mary for a short spell in 1583 and 1584, and he was known to have sold Catholic polemical texts from the French embassy at this time, but he noted that the young man had stepped back from the network around Mary. Perhaps he could be recruited like Gifford and planted back into Mary's web as a mole? In early 1586 the young man struck up connections with other figures on the spymaster's watchlist, making him very much a person of interest. His name was Anthony Babington.

LIKE HIS COUNTRYMAN Francis Throckmorton, Anthony Babington unwittingly gave his name to a fatal scheme, one which echoed down through time and has become inextricably linked to Mary, Queen of Scots. The Babington Plot was the final scheme that Mary involved herself in and led directly to her execution. It began, like all the others that had swirled around Mary over the years, as an intention to free her from her English captivity and liberate Catholics from the persecution they suffered under the current regime. Babington, with his connections to Mary and his experience selling Catholic books, was drawn into the plot by his sympathies for both aims. But for all that the plot ended up taking his name, Babington was not the driver of the scheme. The Babington Plot, in reality, was one conceived by Thomas Morgan from his prison cell in the Bastille. While he had failed to get Parry to shoot Elizabeth in 1585, Morgan remained convinced that the only way to finally liberate Mary was to get rid of Elizabeth. It was never going to be possible otherwise to free Mary, even with a force of armed men storming her prison. And so, in 1586 Morgan once more began to devise a plot, one that would not only free Mary and save the English Catholics but would this time assassinate Queen Elizabeth.

Such an ambitious scheme needed foreign support. This time, Morgan turned not to France for aid, but to Spain. He collaborated with Mendoza, former Spanish ambassador to England who had been expelled when his knowledge of the Throckmorton Plot was discovered in 1584. Mendoza had been posted to Paris where he became, if anything, even more committed to Mary's cause, using his connections and influence in support of her. He and Morgan became close associates, with Mendoza writing to King Philip II of Spain requesting aid for this new intervention.

Although Philip had been aware of several of the previous plots, and had given some support to the various schemes, this time he was more encouraging. Spain had been emboldened by the assassination of the Protestant William of Orange, leader of the rebels in the Spanish Netherlands since 1567. Elizabeth had sent support in the form of troops and finances to the Dutch rebels and his death on 10 July 1584 had been a blow. Moreover, France was once more embroiled in religious civil wars and was unlikely to be able to offer England any support. Mary, too, recognized that the death of Orange and the distractions faced by France gave Spain an edge. She wrote a letter disguised in code to Charles Paget explaining that: 'I can see no other meanes to that end except the King of Spain now being pricked in his particular by the attempt made on Holland and the course of Drake would take revenge of the Queen of England while France (occupied as it is) cannot help Her.'[6]

She had been open to Spanish aid for a long time, with Walsingham recognizing as early as 1574 that Mendoza was plotting on Mary's behalf.[7] Though the negotiations for her marriage to Don Juan had come to nothing with his early death, she was quick to acknowledge that now the best chance of foreign intervention would come from Spain, not France. In a letter to Mauvissière, the French ambassador to England, dated 31 July 1581, she had bluntly told the ambassador that she would be within her rights to negotiate with Spain because France was not offering enough support.[8] Though there was a temporary volte-face back towards France during the Throckmorton Plot, which was led by her cousin the Duke of Guise, Spain was not entirely out of the picture. Mary praised Mendoza's involvement, going so far as to suggest in a ciphered letter to him that she would have preferred that he was the leader of the scheme 'now that the irons are becoming hot and the blows stronger'.[9]

Following the failure of the Throckmorton Plot, Guise made one final attempt to arrange a rescue in 1585, but this would have relied on Spain giving significant funds to both Mary and the Scottish Catholics. It ultimately came to nothing, and Mary was now determined to rely on Spain.

She wrote extensively to Mendoza using cipher and while several of their letters were intercepted, many more did reach him, and there are even some examples that remain undeciphered.[10] It is likely that several different routes and couriers were used that did not involve the French embassy channel. She herself noted that there could never be too many means of communication between them.[11] The Jesuit de Samarie, who managed to visit her in disguise on several occasions, was probably one of these means. In comparison with Mauvissière, Mary was slightly more open and less commanding with Mendoza in her letters.[12] She regularly thanked him 'affectionately for the trouble you take to keep me well informed of events and for your good advice respecting my own affairs.'[13] At the same time that Mary was chastizing Mauvissière for failing to find the mole in the French embassy, she was complaining to Mendoza of his performance: 'I judge your proceedings towards Mauvissière to be well founded as his own designs are questionable.'[14]

To prove herself to Philip, she made a dramatic offer: if he would take her 'entirely under his protection' and stand fully behind her, providing money and troops, she would sign over her rights to the English crown to Philip. This would mean disinheriting her son, James. Though she admitted that she wept at the thought of this, she could not in good conscience allow him to inherit the English throne while he remained a 'heretic'. She had little hope of his return to the Catholic faith and worried that if he came to the English throne, it would be even more difficult for the Church to triumph there.

She wrote to Mendoza, begging him to keep this offer secret, because if it became known 'it will cause the loss of my dowry in France and bring about an entire breach with my son in Scotland, and my total ruin and destruction in England'.[15] Mendoza wrote immediately to Philip informing him of Mary's decision despite being in horrible pain following an operation to relieve his cataracts.[16] Mary might lament her actions against James, but she was no doubt influenced by his decision in March 1585 to negotiate directly with Elizabeth for a new association, which excluded Mary from the Scottish crown. With this any last hope of Scottish help fell away.

Philip II of Spain, meanwhile, had agreed that he would provide troops for an invasion of England. He was confident that this new plot could succeed – largely influenced by Mendoza who never missed a chance to emphasize to his King the merits of the conspirators and their cause. Philip informed the ambassador that he would only send the troops once the plotters had succeeded in assassinating Elizabeth, otherwise his men would be pushed back by the English. He cautioned Mendoza that 'it is difficult to keep a secret entrusted to so many people, it is a cause for anxiety that it should be so widespread' and feared that the plans would be discovered, leading not only to the deaths of the instigators but causing serious repercussions for the innocent English Catholic people.[17]

MORGAN AND MENDOZA had recruited other English Catholics to their new scheme. John Ballard was a priest who travelled covertly between England and the continent throughout the 1580s. He had several aliases, including Thompson, Turner, 'Captain Fortescue' and 'Black Fortescue'. He was the first to suggest to Anthony Babington that there were plans afoot for an invasion of England. Babington was initially sceptical, pointing out that the French had failed to arrive once before and were unlikely to manage it this time either. To this Ballard replied that the foreign aid would be coming from Spain instead. Babington was also realistic enough to recognize that there was no guarantee that the English people, including Catholics, would support an armed foreign invasion. He asked Ballard how any plot was expected to succeed while Elizabeth lived – the same question Morgan had asked himself – and Ballard informed him that this time Elizabeth would be removed. Another conspirator, John Savage, would carry out the assassination.

Gifford, who was known to both Ballard and Savage, from their time in Rheims, would be the courier between them and Mary (though, of course, no one knew that he had been turned by Walsingham). Babington was still unsure, and after meeting with some friends to discuss it, he decided it was best to leave England in June 1586. But he was persuaded to reconsider through the efforts of one Robert Poley. A member of the household of Sir Philip Sidney, Poley was placed there apparently by Morgan as a spy because Sidney was Walsingham's son-in-law, but he was also secretly Walsingham's man. Like Gifford, a cover story had been put about that Poley had been interviewed but not deemed a threat. Walsingham had Poley make sure that Babington remained part of the plot, so that he could monitor it firsthand. By July, Babington was back in contact with Ballard and had agreed to the plan. Including the assassination of Elizabeth.

Over the summer of 1586, Babington helped to recruit other young noblemen to the plot, though the plan to assassinate Elizabeth was known only to himself, Savage and Ballard. Yet it was still not clear that this latest plot would ever come to anything at all: Babington regularly got cold feet and tried to pull back from involvement. As John Bossy puts it, the Babington Plot was 'short-lived, totally theoretical, riddled with holes and hamstrung by Babington's own political and theological doubts, but it certainly existed'.[18] And this existence – the very fact that a wealthy English Catholic gentleman should implicate himself in a plot to kill the queen – was enough for Walsingham. He was determined to turn this opportunity to his advantage. Poley was told to encourage Babington to stay the course and stick with the plot until Walsingham had gathered evidence of Mary's knowledge and involvement. The best way to prove it? By letter of course.

JUST AS MORGAN was coming to the conclusion that Mary could only be free if Elizabeth were out of the picture, Walsingham had decided that action must be taken to rid Elizabeth permanently of Mary. While there had been efforts led by Cecil and other members of parliament to try and have Mary executed for her involvement in the plots of the past seventeen years, Elizabeth had always held back. She was reluctant to take the final step, fearing the reaction of her own subjects and the international response should an anointed queen be put to death. She clung to the lack of evidence in Mary's own hand; without it there was nothing she could do. And her ministers would just have to accept it. Now though, Walsingham realized that he might, finally, after years of 'almost', 'nearly' and 'not quite', as well as the continual dashed hopes and the frustrations of intelligence gathering, be able to produce the crucial evidence. If he could somehow use the Babington plotters and make the most of the inside man Gifford, a letter from Mary with her discussing the plans might make its way into his hands. Such a letter would break the case against her wide open. In 1585, Mary had signed in her own hand, and attached her royal seal to, the Act of Surety for the Queen. This bill ensured that any person found guilty of involvement in any action against the queen would forfeit any right to the succession of the English throne.

Though Elizabeth's councillors had tried to frame it as a response to foreign threats against Elizabeth, it was widely understood that the act was directed purposely towards Mary. If she were implicated in any rebellion, invasion or plot against Elizabeth, she would not only be liable to be tried for treason but she would instantly give up any right to the English crown. It also

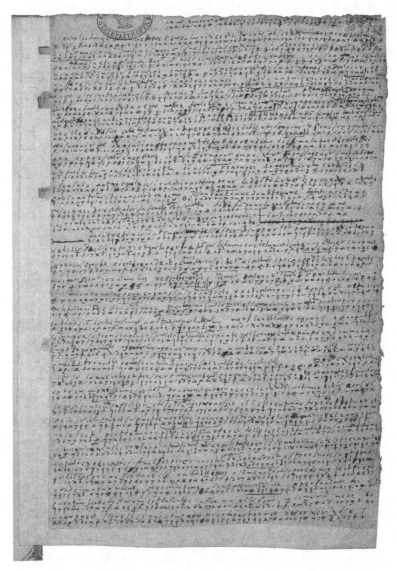

This letter from Mary to a Scottish supporter Patrick, Master of Gray in 1584, shows the intricate code being deciphered above the lines by Walsingham's cryptographer Thomas Phelippes. A full translation of the contents is preserved alongside the original coded letter.

helped secure the association between Elizabeth and James, which excluded her because the act had a clause added that specifically allowed for his inheritance, even if Mary were ever found guilty of any such scheme. Mary's hand was forced – she had little choice by 1585 but to sign it, with her son effectively cutting himself off from her and her captivity creeping ever closer to the twenty-year milestone. For Walsingham, the new legislation meant that now was as good a time as ever to push for the evidence of Mary's complicity in plots against Elizabeth. That this latest scheme sought Elizabeth's death was even better. If he could get hold of the necessary evidence, there would be no coming back for Mary.

Gifford made sure that letters from the conspirators to Mary and her replies were taken to Thomas Phelippes, Walsingham's expert cryptographer. Phelippes had been employed in intelligence for Walsingham since at least 1578 but had become his right-hand man from 1583 as the Throckmorton Plot had been brewing. He was devoted to his work, believing it was for God, Queen and country. He had a remarkable mind and the patience to spend hours decoding texts, as well as being fluent in several languages including Latin, Italian, French, Spanish and German. He was recognized even by his enemies as 'unequalled in deciphering'.[19] Phelippes also acted as the point of contact for several intelligence agents in Walsingham's networks, often paying them out of his own pocket when funds were late. He kept a small circle of close friends, all of them men loyal to Walsingham. Mary saw him when he was sent to Chartley on a brief mission in summer 1586. She described him in a coded letter to Morgan as a man 'of low stature, slender every way, dark yellow haired on the head and clear yellow bearded', though she noted his face was marked by smallpox.[20]

Anthony Babington signs to confirm that this cipher was used by him and Mary to communicate secretly, admitting 'this last is the alphabet by which only I have written unto the Queen of Scots or received letters from her'.

She guessed he was about thirty years old, and she was right: Phelippes was born around 1556. He was married and later in life when he was suffering from eyesight troubles or was imprisoned for debts, his wife, Mary, took over his intelligence network, doing the decryption work herself.

Phelippes used several aliases himself, going by Cornelys at times, and was not above forging letters. When an agent went missing, he took on their persona and wrote to Mary's Scottish secretary, Gilbert Curle.[21] He pretended to be Thomas Barnes, a young man who sometimes acted as courier when Gifford, who was in fact his cousin, was unavailable. Barnes had panicked and vanished, torn between his genuine support for Mary and his fear of Walsingham. Phelippe's 'delicate and secret ventriloquism' was put to good use by Walsingham in Mary's letters, too.[22]

Over the course of the summer of 1586, Walsingham watched as the new plot picked up speed. Morgan had recommended Babington to Mary back in July 1585, emphasizing that he had many friends and servants in the areas where she was being held. However, it was not until spring 1586 that Babington himself seems to have made direct contact with her.[23] Mary first checked with Morgan whether Babington could be relied upon; Morgan sent her a coded letter assuring her that he could be trusted.[24] She admitted in a coded reply that she had agreed to entertain Babington's offers, sending him two letters.[25] Her French secretary, Claude Nau, also wrote to Babington, letting him know that Mary had received his correspondence.[26]

Walsingham's first real proof that Mary knew about this latest plot came in a ciphered letter of July 1586 that was intercepted on its way to Charles Paget in Paris. Phelippes quickly decoded the message, making a copy and sending on the original so that suspicions wouldn't be raised among the conspirators. Mary was cautious and reluctant to authorize any action at this stage. She urged Paget to make sure that this new plan had as much backing as possible from the King of Spain and the Pope before any moves were made 'for otherwise they will but overthrow themselves without any profit'.[27] Nevertheless, she admitted that she had given the men 'ample direction', advising them 'point by point to bring their designs to good effect'. Walsingham's heart must have leapt! Here was Mary admitting that she not only had knowledge of a plot but that she had advised the conspirators.

THE BABINGTON PLOT progressed quickly over the summer of 1586. Gifford checked on the brewer at the start of July, confirming that the route was still reliable. Under pressure from Walsingham to find out specifics of the plot, he met with Ballard and asked him outright about the conspirators' plans. The priest told him that they would not take direct action until they had got Mary's own authority; they wanted something in her own hand to validate their next steps. Gifford was flabbergasted. How on earth was such a thing ever to be done? Mary had never been so reckless as to put her own hand to such incriminating documents. He immediately reported back to Walsingham, who once again saw an opportunity to turn things to his own advantage. This was exactly what he, and Elizabeth's ministers, had been seeking for years. If the conspirators got Mary's authorization in writing, Walsingham was in place to intercept it through Gifford. The double agent was told, as was Poley, to encourage Babington to do as Ballard wanted, and ask Mary to give some written confirmation of her agreement.

Babington stepped right into Walsingham's trap. He wrote to Mary that month setting out the plan: there would be an invasion of England and she must be ready at a moment's notice for he would lead one hundred men to rescue her. Damningly, he told her that 'six gentlemen, all of them your friends will undertake the tragic execution of the dispatch of the usurper'.[28] Mary took ten days to reply. She debated whether the risk was too great. She also wrestled with the admission that Elizabeth would be killed. Though this charge had been levelled at her throughout her captivity, Mary had only ever attempted to free herself. She had not sought Elizabeth's death.

In the end though, she did reply to Babington. Her hopes of returning to Scotland had died with her son's betrayal. Her French relatives were never coming to rescue her. King Philip II of Spain seemed to genuinely support this scheme though, and it might just succeed with his help. She had been in an English prison for almost twenty years. Even if she only acknowledged the plot and didn't encourage it, enough had been shared that by the terms of the new act of parliament she was likely to be interrogated anyway. She was in constant pain from the arthritis that riddled her body. And she was at risk of being forgotten; left to wither away, with a dwindling household, and fewer and fewer letters arriving. The time had come to throw caution to the wind. How could she be sure another chance would ever come again?

A letter was drawn up and sent to Babington. Mary was careful to destroy any notes and she made sure not to pen a draft in her own hand. Her words were dictated to her secretaries; Claude Nau wrote a copy in French and Gilbert Curle translated it into English, then into cipher. She started by commending Babington's zeal for the Catholic faith and the affection he had shown towards her cause and spent quite some time setting out why his actions were so important to the Catholics of England who had been 'exposed to all sorts of persecution and cruelty'.[29]

Turning to the specifics of the plot, she urged him to turn to Mendoza for advice. She asked for detailed information about the number of horses and the number of men he planned to raise, what ports had been scouted for the landing of Philip's troops, where he planned to raise his men openly, how much armour he had gathered and how he planned to finance weapons, offering to give him funds if he needed. She also advised him that they would have better chance of success if an uprising was begun in Ireland at the same time because this would distract the English authorities. She requested to know how the conspirators planned to set her free, giving suggestions of her own for the best way of managing this. Fatally, she also asked 'by what means do the six gentlemen deliberate to proceed'. With this one question she sealed her fate. She had directly responded to Babington's proclamation about these 'six gentlemen' who were planning to kill Elizabeth and she asked for further details, entangling herself irreversibly in the conspiracy to assassinate the English queen.

This was it. Walsingham had cracked it. But something niggled at him. He knew that Elizabeth would only accept the most explicit proof. If there was any chance that Mary could wriggle out of things, Elizabeth was liable to succumb and let her off the hook. He had to be absolutely certain. As Phelippes noted, Walsingham was torn between joy and caution, fearing that Elizabeth would not be bold enough to take the necessary steps:

> *If it please God to inspire her majesty with that heroic*
> *courage that were meet for avenging God's cause and*
> *the security of herself and this state.*[30]

And so, Walsingham had Phelippes put his expert skills as a forger to good use once more. Using Babington's cipher, they added in a crucial phrase to Mary's original request to know how the men planned to proceed: 'I would be glad to know the name and qualities of the six gentlemen which are to accomplish the designment.'[31] If Babington replied giving these extra details, then Walsingham could be sure that he had concrete evidence of Mary's involvement and her authorization of the plot to kill Elizabeth. Phelippes called this doctored version 'the bloody letter' knowing it would seal Mary's fate. He even drew gallows on the address leaf.

Mary could do little but wait for Babington to get back to her. As always, she was forced to rely on those around her to gather intelligence and those outside her prison walls to carry out her instructions. Walsingham was waiting with bated breath for Babington's reply too. As July drew to an end, Babington showed no sign that he had even received the letter, however. He and his friends, several of them drawn into the conspiracy, often met for dinner at his favourite tavern The Castle on Cornhill in the heart of the city of London. Finally, on 29 July 1586, he took delivery of the fatal message. It was handed to him by a boy he had never seen before, but this wasn't necessarily concerning – it was commonplace for street children to be paid a small price to deliver messages. This particular young boy, though, was being paid by Thomas Phelippes.

Realizing that Babington had finally received the letter, Walsingham had Poley encourage him to commit himself to the plot as soon as possible. Babington, though, had other ideas: he hoped that he could use Poley to communicate with Walsingham and arrange a meeting where he might be able to confess what he knew. Giving this intelligence might buy himself some leniency. His old fears were once more raising their head – maybe it might be best to ask for a passport out of England? He didn't necessarily plan to give over the names of his fellow conspirators, but simply inform Walsingham that something of significance was being planned. Of course, he had no idea that Walsingham already knew all about the plot. It was too late for deals.

Walsingham agreed to meet Babington but kept pushing back the actual date. He was determined to wait until Mary's letter had a reply, then they would meet, and he could pounce with the evidence. Poley was forced to give excuses to an increasingly anxious Babington and assure him that sticking with the plot was the right thing to do. It seemed he had succeeded when at the start of August Babington wrote to him. Addressing his friend as 'sweet Robin', he reiterated his decision to go through with the plan: 'The furnace is prepared wherein our faith must be tried.'[32] And then, disaster struck. On 4 August 1586, Poley's chambers were raided. Babington watched in terror as Ballard was arrested and taken to the Wood Street prison. While Poley tried his hardest to convince Babington that this was a usual rounding up of suspected priests and had nothing to do with the conspiracy, things were too close for comfort now. There would be no more waiting to speak to Walsingham. For Babington there was only one option: flee.

The conspirators managed to evade the authorities for ten days. Their families and servants were brought in for questioning.[33] Savage, the man who would have wielded the blade against Elizabeth, was taken first. He was interviewed personally by Walsingham but didn't yet reveal the location of his fellows. In the end, the young men were forced to beg for food after spending more than a week in the countryside outside the city. Babington and most of the other men were arrested on 14 August and taken to the Tower of London the next day. Ballard had, by this point, confessed and confirmed the identities of the others involved. Babington was examined nine times while in the Tower between 18 August and 9 September 1586. He was shown copies of the letters between him and Mary and certified that these were true copies of their correspondence. His interrogators brought in samples of the ciphers and Babington wrote underneath them in his own hand: 'This last is the alphabet by which only I have written unto the Queen of Scots or received letters from her.'[34]

These would be crucial pieces of the evidence levelled against Mary, though Walsingham was also hopeful that other proof could be found. At the start of September, Paulet had offered Mary a rare chance to ride out, claiming that the late summer weather was too nice to waste. Mary of course jumped at the chance. She was dressed and ready to go within the hour. She was about one mile from the house at Chartley when she was surrounded by men. They informed her that she was to be moved to another property and that her secretaries were being made prisoners. She was taken immediately to Fotheringhay in Nottinghamshire while

Nau and Curle were escorted to Windsor to be interrogated. Her rooms at Chartley were searched carefully and chests and boxes were broken. Not only were many of her letters seized, but several ciphers were found and taken away, including a stash that had been buried in the gardens.[35]

Mary's secretaries were closely questioned. They were asked if Mary had composed the 'bloody letter' and Nau at least admitted that she had written a rough draft in her own hand in French. Walsingham pounced on this and ordered the men going through Mary's things back at Chartley to find it at once. No evidence of this was ever discovered. Much to Walsingham's disappointment it seems Mary had destroyed any incriminating notes. Curle also confessed that he had deciphered Babington's letters and had translated Mary's reply from French into English and then into cipher. Like Babington, the two secretaries were shown copies of the letters and certified that they were reliable. Walsingham, though, was careful never to show them the section that Phelippes had added, realizing that the men might point out this was not in the original and thereby weaken his case.

The conspirators were tried between 13 and 15 September 1586. There was no question of them being found innocent. All were pronounced guilty of conspiring to free Mary, to help an invasion of England and of plotting to kill the queen. Babington wrote to Elizabeth begging for mercy for his wife, his young daughter and his family:

> Since there can be no proportion betwixt the quality of
> my crime and any human consideration, shew, sweet
> Queen, some miracle upon a wretch lying prostrate

Anthony Babington's letter to Queen Elizabeth pleading for mercy for his wife and young child, beseeching her to recognize that though his 'own most heinous treachery' deserves punishment, his family are 'guiltless'.

in your prison grievously bewailing his offences and
imploring such comfort at your anointed as my poor
wife's misfortune doth beg, my child's innocence doth
crave, my guiltless family doth wish, and my own most
heinous treachery doth least deserve.[36]

At St Giles-in-the-Fields on 20 September, Anthony Babington, John Ballard, John Savage and Chidiock Tichborne were hung, drawn and quartered. Mendoza recorded the grisly events in a letter to the King of Spain, detailing that the rope wound around Babington's neck to hang him, suddenly snapped and that his chest was cut open while he was still conscious. As the executioner removed his heart, he was heard to have whispered 'Jesus' three times.[37]

And what of the men who ensured Walsingham's plan succeeded? Gilbert Gifford fled to Paris. He continued to work for Walsingham, but in order to keep him safe (and useful) he was denounced publicly as a traitor. His father, thinking that his son was a wanted criminal and not knowing that Gifford was in fact still secretly working for the authorities, condemned his actions.[38] In 1587, he was found in a brothel and was held for several months before being taken before the papal investigators. Walsingham seems to have made sure that his role as a spy for the English authorities was genuinely kept quiet because no verdict was pronounced against Gifford. He was, however, kept in prison in Paris. He died there in 1590.

Robert Poley was dragged in for questioning as a suspected conspirator. His role as Walsingham's man had to be kept secret and he was forced to give a very detailed confession of everything he knew about the plot. He admitted to being friends with Babington and of hearing from him and his friends of their designs to free Mary, but denied knowing of any plot to kill Elizabeth. Walsingham had drawn up a list of questions to be used in Poley's interrogation; he was to be asked why he had paid for Babington's dinner in the Castle tavern![39] He was clearly trying to keep things easy for the young man, but without revealing that he had been Poley's actual master. Poley spent two years in the Tower before being released. He continued in Walsingham's employ but was able to move more openly and took on more official tasks. Even after Walsingham's death, he was an agent of the crown and travelled across Europe. Poley would later be implicated in the death of the renowned playwright Christopher Marlowe in 1593.

FOR MARY, THE discovery of the Babington Plot was disastrous. Just as Walsingham had intended, there was no way she could deny her own involvement. Not with any real effect anyway. Just like almost twenty years ago, Mary was once more put on trial. This commission also sought to investigate her knowledge of the attempted killing of a monarch. Mary protested yet again that she could not be tried by a foreign court, but Walsingham was having none of it. Because this latest scheme had aimed to kill the English queen, then the English state could, and would, investigate. The severity of the crimes – the assassination of a lawful monarch and the invasion of England by foreign forces – also overcame any concern about her own royal status. For Walsingham, Cecil and most other English courtiers, Mary had been a 'guest' in Elizabeth's realm for years and this was how she repaid such kindness.

The trial was to be held at Fotheringhay between 12 and 15 October 1586. Unlike the last time when a small number of nobles were chosen to oversee the commission against Mary, this time a large panel was prepared. There were more than forty attendees, including ten earls, one viscount and twelve barons. Long benches were moved into the great hall of the house, lined on either side of the room. A table and chairs were placed in the centre for two crown officers and public notaries to take detailed notes. The entire trial was conducted under the great cloth of state showing Elizabeth's arms. Royal justice was on display here; Elizabeth's authority was made clear.

Though Mary refused to recognize the authority of the commission, she did attend in person. She was not allowed a lawyer or permitted to examine the documents that were used in evidence against her, but this was common in treason trials. Instead, the proofs were read aloud. When it came to the incriminating letter to Babington, Walsingham made sure that the fateful postscript added by Phelippes was left out. It was felt that they had enough evidence from the original letter and the testimonies of the conspirators and Mary's secretaries. It was not worth the risk of any detailed questions about the postscript. Though Mary tried to deny knowing Babington and claimed she had no knowledge of any plot against Elizabeth, it was evident from her own correspondence that she had written to Elizabeth's enemies about the events planned. Reference was made to a ciphered letter she had sent to the Archbishop of Glasgow in May 1586, which asked for an update on Spanish preparations for the 'enterprise in England' and instructed him to thank Mendoza for sending on money to her.[40]

When faced with the confessions of Curle and Nau, Mary quickly responded that they were only trying to save themselves and had spoken through fear. She also mocked Walsingham by reminding him that in fact he had found no letters in her own hand. She asked outright to see any letters in her handwriting but, of course, no such documents could be produced. This allowed her to claim that anything that had been put in the ciphered letter to Babington had been altered, either by her secretaries or by other unknown parties. Walsingham, knowing full well that the letter had indeed been doctored on his orders, kept quiet. But even disregarding the letter as evidence, the confessions of the conspirators and the numerous letters intercepted and copied over the past year still built a strong case against Mary. She might implausibly deny knowing Babington, but her letters to Mendoza and Morgan showed this was untrue. When pushed on this point, she agreed that she had sought intelligence from friends and that people sent her news regularly, but snapped that this was only natural for one held in such difficult conditions. She quietly but calmly spoke directly to Walsingham, telling him that no spy was ever truly trustworthy: they all turn on their master. She was telling him she knew that he had turned her men against her while warning that the same could happen to him.

As the questioning dragged on, Mary became frustrated. She would occasionally weep as she listened to the evidence against her. But she remained sharp and directly turned on Walsingham asking him: are you an honest man? Though he had been quite ill right up to the start of the commission, he stood and addressed her. He proclaimed that in his private life he was an honest man, but he had no shame in admitting that when it came to the safety of Elizabeth and the future of England, he had undertaken all actions that were necessary. Mary began to cry on hearing this. She knew then that her cause was lost. If Walsingham could stand in court and admit that there was no action deemed dishonourable if done to protect Elizabeth, the men around him would not disagree. There were to be no allies here. Standing suddenly, she withdrew and refused to return.

Though the commission continued in her absence, Elizabeth intervened and ordered Cecil to make sure that there was no pronouncement of guilt against Mary. Walsingham must have been irate – after all his careful work, here was Elizabeth once more dodging the decision of action against Mary. The trial was adjourned for ten days. It reconvened in the Star Chamber in Westminster, but Mary was not present this time as she was still held in Fotheringhay. Curle and Nau were brought in and both swore to the accuracy of the documents they had been shown and once more certified that their testimonies were true. At this point, Curle went further, adding that he had actually warned Mary of the danger of responding to Babington's first letter to her. He claimed that Mary had ignored his concerns and ordered himself and Nau to draw up the reply. Walsingham and Cecil cajoled Elizabeth, and eventually she agreed that the commission could pass sentence against Mary. She was found guilty of knowledge of a plot that sought the death of Queen Elizabeth I of England.

Writing to Mendoza after the sentence was pronounced against her, Mary described herself as a 'free Catholic princess and obedient daughter of the Church … for which I have publicly offered my life'.[41] Astutely, she asked him to make sure that her side of the story was made public, for she suspected that 'these people may make things appear different from what they were'. As such, she emphasized that she had never tried to seek Elizabeth's death but insisted that she was found guilty because her faith and her right to inherit the English crown were too threatening to the English authorities. To Mendoza, she made no attempt to hide her involvement in the Babington Plot – how could she when she had asked him to help the 'poor English gentlemen whom I cannot help recommending to you directly'?[42] Instead, she confessed that she had been 'duty bound to seek my deliverance since I had tried by fair means unsuccessfully and was obliged therefore to listen to other proposals made to me with the same object.' She lamented that out of spite Paulet had taken away her dais and pulled down her cloth of state. She was addressed only as Mary now, her royal status no longer recognized. She had asked for a Catholic priest to comfort herself and her women, but this was refused, though she would not accept a minister of the English Church. She closed by apologizing to him for the poor quality of her letter, admitting she was 'writing in pain and trouble'.

For Walsingham, only part of the battle was won, however. Elizabeth might have allowed Mary to be found guilty, but it didn't mean she would permit any action against her. Though she was badgered by her courtiers and harassed by parliament to execute Mary, Elizabeth was wracked with indecision. She still could not bring herself to kill a fellow monarch. Yet she had been persuaded by her nobles' argument: Mary was a threat to her and would eventually ensure her own destruction. Elizabeth secretly asked Mary's jailor Paulet to have her quietly killed. For all that

Mary had feared that very thing, Paulet was astonished. To his credit, he refused, claiming such an action would forever stain his soul. Finally, in February 1587, Elizabeth signed the warrant for the execution of Mary, Queen of Scots. Before she could change her mind again, Cecil had it sent to Fotheringhay.

Mary was not given long to prepare for her death. She was informed on 7 February that she was to be put to death. She retreated to her rooms. There she comforted her women and servants and spent hours praying. She wanted to make sure that her final will and testament was in order, but she was not allowed access to her papers. That night she turned to writing letters, as she had done for the past twenty years. Writing in her own hand, her secretaries not having been allowed to come back to her after the trial, she wrote to her French relatives. To King Henri III of France, she asked for help for her servants. She condemned Elizabeth for holding her as a captive for all these years. She claimed that it was only because she would not give up her right to the English throne and because of her Catholic faith that she was to be executed. She was disgusted that she was to be killed 'like a criminal'.[43] Despite French sympathy, Elizabeth sent a special ambassador to Paris to combat resistance to the trial and sentence against Mary. Edward, Baron Wotton's mission was to convince the French that Mary had betrayed them and turned to Spain. Copies of her letters were shown and her decision to leave her inheritance rights to Spain was emphasized. Thus French efforts to stop the process against Mary were more half-hearted than she might have hoped for.

On 8 February 1587, Mary walked calmly to a platform raised in the great hall where she had been tried almost six months earlier. George Talbot, Earl of Shrewsbury, the man who had been her custodian for so long, was there to watch her life come to an end. She had two ladies with her, Elizabeth Curle and Janet Kennedy. The young women wept as they ascended but Mary quietly consoled them. They helped her remove her outer garments and tied the blindfold around Mary's eyes. As she knelt, she was heard to speak the words '*In manus tuas Domine commendo spiritum meum*' (Into thy hands O Lord I commend my spirit). Her head was then removed from her body. She was forty-four years old. Mary accepted her fate and had tried her best to ensure her memorialization. We know this because of her letters. We can end our journey with one of Mary's very last ciphered letters:

> *God has given me courage to accept cheerfully this*
> *very unjust sentence from the heretics because of the*
> *happiness I feel at shedding my blood at the bidding of*
> *the enemies of the Church, who do me the honour of*
> *saying they cannot continue without disturbance whilst*
> *I live.*[44]

That Mary had the measure of her English adversaries is shown in a ballad that was published in London in 1586. It set out the conspiracy and condemned the various men involved in the plot. It urged the people of England to 'rejoice in heart' and to thank God who 'hath preserved us by his power from traitors' tyranny'. Just as Mary had said, this popular cheap print decried the 'rage of Rome, the fruits of Popish plants'.[45] Walsingham and Cecil might have succeeded in their quest to bring down Mary and remove what they perceived as the threat she embodied to the safety of the realm and the future of England. But, in reality, her death simply sparked a new danger: Philip II of Spain realized that the time had come for him to go it alone against Elizabeth. There would be no French help, and no Scots support. Instead, he needed an immense fleet. War with Spain was now inevitable.

'Your Humble and Obedient Son'

₁

Begging you very humbly to believe that I shall always remain your very humble and very obedient son, and as long as I live I will bear you the honour and duty that I owe you; believing you will also honour me always with your maternal affection, and that you will recognize me as such.[2]

ARY NEVER SAW her son before her death. James had been brought up in the care of the Earl and Countess of Mar at Stirling Castle from infancy. When she visited him there on 21 April 1567, Mary had no idea that they would never set eyes on one another again. She wrote to his guardians ceaselessly asking for updates on his physical health and his wellbeing. She sent gifts as often as she could – dogs and ponies when she was able, toys and books regularly – though his guardians rarely allowed him to receive these. Though her relationship with James was kept at a physical distance, she took great pleasure in speaking about him. Her letters from her years of English captivity are filled with comments on her son. As we saw, shared care and concern for James was one of the main reasons why Mary reconciled with her mother-in-law, Margaret Douglas.

As a child, James struggled to push back against the advisors and men around him, men who were unwilling to encourage a close relationship between mother and son. He inevitably heard the criticisms levelled at his mother by her adversaries in Scotland. His tutor George Buchanan, writer of the attack on Mary used to such effect by Cecil in 1571, was a hard disciplinarian, but brought the young king to appreciate learning. He was brought up in the strict presbyterian faith of Buchanan and his nobles, taught to disdain if not outright despise his mother's Catholic faith. Of his personal feelings we can know little during these years, while his political decisions were dominated by the various Regents.

The arrival of Esmé Stuart, 6th Seigneur d'Aubigny, in Scotland was an opportunity, Mary thought, to bring her son back to her. Here was a French supporter who could challenge her enemies at the Scottish court. Yet the Scots nobles had come to the same conclusion and were unwilling to allow Lennox to set back their own causes. Though Lennox succeeded in bringing down the Regent, the Earl of Morton, he himself was forced out of power following the dramatic events of the Ruthven Raid in August 1582 when James was kidnapped. As we have seen, this event had a deep impact on James, convincing him that he must step out from under the influence of others and rule in his own right. This proved disastrous for Mary because it led to the failure of the negotiations for an association that would have seen her set at liberty to return to Scotland to rule jointly with her son. French diplomats despaired that James could so easily, it appeared, turn his back on his mother. But this was a young man who had had no physical contact with his mother since he was an infant and who had been brought up to believe the very worst of her character. Despite the best efforts of his nobles and advisors, he did not hate Mary but was at times indifferent to her predicament. He was often dealing with serious challenges to his rule himself.

In the early 1580s, Mary repeatedly requested that either of her secretaries, Claude Nau or Gilbert Curle, be allowed to travel to Scotland to speak to her son more openly. Writing a letter to James, she urged him to beseech Elizabeth to agree to this visit 'in as much as you hold my benediction dear'.[3] She was permitted to send someone in 1582, but when she asked a second time the passport for such a journey was never granted. Instead, she had to rely on men such as William Fowler and Archibald Douglas, men who were eventually corrupted by Walsingham. She also turned to Patrick, Lord Gray, as a means to communicate with her son. Gray had travelled to France where he converted to Catholicism and joined Mary's cause. For several years he was a useful ally, being able to ensure messages reached Scotland. But in 1583, he encouraged James not to go ahead with the proposed association for joint rule. He may have genuinely believed the bond to have been against James's interests – certainly several Scots nobles felt that it was unnecessary – especially after the young king had broken free of the yoke of domineering guardians. To Mary though, this was yet another betrayal. She was not particularly impressed with James's decision to send Gray to negotiate with Elizabeth over her fate in late 1586. Though outwardly still a supporter of Mary, his speech did little to persuade the English to change their minds over her sentence following the Babington Plot.

Some letters survive between James and Mary. He wrote to her in his own hand, but this was an expected practice of letter-writing culture; children should write in their own hands to parents as a mark of respect. He often wrote in French, which may have been a way of accommodating his mother, using her preferred language, but this can also be seen as a pointed marker distancing her from her position as Queen of Scots. He used a beautiful italic hand, showing off his learning and writing skills. And he made sure to always use deferential language, emphasizing his duty and devotion to his mother, signing with the phrase 'I shall always remain your very humble and very obedient son'.[4]

In his letters James did a good job of appearing to be a dutiful son. He assured Mary that he was doing his utmost to have the association confirmed. He was willing to do everything in his power to secure her deliverance, which he claimed he wished for 'above all the happiness of this world'.[5] Yet behind the scenes, his direct negotiations with Elizabeth and her advisors would lead to him signing a separate agreement that cut out Mary entirely. He nevertheless wished to be seen by the outside world as a good son. In a letter to Mary from 1581, he reveals his concern that others were developing a negative opinion of him and his efforts to support his mother:

> *I was very much displeased that anyone should think I would not bear you the honour and duty I owe you [...] knowing well enough that above Him all the honour I have in this world I hold from you.*[6]

We do not know if Mary wrote to James on the eve of her execution as she did to other relatives. Perhaps a letter reached him, or maybe she chose not to write, their relationship having become too distant by this time. Different reports circulated after he was informed of his mother's execution: James gave little reaction or he retreated to his private chambers. Diplomatic contact with England was not severed, but his letters to Elizabeth were cool. He did accept Elizabeth's rebuttal of her own involvement, pushing blame onto the messenger who had carried the warrant. We cannot be too harsh on James of course, knowing the trials he had faced growing up, and the opportunity he had to succeed to the English throne. It is also important to remember that Mary had herself given up his rights of inheritance, offering the English succession to King Philip II of Spain.

When he ascended as King of England in 1603, James had Mary moved from her tomb at Peterborough Cathedral and reinterred in Westminster Abbey. He also had a new edition of Buchanan's *Ane detectioun of the duinges of Marie Quene of Scottes* published with a dedicatory chapter of sorts included, honouring his mother's sufferings. In one of his own texts, the *Basilikon Doron*, he savaged his uncle the Earl of Moray, who had gained the regency at Mary's expense after her forced abdication. Whether these were all the efforts of a loving and slightly guilty son or whether James was simply keen to ensure that the wider world saw his efforts as those of a suitably dutiful son, we can but guess.

Chronology

8 December 1542: Mary is born at Linlithgow Palace.

14 December 1542: Mary's father King James V dies at Falkland Palace.

1 July 1543: Treaty of Greenwich signed between Scotland and England, agreeing the marriage of Mary and Henry VIII's heir Prince Edward.

9 September 1543: Mary crowned Queen of Scots at Stirling Castle.

19 January 1544: Francis, Dauphin of France, and Mary's future first husband, is born.

3 May 1544: Edward Seymour, Earl of Hertford leads an army into Scotland following the Scots rejection of the Treaty of Greenwich, beginning the 'Rough Wooing'.

27 February 1545: Battle of Ancrum Moor. Scots defeat a larger English army.

7 December 1545: Henry Stuart, Lord Darnley is born.

28 January 1547: Death of Henry VIII of England. His son succeeds him as Edward VI.

10 September 1547: Battle of Pinkie Cleugh. English forces defeat Scots.

7 July 1548: Mary is betrothed to the Dauphin Francis.

29 July 1548: Mary boards a ship at Dumbarton and leaves for France.

6 July 1553: Edward VI of England dies. Mary Tudor eventually succeeds to the throne of England following the nine-day reign of Lady Jane Grey.

25 July 1554: Mary Tudor, Queen of England marries the son of Emperor Charles V, Philip of Spain.

16 January 1556: Philip inherits the Spanish throne at his father's command, becoming King Philip II of Spain.

24 April 1558: Mary, Queen of Scots marries the Dauphin Francis at Notre-Dame Cathedral, Paris.

17 November 1558: Mary Tudor dies. She is succeeded by her half-sister Elizabeth I.

22 November 1558: William Cecil appointed Secretary of State to Queen Elizabeth I.

10 July 1559: King of France, Henri II, dies following injuries sustained during a jousting tournament. Francis becomes King of France and Mary, Queen of Scots becomes Queen of France.

1560: Protestant church formally established in Scotland.

11 June 1560: Marie de Guise, Mary's mother and Regent of Scotland, dies at Edinburgh Castle.

5 December 1560: King Francis dies of an ear infection which may have caused meningitis, leaving Mary as dowager queen of France. His brother succeeds as Charles IX.

April 1561: Mary meets her half-brother, James Stewart, future Regent of Scotland, at St Dizier, France and agrees to return to Scotland.

19 August 1561: Mary arrives in Leith, having departed France less than a week earlier. She is joined by French ambassador Michel de Castelnau, Sieur de la Mauvissière.

24 August 1561: Mary hears a private mass at the Palace of Holyroodhouse, outraging the Protestant leaders.

2 September 1561: Mary hosts a state banquet and parades through Edinburgh.

11–29 September 1561: Mary undertakes a progress through the north-east of Scotland.

8 February 1562: Mary's half-brother James Stewart marries Annas Keith, daughter of the Earl Marischal at St Giles Cathedral, Edinburgh. Mary privately appoints her brother to the title of Earl of Moray.

3 March–14 May 1562: Mary makes a progress through Fife, staying briefly at Lochleven Castle.

11 August–22 November 1562: Mary goes on progress once more, travelling through the north-east and Perthshire.

September 1562: Mary is refused entry to Inverness Castle by the Captain there, a follower of George Gordon, Earl of Huntly. After a three-day siege, the castle is captured and the Captain hanged from the battlements. Sir John Gordon, Huntly's son, leads a force to kidnap Mary, but they are repulsed. James Stewart's title of Earl of Moray is proclaimed publicly.

16 October 1562: George Gordon, Earl of Huntly and his son Sir John Gordon are declared outlaws.

28 October 1562: Battle of Corrichie, Aberdeenshire. Mary's forces, led by her half-brother James Stewart, Earl of Moray, defeat the forces of Huntly and his son. Huntly suffers a seizure or stroke and dies on the battlefield.

2 November 1562: Sir John Gordon executed at Aberdeen, with Mary reluctantly looking on.

May 1563: Huntly's embalmed corpse is tried and declared traitor.

March 1564: Michel de Castelnau, Sieur de la Mauvissière, returns to Scotland as French ambassador.

25 February 1565: The courtship of Mary and Henry Stuart, Lord Darnley begins during a dance at the Palace of Holyroodhouse.

29 July 1565: Mary marries Darnley at the Palace of Holyroodhouse.

August–October 1565: During the 'Chase-about Raid' Mary rides out to capture the Earl of Moray after his rebellion. He flees to England.

9 March 1566: Mary's favoured secretary, David Rizzio, is murdered in her private apartments at the Palace of Holyroodhouse.

19 June 1566: Mary gives birth to her son, the future King James VI of Scotland and I of England, at Edinburgh Castle.

17 October 1566: Mary suffers a severe illness and almost dies while at Jedburgh.

17 December 1566: Prince James is baptized at Stirling.

21 January 1566: Mary visits Darnley at Glasgow, where he is recovering from illness.

10 February 1567: Darnley is murdered at Kirk o' Field, Edinburgh, in the early hours of the morning.

12 April 1567: Bothwell is acquitted of Darnley's murder despite Darnley's father, the Earl of Lennox's, protests.

24 April 1567: Mary is abducted by Bothwell and taken to Dunbar Castle.

15 May 1567: Mary marries Bothwell.

15 June 1567: Mary surrenders to her nobles at the Battle of Carberry Hill, near Musselburgh. Bothwell flees.

17 June 1567: Mary is imprisoned at Lochleven Castle, Perthshire.

24 July 1567: Mary is forced to abdicate in favour of her son, James VI.

29 July 1567: James VI is crowned at Stirling.

22 August 1567: James Stewart, Earl of Moray, Mary's half-brother, is proclaimed Regent of Scotland.

August 1567: Bothwell escapes to Norway via Orkney and Shetland.

January 1568: Bothwell is captured and taken to Malmö Castle, Sweden.

2 May 1568: Mary escapes from Lochleven Castle. She is taken to George, Lord Seton's property at Niddrie.

10–11 May 1568: Mary is sheltered at Hamilton Castle and Craignethan Castle.

13 May 1568: Mary is defeated at the Battle of Langside, outside Glasgow, by forces led by her half-brother James Stewart, Earl of Moray and Regent of Scotland.

16 May 1568: Mary flees from Dundrennan Abbey, crossing the Solway Firth to arrive at Workington in Cumbria. She is sheltered at Workington Hall, home of Sir Henry Curwen.

18 May 1568: Mary is escorted to Carlisle Castle.

21 May 1568: Thomas Percy, 7th Earl of Northumberland visits Mary at Carlisle and attempts to take her into his personal protection.

13 July 1568: Mary is moved from Carlisle Castle to Bolton Castle.

October–December 1568: Commissions to assess whether Mary was guilty of the murder of her husband Darnley, held first at

York, then Westminster and finally Hampton Court. The Casket Letters are produced by James Stewart, Earl of Moray and Regent of Scotland.

10 January 1569: The Commissions end with no formal conclusion.

26 January 1569: Mary is moved to Tutbury Castle, Staffordshire and is placed in the custody of George Talbot, Earl of Shrewsbury.

20 April 1569: Mary enjoys time away from Tutbury, moving to Wingfield Manor in Derbyshire.

25 May 1569: Mary is moved once more, this time to Chatsworth House.

21 September 1569: Mary returns to Tutbury.

November–December 1569: Northern Rebellion led by Thomas Percy, 7th Earl of Northumberland and Charles Neville, 6th Earl of Westmorland. Thomas Howard, 4th Duke of Norfolk is implicated and held in the Tower of London.

25 November 1569: Mary is taken to Coventry to keep her out of reach of the rebels in the north.

2 January 1570: Mary moves back to Tutbury.

23 January 1570: James Stewart, Earl of Moray and Regent of Scotland assassinated in Linlithgow.

25 February 1570: Pope Pius V issues a bull of excommunication against Elizabeth I of England.

11 July 1570: Darnley's father, Matthew Stewart, Earl of Lennox, is appointed Regent of Scotland.

August 1570: Thomas Howard, Duke of Norfolk is released from the Tower of London.

October 1570: William Cecil and Sir Walter Mildmay visit Mary at Chatsworth.

28 November 1570: Mary is moved to Sheffield Castle.

April 1571: Sir William Kirkcaldy of Grange occupies Edinburgh Castle on behalf of Mary, establishing it as a site of resistance for her supporters against those nobles who support James VI and his regents.

4 September 1571: Regent Lennox is killed at Stirling during a skirmish with the Earl of Huntly's men. John Erskine, Earl of Mar replaces Lennox as Regent.

September 1571: Ridolfi plot is discovered.

7 October 1571: Battle of Lepanto. Catholic states defeat an Ottoman fleet. Don Juan of Austria, half-brother of King Philip II of Spain, is admiral of the Catholic fleet.

November 1571: The Casket Letters are published as part of *Ane detectioun of the duinges of Marie Quene of Scottes*.

1 May 1572: Pope Pius V dies and is succeeded by Pope Gregory XIII.

2 June 1572: Thomas Howard, Duke of Norfolk is executed for his involvement in the Ridolfi Plot.

13 July 1572: William Cecil is appointed Lord High Treasurer of England.

22 August 1572: Thomas Percy, 7th Earl of Northumberland is executed for his role in the Northern Rebellion of 1569 after being returned to England from Scotland.

23 August 1572: St Bartholomew's Day Massacre sees thousands of Protestants killed in Paris and across France.

28 October 1572: John Erskine, Earl of Mar and Regent of Scotland dies. James Douglas, Earl of Morton becomes the next Regent of Scotland.

24 November 1572: John Knox, leader of the Scottish Reformation, dies.

17 May 1573: Edinburgh Castle is finally taken from Kirkcaldy of Grange, falling to the Regent's men after a twelve-day bombardment.

25 April 1573: Mary moves to Sheffield Manor.

June 1573: Bothwell is moved to Dragsholm Castle, Denmark.

22 August 1573: Mary travels to Buxton to visit the spa.

27 September 1573: Mary is returned to Chatsworth.

20 December 1573: Sir Francis Walsingham appointed Secretary of State by Elizabeth I after he returns from his post as ambassador to France.

30 May 1574: King Charles IX of France dies and is succeeded by his brother Henri III.

June 1574: Mary visits Buxton again.

July 1575: Mary is permitted to visit Buxton once more.

September 1575: Michel de Castelnau, Sieur de la Mauvissière is appointed French ambassador to England.

March 1576: Mary is moved to Sheffield Manor.

June 1576: Mary visits the spa at Buxton.

July 1576: Mary returns to Sheffield Manor.

11 February 1577: Mary writes up her will.

May 1577: Mary moves to Chatsworth.

November 1577: Mary returns to Sheffield Castle.

March 1578: A papal fleet sets out for Ireland led by English exile Sir Thomas Stukely, aiming to establish a base there from which invade England.

14 April 1578: Bothwell dies, after suffering years of insanity, in prison at Dragsholm Castle, Denmark.

August 1578: Mary is taken to Chatsworth once more.

5 October 1578: Mary returns to Sheffield Manor.

1578: Don Bernardino de Mendoza arrives in London as the new Spanish ambassador, replacing Antonio de Guarás.

1 October 1578: Don Juan of Austria, Governor of the Spanish Netherlands, dies of a fever.

1579: Esmé Stuart, Seigneur d'Aubigny arrives in Scotland and becomes a close confidant of the young James VI.

June 1579: Mary is again at Chatsworth.

September 1579: James VI begins his personal rule in Scotland.

25 March 1580: King Philip II of Spain becomes King of Portugal in the union of the Iberian crowns.

26 July 1580: Mary visits the spa at Buxton.

16 August 1580: Mary returns to Sheffield Manor.

2 June 1581: James Douglas, Earl of Morton, former Regent of Scotland, is executed for his role in the murder of Darnley.

5 August 1581: Esmé Stuart, Seigneur d'Aubigny created Lord Aubigny and Duke of Lennox.

23 August 1582: James VI of Scotland is kidnapped by disaffected nobles led by William Ruthven, Earl of Gowrie. Aubigny is forced to leave Scotland and return to France.

26 May 1583: Esmé Stuart, Lord Aubigny and Duke of Lennox dies in France.

July 1583: James VI escapes his abductors and reaches his own men at St Andrews Castle.

November 1583: Throckmorton Plot is discovered.

January 1584: Don Bernardino de Mendoza, Spanish ambassador to England is expelled following his involvement in the Throckmorton Plot.

May 1584: William Ruthven, Earl of Gowrie is executed.

July 1584: Mary visits Buxton. Francis Throckmorton and his fellow plotters are executed for the conspiracy against Queen Elizabeth.

10 July 1584: William of Orange, leader of the Protestant rebels in the Low Countries, is assassinated.

8 August 1584: Mary returns to Sheffield Manor.

August 1584: Sir Ralph Sadler replaces George Talbot, Earl of Shrewsbury as Mary's keeper.

October 1584: Bond of Association is proposed.

4 January 1585: Sir Amyas Paulet is named as Mary's new keeper.

March 1585: The Act for the Queen's Safety proclaimed, ensuring that anyone implicated in plots against Queen Elizabeth will be guilty of treason.

19 April 1585: Paulet arrives at Tutbury Castle.

September 1585: Michel de Castelnau, Sieur de la Mauvissière is recalled to France and is replaced as ambassador by Guillaume de l'Aubespine, baron de Châteauneuf.

24 December 1585: Mary is taken to Chartley Castle.

April–August 1586: Babington Plot begins to take shape.

6 July 1586: Treaty of Berwick agrees mutual military support between Queen Elizabeth and James VI.

17 July 1586: Mary writes to Babington regarding the plot.

4 August 1586: The Babington Plot is uncovered publicly.

11 August 1586: Mary removed from Chartley and her papers are seized.

25 August 1586: Mary returned briefly to Chartley.

20 September 1586: The Babington plotters are hanged, drawn, and quartered in London.

25 September 1586: Mary arrives at Fotheringhay Castle in Northamptonshire.

11 October 1586: Commissioners arrive at Fotheringhay Castle to begin the trial of Mary.

12 October 1586: The trial against Mary begins.

14 October 1586: Mary appears at the trial.

15 October 1586: The trial is adjourned.

25 October 1586: The trial restarts and Mary is found guilty of treason.

4 December 1586: A proclamation announcing Mary's involvement in the Babington Plot is released.

1 February 1587: Queen Elizabeth finally signs the warrant for Mary's execution.

3 February 1587: Privy Council sends the warrant without informing Elizabeth as she has begun to have second thoughts.

7 February 1587: George Talbot, Earl of Shrewsbury informs Mary that she is to be executed the following morning.

8 February 1587: Mary is executed at Fotheringhay.

Notes

PREFACE

1   Cipher symbol for 'practise' from a page of ciphers used by Mary, Queen of Scots, c.1586, The National Archives (TNA), SP53/22 f. 1.

2   Mary, Queen of Scots to Guillaume de l'Aubespine de Châteauneuf, 31 January 1586, deciphered copy, TNA, SP 53/17.

3   Mary to Don Bernardino de Mendoza, 23 November 1586, *Calendar of State Papers, Spain (Simancas)* Vol. 3, 1580–1586, edited by Martin A. S. Hume (London, 1843–1910) (*CSP*), p. 663.

4   For the complexities of authorship and authority in editing Mary's letters see: Jade Scott, 'Editing the Letters of Mary, Queen of Scots: The Challenges of Authorship,' in *Women's Writing*, 30(4), 2023, pp. 353–368.

5   Nadine Akkerman, *The Correspondence of Elizabeth Stuart, Queen of Bohemia,* Vol. I (Oxford: Oxford University Press, 2015).

6   George Lasry, Norbert Biermann and Satoshi Tomokiyo, 'Deciphering Mary Stuart's Lost Letters From 1578–1584', *Cryptologia*, 47(2), 2023, pp. 101–202.

7   Mary to Michel de Castelnau, Sieur de la Mauvissière, 2 May 1578, Bibliothèque nationale de France (BnF), Fr. 2988 f. 87; Mary to Mauvissière, 8 November 1579, BnF, Fr. 20506, f. 241; Lasry et al., 'Deciphering Mary Stuart's Lost Letters', p. 137–9.

8   Francis, Duke of Alençon was named Hercule but changed his name to honour the death of his brother Francis II of France. It was also claimed that he did not suit his birth name Hercule and he was keen to change it anyway.

9   John Bossy, *Under the Molehill: An Elizabethan Spy Story* (London: Yale University Press, 2002), p. 33.

10 Mary to Mauvissière, 25 February 1584, British Library (BL), Harley MS 1582, f. 311. The newly decoded original cipher letter is at BnF, Fr. 2988, f. 58; Bossy, *Under the Molehill*, p. 106.

11 Bossy, *Under the Molehill*, pp. 66–81.

INTRODUCTION

1 Cipher symbol for 'Queen of Scotland' from a page of ciphers used by Mary, Queen of Scots, c.1586, TNA, SP53/22 f. 1.

2 Mary, Queen of Scots to Queen Elizabeth I of England, 29 September 1585, from Tutbury Castle, Staffordshire, British Library (BL), Cotton MS Caligula C/VII f. 140. Original letter in Mary's own hand, written in French. Translation my own.

3 A letter written in French and in her own hand by Mary to King Henri III of France, the brother of her first husband, Francis II. This is traditionally accepted as the last letter that Mary wrote before her execution, though we can't be certain that others weren't prepared at the same time or even later, during the very last minutes before she was taken to her execution. We certainly know she wrote this one at 2 o'clock in the morning on Wednesday 8 February 1587 while at Fotheringhay Castle, Northamptonshire. The letter is held in the National Library of Scotland (Adv.MS.54.1.1) and can be viewed online at https://digital.nls.uk/mqs/index.html.

4 This example was a letter sent by Mary to Bertrand de Salignac de la Mothe-Fénelon, French ambassador to England from 1568 to 1575. She wrote it on 26 June 1568 while she was at Carlisle Castle, six weeks after first arriving in England. The letter is in French and in the hand of a secretary but includes a postscript in Mary's own hand in which she asks him to secure a passport so that a supporter, George Douglas, can travel safely to France. Douglas had helped engineer Mary's escape from Lochleven Castle. https://www.bbc.co.uk/news/uk-england-cumbria-60241735.

5 Sir Ralph Sadler to William Cecil, 11 January 1572, TNA, SP 53/8 f. 9.

6 In The National Archives, Kew, London, there are 75 examples of ciphers attributed to Mary, Queen of Scots spanning the mid-1570s to 1586, TNA, State Papers [SP] 53/23.

7 William Maitland of Lethington to Agnes Fleming, Lady Livingston, TNA, SP 52/43 f. 140.

8   For letters hidden under stones, see George Talbot, Earl of Shrewsbury to Cecil, 28 February 1572, TNA, 53/8 f. 43; for books and fabrics, see Mary to James Beaton, Archbishop of Glasgow, deciphered copy, TNA, SP 53/10 f. 95.

9   List of Mary's household, 30 May 1586, TNA, SP 53/17 f. 91.

10 Some of the most accomplished biographies include Antonia Fraser, *Mary Queen of Scots* (London: W&N, 2018); Retha N. Warnicke, *Mary Queen of Scots* (London: Routledge, 2006); John Guy, *My Heart is My Own: The Life of Mary Queen of Scots* (London: Harper Perennial, 2004).

11 Known as the Craigmillar Bond, after the castle where the nobles met to discuss their plans.

12 Mary to her mother, Marie de Guise, c.1550, National Records of Scotland, SP13/71.

13 Mary to Cecil, 4 December 1569, TNA, SP 53/4 f. 81.

14 The excellent 'Letter locking' project led by Jana Dambroglio and Daniel Starza Smith has reconstructed the physical ways that writers secured their letters in the early modern period. They have a series of videos recreating letters, https://letterlocking.org.

15 Jana Dambrogio, Daniel Starza Smith, Jennifer Pellecchia and Alison Wiggins et al., 'The Spiral-Locked Letters of Elizabeth I and Mary, Queen of Scots', *Electronic British Library Journal*, 11, 2021.

16 Mary to King Henri III of France, 8 February 1587, National Library of Scotland, Adv.MS.54.1.1.

17 Nadine Akkerman, 'Enigmatic Cultures of Cryptology', in *Cultures of Correspondence in Early Modern Britain*, ed. Daybell and Gordon, pp. 69–84.

18 Mary to her mother, Marie de Guise, April 1550, National Records of Scotland, SP13/79. It is difficult to say conclusively whether the letter was folded in this style because of the conservation of the paper laid out flat, but initial examination suggests several narrow folds indicative of the plaiting style.

19 *Oxford English Dictionary*: 'friend' https://www.oed.com/dictionary/friend_n?tab=meaning_and_use#3721913

20 Mary to Cecil, 9 November 1569, TNA, SP 53/4 f. 57.

21 In one of her late letters to Cecil dated 2 May 1585, in the heat of the Throckmorton Plot, Mary signed off 'vostre entierement meilleur amye' [your entirely best friend].

22 Mary to Annas Keith, Countess of Moray, 23 March 1570, National
    Register of Archives for Scotland, NRAS217 Stuart Family, Earls of
    Moray.

CHAPTER ONE

1   Cipher symbol for 'Queen of England' from a page of ciphers used by
    Mary, Queen of Scots, c.1586, TNA, SP53/22 f. 1.
2   'Quhair as ye wrait to us that we in former letters blamit thame that
    keipis nocht promissis both thinkis ane thing and dois ane other: we
    wald ye sould remember the same' Mary to Elizabeth, 15 March 1566,
    TNA, SP 52/12 f.58.
3   Agnes Strickland, *Life of Mary Queen of Scots*, (1873), vol 2, p. 84.
4   James Melville, *Memoirs*, p. 134
5   Thomas Randolph to William Cecil, 27 February 1565, TNA, SP 52/10
    f. 30.
6   Queen Elizabeth I of England to Mary, Queen of Scots, 27 June 1568,
    TNA, SP 52/10 f. 133.
7   'At first hes takin our house, slane our maist spetial servand in our
    awin presence, and thair eftir haldin our propper personis captive
    tressonneblie quhair by we war constranit to escaipe straitlie about
    midnycht out of our palice of Halliruidhouss, to the place quhair we are
    for the present, in the grittest danger, feir of our lywis, and ewill estate
    that evir princes on earth stuid in' Mary to Elizabeth, 15 March 1566,
    TNA, SP 52/12 f.58.
8   'We ar assurit, and nocht sua disprovit, both utheris princes that will
    heir of our estate, consideering the samin, will favour us sa meikle as to
    help and support us (gif neid beis) to defend us and our realme [and]
    the Word of God quhilk commandis that all princes sould favour and
    defend the just actiouns of uther princes als wele as thair awin.' TNA, SP
    52/12 f.58.
9   Confession of the Laird of Ormiston, 13 December 1573 in R. Pitcairn,
    Ancient Criminal Trials in Scotland, (1833), p. 512.
10 Depositions on the King's murder, 11 February 1567, British Library (BL),
    Add. MS 33, 531, f. 37.
11 Elizabeth to Mary, 24 February 1567, TNA, SP52/13 f. 17.
12 Named for the tavern in which the men were gathered when they
    signed.

13 Elizabeth to Mary, 23 June 1567, TNA, SP 52/13 f.71.

14 Strickland, *Life of Mary Queen of Scots*, vol. 2, p. 80.

15 A commendator was someone who was responsible for a religious property: the position was taken up after the Reformation in Scotland to replace the Catholic titles. Technically, a commendator owed his position to the monarch and as such can be seen as a more secular role.

16 The 'Luck of Workington Hall' was put up for auction in 2023: https://www.sothebys.com/en/buy/auction/2022/treasures-2/the-luck-of-workington-hall-an-agate-cup-probably

17 Mary to Elizabeth, 17 May 1568, TNA, SP 53/1 f.1.

18 Richard Lowther to Cecil, 22 May 1568, TNA, SP 53/1 f. 10.

19 Memorial of William Cecil, May 1568, BL, Cotton MS Caligula C. I. f. 97.

20 Memorial of William Cecil, May 1568, BL, Cotton MS Caligula C. I. f. 97.

CHAPTER TWO

1 Cipher symbol for 'Sir William Cecil' from a page of ciphers used by Mary, Queen of Scots, c.1586, TNA, SP53/22 f. 1.

2 'Our rebellis, for quhat offeris thai can mak, will nocht get the support fra this cuntrey that thai pretend; and of our part we will assure yow that […] we hoip to gett sic sufficient socours of freindis to impesche the malheureux intentioun of oure rebellis and cause thame knaw thair dewitie to our honour.' Mary, Queen of Scots to Gilbert Kennedy, Earl of Cassilis, 17 January 1569, TNA, SP 53/3 f. 12.

3 *The Records of the Parliaments of Scotland to 1707*, K.M. Brown et al eds (St Andrews, 2007-2024), A1567/12/18. Date accessed: 2 February 2024.

4 *The Records of the Parliaments of Scotland (RPS)*, A1567/12/18.

5 *RPS*, A1567/12/18.

6 *RPS*, A1567/12/18.

7 Queen Elizabeth I of England to Moray, edited by William Cecil, 20 September 1568, TNA, SP 52/15 f.132

8 Guy, *My Heart is my Own*, p. 388.

9 Mary to Elizabeth, contemporary copy by Wiliam Cecil's clerk, 5 July 1568, BL, Cotton MS Caligula C. I. f. 160.

10 Mary to Bishop of Ross, 5 October 1568, TNA, SP 53/2.

11 Mary to Elizabeth, contemporary copy by William Cecil's clerk, 5 July 1568, BL. Cotton MS Caligula C. I. f. 160.

12 Mary to Elizabeth, contemporary copy by William Cecil's clerk, 5 July 1568, BL. Cotton MS Caligula C. I. f. 160.

13 Mary's instructions to Robert Melville, Alexandre Labanoff, ed., *Lettres, Instructions et Memoires de Marie Stuart, Reine d' Ecosse* (London, 1844), vol. 2, pp. 44–49.

14 The best detailed deconstruction of the Casket Letters remains Guy's, *My Heart is My Own*, ch. 25 and 26; Casket Letter 1: TNA, SP 53/2 f.62.

15 Casket Letter 2: TNA, SP 53/2 f. 65.

16 Casket Letter 3: TNA, SP 53/2 f. 66; Casket Letter 4 (English translation): Cecil Papers CP 352/4; Casket Letter 4 (French transcription): CP 352/3; Casket Letter 5: TNA, SP 53/2 f. 64.

17 Casket Letter 6 (French transcription): CP 352/1; Casket Letter 6 (English translation): 352/2; Casket Letters 7 and 8 have no surviving manuscript transcription and are generally taken from printed versions which appeared later in 1572, see BL, Add. MS. C.55.A.26.

18 'dowtfullyst and dangerowst that ever I dealt in; yff you sawe and harde the constante affyrmyng off bothe sydes not withowte great stowtnes you wolde wonder!' Thomas Howard, Duke of Norfolk to Cecil, 16 October 1568, TNA, SP 53/2 f. 19.

19 'seke hollye to sarve their owne partyculer turnes' and 'they care not what becumes nether off quene nor of kynge'. They 'play att no small game, they stande for their lyves, lands and goods', TNA, SP 53/2 f. 19.

20 Guy, *My Heart is My Own*, p. 431.

21 'And wyth Goddis grace we shall first mak sic ansuer thairto that oure innocencie salbe knowen to oure goode sister and all utheris princes, and siclyke shall charge thame as authoris, inventaris and doaris of the said cryme they wold imput to ws,' Mary to her Commissioners, 19 December 1568, BL, Cotton MS Caligula B. IX, f. 344.

22 Sir Francis Knollys to Cecil, 21 September 1568, TNA, SP 53/1 f.60.

23 Though there were several brief moments when she was more robust in supporting Catholicism in Scotland, notably the so-called 'Catholic Interlude' during the marriage negotiations with England and her subsequent wedding to Henry Stuart, Lord Darnley. See Julian Goodare, 'Queen Mary's Catholic Interlude', *Innes Review*, 38, 2010, p. 154-170.

24 Labanoff, vol. 2, pp. 237–241.

25 Mary to Archbishop of St Andrews, 18 January 1569, BL, Add. MS. 33531, f.73.

26 TNA, SP52/15 f. 87.

27 See Jane Dawson, *The Politics of Religion in the Age of Mary, Queen of Scots: The Earl of Argyll and the Struggle for Britain and Ireland* (Cambridge University Press, 2002).

CHAPTER THREE

1 Cipher symbol for Thomas Percy, 'Earl of Northumberland', from a page of ciphers used by Mary, Queen of Scots, c.1586, TNA, SP53/22 f. 1.

2 Mary, Queen of Scots to Thomas Howard, Duke of Norfolk, deciphered copy, 25 [unknown month] 1569, British Library (BL), Harley MS 290, f. 94.

3 Queen Elizabeth I of England to Mary, 20 January 1569, TNA, SP53/5 f. 18.

4 Instructions for the Scots Queen's accommodation, TNA, SP53/3 f. 19.

5 Sir Francis Knollys to William Cecil, 29 January 1569, TNA, SP53/3 f. 32.

6 Knollys to Privy Council, 29 January 1569, TNA, SP53/3 f. 31.

7 Knollys to Cecil, 1 February 1569, TNA, SP53/3 f. 35.

8 List of persons attached to or attendant on Mary, February 1569, TNA, SP53/3 f. 57.

9 'willing to leiff and deall uprychtlie in all thair adois', Bishop of Ross and Lord Boyd to Cecil, 20 February 1569, TNA, SP53/3 f. 52.

10 Elizabeth to Shrewsbury, 21 February 1569, TNA, SP53/3 f. 34.

11 Instructions from Elizabeth to Shrewsbury with his reply, 26 January 1569, TNA, SP53/3 f. 23.

12 'Sathane and his ministeris nocht contentit to God's will', Regent's Proclamation, March 1569, TNA, SP52/14 f. 160a (wrongly catalogued as 1568).

13 Mary to Cecil, 13 March, 1569, TNA, SP53/3 f. 61.

14 Shrewsbury to Cecil, 13 March 1569, TNA, SP53/3 f. 62.

15 Bishop of Ross to Elizabeth, 15 March 1569, TNA, SP53/3 f. 63.

16 Alexander Leslie to Bishop of Ross, 6 April 1569, TNA, SP53/3.

17 Shrewsbury to Cecil, 27 April 1569, TNA, SP53/3 f. 75.

18 Articles devised by Bishop of Ross at the Queen of England's command, 8 May 1569, TNA, SP53/3 f. 78.

19 Mary had in fact signed over the inheritance of the Scottish crown and her claim to the English throne prior to her wedding to the dauphin Francis in 1558, but this was not widely known and with the death of Francis and her return to Scotland it became void.

20 Shrewsbury and others to the Council of the North, 27 September 1569, TNA, SP53/4 f. 27.

21 Mary to Elizabeth, 1 October 1569, BL, Cotton MS Caligula C. I. f. 444.

22 Examination of John Hameling, 18 April 1570, CP157/30.

23 Shrewsbury to Cecil, 13 August 1571, TNA. SP53/7 f. 20.

24 Sussex to Elizabeth, 10 November 1569, TNA, SP15/15 f. 29.

25 Nicholas White to Cecil, 26 February 1569, CP155/100.

26 Krista J Kesselring, 'Mary Queen of Scots and the Northern Rebellion of 1569,' p. 52.

27 Hunsdon to Cecil, 26 November 1569, TNA, SP15/15 f. 87; Sir Cuthbert Sharp, *Memorials of the Rebellion of 1569* (London, 1841).

28 Mary to Elizabeth, contemporary copy by William Cecil's clerk, 5 July 1568, BL, Cotton MS Caligula C. I. f. 160.

29 Jane Dawson, *Scotland Re-formed 1488–1587* (Edinburgh, Edinburgh University Press, 2007), p. 270.

30 Chatsworth was one of the most luxurious properties that Mary was held in. It belonged to Bess of Hardwick, Shrewsbury's wife, and had been extensively remodelled with the most stylish architecture and furnishings.

31 Jade Scott, *The Life and Letters of Lady Anne Percy, Countess of Northumberland (1536–91)* (Suffolk: Catholic Record Society, Boydell and Brewer, 2024), p. xxx.

32 Confession of John Hall, May 1571, CP157/122; John Beaton's brother Andrew had previously been Mary's master of the household during the personal reign.

33 Antonia Fraser, *Mary Queen of Scots*, p. 577.

34 Mary to Norfolk, deciphered copy, 1569, Labanoff, vol. 2, p. 369; BL, Harley MS 290, f. 94.

35 Cecil to Elizabeth, 6 October 1569, BL, Cotton MS Caligula, C. I. f. 456.

36 Mary to Elizabeth, 1 October 1569, BL, Cotton MS Caligula, C. I. f. 444.

37 Maureen Meikle, *Scotland's People*, p. 227.

38 Guy, *My Heart is My Own*, p. 464.

39 Charles Bailly to Bishop of Ross, 26 April 1571, Cecil Papers, Hatfield House, CP5/116.

40 Sir Ralph Sadler to Cecil, 9 January 1582, TNA, SP 53.8 f. 7.

CHAPTER FOUR

1 Cipher symbol for George Talbot, 'Earl of Shrewsbury', from a page of ciphers used by Mary, Queen of Scots, c.1586, TNA, SP53/22 f. 1.

2 Mary, Queen of Scots to Queen Elizabeth I, contemporary copy made by a clerk, 2 May 1580, TNA, SP 53/11 f. 22.

3 List of Mary's household, 30 May 1586, TNA, SP53/17 f. 91.

4 John Somer to William Cecil, 1 March 1585, TNA, SP53/15 f.48.

5 Labanoff, vol. 6, pp. 165–167.

6 Mary to Mauvissière, 12 March 1575, TNA, SP53/10 f. 78.

7 Shrewsbury to Cecil, 7 June 1573, TNA, SP53/9 f. 8.

8 Mary to Mauvissière, 12 March 1575, TNA, SP53/10 f. 78; Shrewsbury to Elizabeth, 9 November 1569, TNA, SP53/4 f. 58.

9 Shrewsbury to Cecil, 7 June 1573, TNA, SP53/9 f.8.

10 Guy, *My Heart is My Own*, p. 447.

11 Mary to Elizabeth, 30 July 1576, TNA, SP53/10.

12 Elizabeth to Shrewsbury, 18 August 1573, TNA, SP53/9 f. 10.

13 Mary to Cecil, January 1570, TNA, SP53/5 f. 1.

14 This may be the man referred to as 'Andrew Makeson' in a note of Mary's servants from 1571 (or perhaps a relation of his), Shrewsbury to Cecil, 4 May 1571, TNA, SP53/6 f.103; Mary to Ross, 18 August 1570, TNA, SP53/5 f. 121.

15 Mary to Ross, 17 August 1571, TNA, SP53/7 f.31.

16 Shrewsbury to Cecil, 4 May 1571, TNA, SP53/6 f.103; Shrewsbury to Walsingham, 26 April 1576, British Library (BL), Cotton MS Caligula, C/ IX f.95.

17 Mary's request for passports, 22 July 1578, TNA, SP53/11 f. 9; Mary to Elizabeth, 2 May 1580, TNA, SP53/11 f. 22.

18 Jean Scott, Lady Ferniehurst to Mary, deciphered copy, 4 November 1583, BL, Cotton MS Caligula C/VI f. 338; Lady Ferniehurst to Mary, deciphered copy, 25 November 1583, TNA, SP53/12 f. 93.

19 G. R. Hewitt, 'Stewart, John, fourth earl of Atholl,' *Oxford Dictionary of National Biography*, online ed. 2006.

20 Rosalind K. Marshall, 'Queen's Maries', *ODNB*, online ed. 2004; Rosalind K. Marshall, *Queen Mary's Women*, p. 151.

21 Inventory of Mary's goods, Labanoff, vol. 7, pp. 254–274.

22 Mary's requests presented by Claude Nau, 28 November 1584, TNA, SP53/14.

23 Maitland to Lady Livingston, 23 February 1573, TNA, SP52/54 f.140.

24 Margaret Douglas, Countess of Lennox to Mary, 10 November 1575, TNA, SP53/10 f.71.

25 Bess to Mary, December 1574, TNA, SP53/9 f. 195.

26 Mary to Guillaume de L'Aubespine, deciphered copy, 31 May 1586, TNA, SP53/17 f.88.

27 Mary's testament of 1577, Labanoff, vol. 4, p. 358; seventeenth-century copy of Mary's testament of 1587, Labanoff, vol. 5, p. 488.

28 Copy testament, Labanoff, vol. 5, p. 491.

29 Mary to James Beaton, Archbishop of Glasgow, 22 September 1574, Labanoff, vol. 4, p. 229.

30 Labanoff, vol. 7, p. 258.

31 Commodities for Tutbury, 1 February 1585, TNA, SP53/15 f. 30i.

32 Inventory of items sent from France, 21 July 1579, BL, Cotton MS Caligula C/IX f.163.

33 List of the victuals for Mary, 1 February 1585, TNA, SP53/15 f. 26; Commodities, 1 February 1585, TNA, SP53/15 f.30i.

34 Guy, *My Heart is My Own*, p. 448.

35 Sir Francis Knollys to Cecil, 28 June 1568, BL, Cotton MS Caligula, B/IX/2 f. 345.

36 Guy, *My Heart is My Own*, p. 440.

37 Knollys to Cecil, 28 June 1568, BL, Cotton MS Caligula B/IX/2 f. 345; Labanoff, vol. 7, pp. 254–274.

38 Knollys to Cecil, 7 July 1568, BL, Cotton MS Caligula B/IX/2 f. 338; Mary to James Beaton, 20 February 1580, Labanoff, vol. 5, p. 121.

39 Labanoff, vol. 7, pp.254–274.

40 Knollys to Cecil, 28 June 1568, BL, Cotton MS Caligula B/IX/2 f. 338.

41 Mary to Elizabeth, 30 July 1576, TNA, SP53/10.

42 Mary to James Beaton, 20 February 1580, Labanoff, vol. 5, p. 121.

43 A muffler was a wrap worn about the neck or lower face either for warmth or to cover the face. List of items taken from Mary's chambers, 1586, TNA, SP53/20 f. 44.

44 Labanoff, vol. 7, pp. 254–274.

45 List of items taken from Mary's chambers, 1586, TNA, SP53/20 f. 44.

46 *A Booke of Secrets: Shewing divers waies to make and prepare all sorts of Inke and Colours*…Translated out of Dutch into English by W. P. (London, 1596), accessed via https://www.english.cam.ac.uk/ceres/ehoc/intro/inkrecipes.html.

47 List of the victuals for Mary, 1 February 1585, TNA, SP53/15 f. 26.

48 Labanoff, vol. 7, pp. 254–274.

49 List of items taken from Mary's chambers, December 1586, TNA, SP53/20 f. 44.

50 Guy, *My Heart is My Own*, p. 447.

51 List of the victuals for Mary, 1 February 1585, TNA, SP53/15 f. 26.

52 List of Mary's household, 30 May 1586, TNA, SP53/17 f. 91

53 Labanoff, vol. 7, pp. 254–274.

54 Ibid.

55 Shrewsbury to Cecil, 18 February 1572, TNA, SP53/8 f. 38.

56 John Somer to Walsingham, 21 October 1584, TNA, SP53/14 f. 14.

57 Instructions for Mary's custody, 1 February 1585, TNA, SP53/15 f. 30.

58 Mary's requests, November 1584, TNA, SP53/14 f. 23.

59 Mary's requests, 3 December 1581, TNA, SP53/11 f. 72.

60 List of Mary's household, 30 May 1586, TNA, SP53/17 f. 91.

61 Shrewsbury to Cecil, 13 March 1569, TNA, SP53/3 f. 62.

62 'thar talk is altogether of indifferent and trifling materes without menstring any signe of secrete dealing or practise', he would 'mak suche straight restrainte therin as shal please hir highnes to command', Shrewsbury to Cecil, 13 March 1569, TNA, SP53/3 f. 62.

63 Remembrances for Shrewsbury, 26 January 1569, TNA, SP53/4 f. 23

64 Labanoff, vol. 7, pp. 254–274.

65 List of Mary's household, 30 May 1586, TNA, SP53/17 f. 91.

66 Sir William Cavendish to Bess, 13 April 1550, Folger Shakespeare Library, Cavendish-Talbot MS, X.d.428 (13); Sir William St Loe to Bess, 12 October 1560, Folger Shakespeare Library, Cavendish-Talbot MS, X.d.428 (76), accessed bessofhardwick.org.

67 George Talbot, Earl of Shrewsbury to Bess, 28 June c. 1568, Folger Shakespeare Library, Cavendish-Talbot MS, X.d.428 (85), accessed bessofhardwick.org.

68 Shrewsbury's request of Elizabeth, 3 December 1581.

69 Mary to L'Aubespine, deciphered copy, 31 May 1586, TNA, SP53/17 f. 88.

70 Fraser, *Mary, Queen of Scots*, p. 510

71 Guy, *My Heart is My Own*, p. 441.

72 Fraser, *Mary, Queen of Scots*, p. 511.

73 Mary to Annas Keith, Countess of Moray, NRAS217/Box15.

74 List of victuals, 1 February 1585, TNA, SP53/15 f. 26.

75 Labanoff, vol. 7, pp. 254–274.

CHAPTER FIVE

1 Cipher symbol for 'Don Juan of Austria' from a page of ciphers used by Mary, Queen of Scots, c.1586, TNA, SP53/22 f. 1.

2 Mary, Queen of Scots to James Beaton, Archbishop of Glasgow, deciphered copy, 6 November 1577, TNA, SP 53/10 f. 95.

3 Cardinal of Lorraine to Mary, 1 February 1574, TNA, SP 53/9 f. 135.

4 William Kincaid to William Cecil, 5 January 1572, TNA, SP 52/22 f. 2.

5 The couple had several sons: François, Louis (who died in infancy), Charles, Henri and Hercule (renamed Francis), Duke of Anjou. They also had three daughters who survived to adulthood: Elisabeth, Claude and Margaret.

6 Henry Killigrew to Cecil, 29 January 1573, TNA, SP 52/24 f. 50.

7 Francis Walsingham to James Douglas, Earl of Morton, Regent of Scotland, 26 February 1577, TNA, SP 70/143 f. 159.

8 Dr Thomas Wilson to Robert Dudley, Earl of Leicester, 18 May 1577, Cecil Papers, Hatfield House, CP9/67.

9 Mary to Bishop of Ross, ciphered letter, TNA, SP 53/6 f. 19.

10 Examination of Robert Melville, 19 October 1572.

11 Lord Seton's Book of Negotiations, February 1572, TNA, SP 53/8 f. 45.

12 Shrewsbury to Cecil, 22 April 1572, TNA, SP 53/8 f. 82.

13 Mary to Thomas Morgan, ciphered letter, 3 August 1577, TNA, SP 53/10 f. 88.

14 Kervyn de Lettenhove, *Relations Politiques*, vol. 6, pp. 8–11.

15 Mary to James Beaton, ciphered letter, 6 November 1577, British Library (BL), Add. MS 48049 f. 284.

16 Sir Francis Englefield to Jane Dormer, Duchess of Feria, 12 November 1574, BL, Cotton MS Caligula C/III f. 513.

17 Mary to Andrew Beaton, 12 August 1577, Labanoff, vol, 4, p. 378.

18 Shrewsbury to Walsingham, 26 April 1577, BL, Cotton MS Caligula C/IX f. 95.

19 Mary to James Beaton, ciphered letter, 31 August 1577, BL, Add. MS 48049 f. 268.

20 Earl of Sussex to Cecil, 1560, TNA, SP 63/2 f. 86.

21 Lord Seton's Negotiations, February 1572, TNA, SP 53/8 f. 45.

22 Examination of Mary, 19 June 1581, Cecil Papers, Hatfield House, CP 11/80.

23 Lady Anne Percy to Thomas Stukely, 21 June 1571, BL, Cotton MS Caligula C/III f. 186.

24 Mary to Michel de Castelnau, Sieur de la Mauvissière, 2 May 1578, Bibliothèque nationale de France (BnF), Fr. 2988 f. 87; Lasry et al. 'Deciphering Mary Stuart's Lost Letters', p. 138.

25 Mary to James Beaton, 18 March 1577, Labanoff, vol. 4, p. 363.

26 Mary to James Beaton, 29 January 1577, Labanoff, vol. 4, p. 344.

27 Interrogatories for Antonio de Guarás, Spanish ambassador to England, 1578.

28 Antonio de Guarás to an unknown recipient, 20 September 1577, BL, Add. MS

29 Mary to Mauvissière, 12 June 1578, BnF, Fr. 20506 f. 227.; Lasry et al. 'Deciphering Mary Stuart's Lost Letters', p. 138.

30 Mary to James Beaton, 15 September 1578, Labanoff, vol. 5, p. 50.

31 Margaret Douglas, Countess of Lennox to Mary, SP53/10 f. 71.

32 Mary to Mauvissière, 2 May 1578, BnF, Fr. 2988 f. 87; Lasry et al. 'Deciphering Mary Stuart's Lost Letters', p. 137

33 Intelligence against Esmé Stuart, 6th Seigneur d'Aubigny, 3 February 1581, BL, Cotton MS Caligula, C/V f.131.

34 Privy Council to Henry Carey, Lord Hunsdon, 10 April 1581, BL, Harley MS 6999 f. 165.

35 Rosalind K. Marshall, 'Stuart [Stewart], Esmé, first Duke of Lennox', *Oxford Dictionary of National Biography*, online ed., 2008.

36 Mary to Mauvissière, 20 October 1581, BnF, Fr. 20506 f. 194; Lasry et al. 'Deciphering Mary Stuart's Lost Letters', p. 146.

37 Esmé Stuart, Duke of Lennox to Mary, 7 March 1582, *Calendar of State Papers, Spain (Simancas), Volume 3,1580–1586*, p. 333.

38 Mary to Don Bernardino de Mendoza, 8 April 1582, *CSP Simancas 1580–1586*, p. 330.

39 Proposed treaty with Mary, 2 October 1583, TNA, SP 53/12 f. 89.

CHAPTER SIX:

1 Cipher symbol for 'Monsieur de Mauvissière' from a page of ciphers used by Mary, Queen of Scots, c.1586, TNA, SP53/22 f. 1.

2 Mary, Queen of Scots to Michel de Castelnau, Sieur de la Mauvissière, deciphered copy, 5 January 1584, TNA, SP 53/13.

3 Bossy, *Under the Molehill*.

4 Shrewsbury to Queen Elizabeth I of England, 28 February 1572, TNA, SP 53/8 f. 40.

5   James Douglas, Earl of Morton to Henry Killigrew, 23 May 1574, TNA, SP 70/131, f. 60.

6   Shrewsbury to Walsingham, 12 June 1574, TNA, SP 53/9 f. 152.

7   Mary to Mauvissière, 15 January 1583, Bibliothèque nationale de France (BnF), Fr. 20506, f. 153; Lasry et al., 'Deciphering Mary Stuart's Lost Letters', p. 160.

8   Mary to Mauvissière, deciphered copy, 25 February 1584, BL, Harley MS 1582 f. 311.

9   Mauvissière to Paul de Foix, 26 September 1566, Bnf, Fr. 15971, f. 12.

10 William Fowler to Walsingham, May 1583, TNA, SP 52/32 f. 41.

11 Mary to Mauvissière, 31 May 1583, BnF, Fr. 2988 f. 26; Lasry et al., 'Deciphering Mary Stuart's Lost Letters,' p. 173.

12 Mary to Mauvissière, 30 October 1584, BnF, Fr. 3158, f. 57; Lasry et al., 'Deciphering Mary Stuart's Lost Letters,' pp. 180–181.

13 Mary to Mauvissière, deciphered copy, 25 February 1584, British Library (BL), Harley MS 1582, f. 311. The newly found original cipher letter is at BnF, Fr. 2988, f. 58;

14 Alison Plowden, 'Throckmorton [Throgmorton], Francis, 1554-1584', in *Oxford Dictionary of National Biography*, online ed. September 2015.

15 *A Discoverie of the Treasons practised & attempted... by Francis Throckmorton* (1584), p. 192.

16 Sir Francis Walsingham to Charles Paget, 4 May 1582, TNA, SP 15/27/1 f. 123.

17 Charles Paget to Queen Elizabeth, 1582, TNA, SP 15/27/1.

18 Bossy, *Under the Molehill*, p. 34.

19 Mary to Mauvissière, deciphered copy, 5 January 1584, TNA, SP 53/13.

20 Thomas Lord Paget to his mother Lady Paget, 2 December 1583, TNA, SP 12/164 f. 6.

21 Stephen Alford, *The Watchers*, (London, 2013), p. 163

22 Mauvissière to Mary, December 1583, BL, Harley MS 1582, ff. 365.

23 Alford, *The Watchers*, p. 172.

24 Bossy, *Under the Molehill*, p. 24.

25 Mary to Mauvissière, 15 June 1583, BnF Fr. 2988 f. 34; Mary to Mauvissière, 10 October 1583, BnF Fr. 2988, f. 30; Lasry et al., 'Deciphering Mary Stuart's Lost Letters,' pp. 175–80; Charles Paget to Mary, 14 February 1584, TNA, SP 53/13/4.

CHAPTER SEVEN:

1 Cipher symbol for 'Sir Francis Walsingham' from a page of ciphers used by Mary, Queen of Scots, c.1586, TNA, SP53/22 f. 1.

2 Mary to James Beaton, Archbishop of Glasgow, deciphered copy, 31 August 1577, TNA, SP 53/10 f. 92.

3 Mary to Mendoza, deciphered copy, 27 July 1586, TNA, SP53/18 f. 165.

4 Mary to Charles Paget, 20 May 1586, TNA, SP53/17 f. 77; for similar complaints see Mary to Sir Francis Englefield, 20 May 1586, TNA, SP53/17 f. 75; Mary to Thomas Morgan, 20 May 1586, TNA, SP53/17 f. 80.

5 Alison Plowden, 'Gilbert Gifford', *Oxford Dictionary of National Biography*, online ed., 2004.

6 Mary to Charles Paget, deciphered copy, 20 May 1586, TNA, SP53/17 f. 77.

7 Walsingham to Killigrew, 18 Jul 1574, TNA, SP52/26/1 f. 78.

8 Mary to Michel de Castelnau, Sieur de la Mauvissière, 31 July 1581, Bibliothèque nationale de France, Fr. 2988 f. 98, Lasry et al., 'Deciphering Mary Stuart's Lost Letters', p. 145.

9 Mary to Mendoza, 29 July 1582, *Calendar of State Papers, Spain (Simancas), Volume 3,1580–1586*, p.392.

10 Mary to Mendoza, July 1586, TNA, SP53/18 f. 194.

11 Mary to Mendoza, 29 July 1582, *CSP Simancas 1580–1586*, p. 392.

12 Bossy, *Under the Molehill*, p. 69.

13 Mary to Mendoza, 14 January 1582, *CSP Simancas 1580–1586*, p. 257.

14 Mary to Mendoza, 13 July 1583, *CSP Simancas 1580–1586*, p. 491.

15 Mary to Mendoza, deciphered copy, 20 May 1586, TNA, SP53/17.

16 Mendoza to Mary, deciphered copy, 26 June 1586, TNA, SP5318 f. 35.

17 Philip II of Spain to Mendoza, 5 September 1586, *CSP Simancas 1580–1586*, p. 614.

18 Bossy, *Under the Molehill*, p. 140.

19 Girolamo Lando, Venetian ambassador to England, to the heads of the Venetian Council of Ten, deciphered copy, 15 April 1622, *Calendar of State Papers Relating To English Affairs in the Archives of Venice, Volume 17, 1621–1623*, p. 289.

20 Mary to Morgan, deciphered copy, Cecil Papers at Hatfield House, CP133/64.

21 Thomas Barnes (Thomas Phelippes) to Gilbert Curle, 16 June 1586, TNA, SP53/18 f. 11.

22 Alford, *The Watchers*, p. 203.

23 Morgan to Mary, deciphered copy, 26 July 1585, Cecil Papers at Hatfield House, CP13/113.

24 Morgan to Mary, deciphered copy, 9 May 1586, Cecil Papers at Hatfield House, CP164/56.

25 CP164/56.

26 Claude Nau to Babington, deciphered copy, 13 July 1586, TNA, SP53/18 f. 87.

27 Mary to Paget, deciphered copy, 27 July 1586, British Library (BL), Cotton MS Caligula C/VIII f. 305.

28 Babington to Mary, deciphered copy, July 1586, TNA, SP53/19.

29 Mary to Babington, copy, 17 July 1586, TNA, 53/18 f. 106.

30 Thomas Phelippes to Walsingham, 19 July 1586, TNA, SP 53/18.

31 TNA, SP53/18 f. 106; Alford, *The Watchers*, p. 218.

32 Babington to Poley, BL, Lansdowne 49/63.

33 Interrogation of Jane Tichborne, SP53/19/34; Confession of Jane Tichborne, SP53/19/35.

34 Cipher with Babington's confession, TNA, SP12/193/54.

35 Mendoza to Philip II of Spain, 26 September, *CSP Simancas 1580–1586*, p. 625.

36 Babington to Elizabeth, 19 September 1586, TNA, SP12/193 f. 122.

37 Mendoza to Philip II of Spain, 20 October 1586, *CSP Simancas 1580–1586*, p. 641.

38 Submission of John Gifford, 28 November 1588, TNA, SP12/218 f. 73.

39 Interrogation questions of for Robert Poley, August 1586, SP53/19 f. 25.

40 Mary to James Beaton, deciphered copy, 28 May 1586, TNA, SP53/17 f. 84.

41 Mary to Mendoza, deciphered copy, 23 November 1586, *CSP Simancas 1580–1586*, p. 663.

42 Mary to Mendoza, deciphered copy, 2 August 1586, TNA, SP53/19 f. 2.

43 Mary to Henri III, 7 February 1587, NLS Adv. MS. 54. 1.1.

44 Mary to Mendoza, deciphered copy, 23 November 1586, *CSP Simancas 1580–1586*, p. 663.

45 *Proper new ballad, briefly declaring the death and execution of 14 most wicked traitors*, (London, 1586), National Library of Scotland, Crawford, EB. 1027.

AFTERWORD:

1   Cipher symbol for 'Prince of Scotland' from a page of ciphers used by Mary, Queen of Scots, c.1586, TNA, SP53/22 f. 1.

2   'Vous supplient tres humblement de croire que Je Vous demeureray a Jamais tres humble et tres obeisent filz et que tent que Je viveray Je Vous porteré lhonneur et le devoir que Je Vous doirs croyent anssy que Vous me honoreres tousiours de v[ot]re bonne afection maternele et que me reconquoistres pour tel', James VI to Mary, Queen of Scots 19 April 1581, TNA, SP 53/11 f. 46.

3   Mary to James VI, 16 April 1582, TNA, SP 53/12 f. 11.

4   James VI to Mary, 19 April 1581, TNA, SP 53/11 f. 46.

5   James VI to Mary, deciphered copy, 23 July 1584, TNA, SP 53/13 f. 107.

6   James VI to Mary, 1581, TNA, SP 53/11 f. 44.

Illustration Credits

Plate Illustrations

Page 1   Mary Stuart (1542–87), by François Clouet (school of),
          Czartoryski Museum, Cracow, Poland. Bridgeman Images

Page 2   (above left) James Stewart, Earl of Moray (c 1531–1570).
          Universal History Archive / UIG / Bridgeman Images

Page 2   (below right) William Cecil, Lord Burghley (1520–1598).
          Lebrecht History / Bridgeman Images

Page 3   (above left) Portrait of Henry Stuart, Earl of Darnley (1545–
          1567), by Adrian Vanson (attr. to), Private Collection.
          Photo © Bonhams, London UK / Bridgeman Images

Page 3   (above left) Portrait of James Hepburn, fourth Earl of
          Bothwell (ca 1534–1578), Prince Consort of Scotland
          (miniature), Edinburgh, National Gallery of Scotland.
          Photo © NPL – DeA Picture Library / Bridgeman Images

Page 3   (below) The Murder of Rizzio, 1787, by John Opie
          (1761–1807), Guildhall Art Gallery / Bridgeman Images

Page 4   (above) Lochleven Castle, in which Mary, Queen of Scots was
          imprisoned (engraving), English School (19th century), Private
          Collection. Image © Look and Learn / Bridgeman Images

Page 4   (below) Dundrennan Abbey (engraving), English School
          (19th century), Private Collection. Image © Look and Learn
          / Bridgeman Images

Page 5   (above) Workington Hall, by Alexander Francis Lydon (1836–1917), English, Private Collection. Image © Look and Learn / Bridgeman Images

Page 5   (below) The Luck of Workington Hall. Photo supplied by courtesy of The Helena Thompson Museum, Workington

Page 6   (above) Portrait of Henry I of Lorraine, Duke of Guise, Dit Le Balafre (1550–1588), French School (16th century), Musee Conde, Chantilly, France. Photo © Photo Josse / Bridgeman Images

Page 6   (below) Michel de Castelnau, Seigneur de Mauvissière, (engraving), French School, Private Collection. Bridgeman Images

Page 7   (above) Elizabeth Hardwick (Bess of Hardwick), Countess of Shrewsbury by Hans Eworth (c. 1525–after 1578), Flemish, Hardwick Hall, Derbyshire, UK. National Trust Photographic Library / Bridgeman Images

Page 7   (below) Lady Margaret Douglas, Countess of Lennox, 1575, Rijksmuseum, Amsterdam, The Netherlands. Bridgeman Images

Page 8   (above) Portrait of the Blessed Thomas Percy, 7th Earl of Northumberland by Steven van der Meulen (fl. 1543–1568), Private Collection. Photo © Philip Mould Ltd, London / Bridgeman Images

Page 8   (below) Portrait of Sir Francis Walsingham by John de Critz the Elder (c. 1552–1642), Flemish, Private Collection. Photo © Philip Mould Ltd, London / Bridgeman Images

Page 9   Ciphers of Mary, Queen of Scots, c.1586 (SP 53/22 f.1). National Archives Kew / State Papers Online

Page 10   (above) Queen Elizabeth I, English School, Compton Verney, Warwickshire, UK. © Compton Verney / Bridgeman Images

Page 10   (below) Portrait of the King of Spain Philip II, 16th century
          by Sofonisba Anguissola (c. 1532–1625), Prado, Madrid,
          Spain. Photo © Photo Josse / Bridgeman Images

Page 11   From The Cecil Papers, reproduced with permission of the
          Marquess of Salisbury, Hatfield House. Image © Hatfield
          House Archives

Page 12   (above) Tutbury Castle (engraving), English School (17th
          century), Private Collection. Photo © Tom Graves Archive
          / Bridgeman Images

Page 12   (below) Mary, Queen of Scots (1542–1587) and John Knox
          (c. 1512–1572) by Samuel Sidley (18229–1896), Towneley Hall
          Art Gallery and Museum, Burnley, Lancashire, UK. Photo
          © Towneley Hall Art Gallery and Museum / Bridgeman
          Images

Page 13   (above) Portrait of Don Juan of Austria by Alonso Sanchez
          Coello (c. 1531–1588), Art Museum, Khabarovsk, Russia.
          Bridgeman Images

Page 13   (below) Babington with his Complices in St. Giles Fields,
          1586 (engraving), English School, Private Collection.
          Bridgeman Images

Page 14   Last Letter written by Mary, Queen of Scots, on 8 February
          1587 (the night before her execution), to her brother-in-law,
          Henri III of France, Adv.MS.54.1.1. © National Library of
          Scotland Archives and Manuscripts Division

Page 15   (above) Fotheringhay Castle (engraving), English School,
          Private Collection. Image © Look and Learn / Bridgeman
          Images

Page 15   (below) The Execution of Mary, Queen of Scots, c. 1613,
          Dutch School, National Galleries of Scotland, Edinburgh.
          Image © National Galleries of Scotland / Bridgeman Images

Page 16   Portrait of Mary, Queen of Scots (1542–1587), Scottish
           School (16th century), Falkland Palace, Falkland, Fife,
           Scotland. Image © Mark Fiennes Archive. All rights
           reserved 2024 / Bridgeman Images

Text Illustrations

Page 76   Mary to Elizabeth. 30 July 1576. MS Records Assembled
           by the State Paper Office SP 53/10. The National Archives
           (Kew, UK). State Papers Online

Page 110   Proclamation by the Regent. 1567. MS Records Assembled
           by the State Paper Office SP 52/14 f.160a. The National
           Archives (Kew, UK). State Papers Online

Page 149   A note of what victual, and other things, is demanded
           for the Queen of Scots and her household. 1 February
           1585. MS Records Assembled by the State Paper Office SP
           53/15 f.26. The National Archives (Kew, UK). State Papers
           Online

Page 221   Queen of Scots to the Master of Gray. November 1584. MS
           Records Assembled by the State Paper Office SP 53/14 f.30.
           The National Archives (Kew, UK). State Papers Online

Page 223   Alphabets or ciphers between the Queen of Scots
           and divers persons. 20 September 1586. MS Records
           Assembled by the State Paper Office SP 12/193 f.123. The
           National Archives (Kew, UK). State Papers Online

Page 232   Babington, Anthony. Anthonie Babington to the Queen.
           19 September 1586. MS Records Assembled by the State
           Paper Office SP 12/193 f.122. The National Archives (Kew,
           UK). State Papers Online

Sources

―――――――――――――― ❧ ――――――――――――――

MANUSCRIPTS AND ARCHIVES

Bibliotheque nationale de France:
Français MSS.

British Library:
Additional MSS.
Cotton MSS.
Harley MSS.
Lansdowne MSS.

Hatfield House Archives:
Cecil Papers

Folger Shakespeare Library:
Cavendish-Talbot MSS.

National Library of Scotland:
Advocates MSS.

National Register of Archives for Scotland:
Moray Muniments, NRAS217.

The National Archives, State Paper Office:
SP 12
SP 52
SP 53
SP 70

PRINTED BOOKS

Anderson, James, *Collections relating to the history of Mary, Queen of Scotland* (Edinburgh, 1727)

Bain, Joseph, et al., eds., *Calendar of State Papers relating to Scotland and Mary, Queen of Scots* (Edinburgh, 1898–1952)

Bain, Joseph, ed., *The Hamilton Papers, Letters and Papers Illustrating the Political Relations of England and Scotland in the Sixteenth Century*, 2 vols (London, 1890–92)

Brown, K. M. et al., eds., *The Records of the Parliaments of Scotland to 1707* (St Andrews, 2007–2024)

Brown, Peter Hume, ed., *Register of the Privy Council of Scotland* (Edinburgh, 1904)

Buchanan, George, *Ane Detectioun of the Doingis of Marie Quene of Scottis tuiching the Murther of hir husband, and hir Conspiracie, Adulterie, and pretensit Mariage with the Erle Bothwell* (St Andrews, 1572)

Calderwood, David, *The True History of the Church of Scotland from the Beginning of the Reformation unto the End of the Reign of King James VI*, 8 vols (Edinburgh, 1842–49)

Calendar of the Manuscripts of the Most Honourable the Marquis of Salisbury (London, 1883–1976).

Camden, William, *The Historie of the Life and Death of Mary Stuart, Queen of Scotland* (London, 1624).

Castelnau, Michel de, *Mémoires*, ed. Michaud, J. F. and J. J. F. Poujoulat (Paris, 1838)

Clifford, Arthur, ed., *State Papers and Letters of Sir Ralph Sadler* (Edinburgh, 1809)

Cokayne, G. E. C., ed., *The Complete Peerage of England, Scotland, Ireland, Great Britain and the United Kingdom*, 6 vols (Gloucester, 1987)

Crosby, Allan J. and John Bruce, eds., *Accounts and Papers relating to Mary, Queen of Scots* (Camden Society, 1867)

Dawson, Jane, ed., *Campbell Letters, 1559–1583* (Edinburgh, 1997)

Forbes-Leith, William, *Narratives of Scottish Catholics under Mary Stuart and James VI* (Edinburgh, 1885)

Fraser, William, *The Lennox* (Edinburgh, 1874)

Hinds, Allen B., *Calendar of State Papers Relating To English Affairs in the Archives of Venice*, vol. 17 (London, 1911)

Hume, Martin A. S., ed., *Calendar of State Papers, Spain (Simancas), Volume 3, 1580–1586* (London, 1843–1910)

Labanoff, Alexandre, ed., *Lettres, Instructions et Memoires de Marie Stuart, Reine d'Ecosse* (London, 1844)

Leslie, John, *A Defence of the honor of the right high, right mighty, and noble princesse Marie queene of Scotlande* (Rheims, 1569)

Macdonald, Alexander, ed., *Letters to the Argyll Family* (Maitland Club, 1839)

Melville, James, *Memoirs of His Own Life by Sir James Melville of Halhill*, ed. Thomson, Thomas (Bannatyne Club, 1827)

Nau, Claude, *The History of Mary Stuart from the Murder of Riccio until her Flight into England*, ed. Joseph Stevenson (Edinburgh, 1883)

Pollen, J. H., *Mary, Queen of Scots and the Babington Plot* (Scottish History Society, 1922)

Seton, George, *A History of the Family of Seton* (Edinburgh, 1896)

Stevenson, Joseph, et al., eds., *Calendar of State Papers Foreign* (London, 1861–1950)

Strickland, Agnes, *Letters of Mary, Queen of Scots and Documents Concerned with her Personal History* (London, 1844)

Teulet, A., *Relations Politiques de la France avec l'Ecosse au XVIe siècle* (Paris, 1862)

Thomson, Thomas and Cosmo Innes, eds., *The Acts of the Parliaments of Scotland* (Edinburgh, 1814–75)

Turnbull, William, trans., *Letters of Mary Stuart, Queen of Scotland* (London, 1845)

Wood, Marguerite, ed., *Foreign Correspondence of Marie de Lorraine, 1548–57* (Scottish History Society, 1925)

Secondary Sources

Akkerman, Nadine, ed., *The Correspondence of Elizabeth Stuart, Queen of Bohemia Vol 1, 1603–1631* (Oxford, 2015)

Akkerman, Nadine, ed., *The Correspondence of Elizabeth Stuart, Queen of Bohemia Vol 2, 1631–1642* (Oxford, 2011)

Akkerman, Nadine and Langman, Pete, *Spycraft: Tricks and Tools of the Dangerous Trade from Elizabeth I to the Restoration* (Yale, 2024)

Alford, Stephen, *All His Spies: The Secret World of Robert Cecil* (London, 2024)

Alford, Stephen, *Burghley: William Cecil at the Court of Elizabeth I* (Yale, 2011)

Alford, Stephen, *The Watchers: A Secret History of the Reign of Elizabeth I* (London, 2013)

Batho, G. R., ed., 'The Execution of Mary, Queen of Scots', *Scottish Historical Review*, 39, pp. 35–42

Bertolet, Anna Riehl, ed., *Queens Matter in Early Modern Studies* (Cham, 2018)

Bezio, Kristin M. S., *The Eye of the Crown: The Development and Evolution of the Elizabethan Secret Service* (Abingdon, 2023)

Bingham, Caroline, *Darnley: A Life of Henry Stuart, Lord Darnley* (London, 1995)

Blakeway, Amy, *Regency in Sixteenth-Century Scotland* (Woodbridge, 2015)

Bossy, John, *The English Catholic Community 1570–1850* (London, 1975)

Bossy, John, *Under the Molehill: An Elizabethan Spy Story* (London, 2001)

Burnet, Andrew, *Mary Was Here: Where Mary Queen of Scots went and what she did there* (Edinburgh, 2013)

Carroll, Stuart, *Martyrs and Murderers: The Guise Family and the Making of Europe* (Oxford, 2011)

Cheetham, Keith, *Mary, Queen of Scots: The Captive Years* (Sheffield, 1982)

Collinson, Patrick, *The English Captivity of Mary, Queen of Scots* (Sheffield, 1987)

Cooper, John, *The Queen's Agent: Francis Walsingham at the Court of Elizabeth I* (London, 2012)

Cowan, I. B., *Mary, Queen of Scots* (Edinburgh, 1987)

Dack, C., *The Trial, Execution and Death of Mary, Queen of Scots* (Northampton, 1889)

Dawson, Jane, *John Knox* (Yale, 2016)

Dawson, Jane, *The Politics of Religion in the Age of Mary, Queen of Scots* (Cambridge, 2002)

Donaldson, Gordon, *All the Queen's Men* (London, 1983)

Donaldson, Gordon, *The First Trial of Mary, Queen of Scots* (London, 1969)

Doran, Susan, *From Tudor to Stuart: The Regime Change from Elizabeth I to James I* (Oxford, 2024)

Drummond, H., *The Queen's Man: James Hepburn, Earl of Bothwell and Duke of Orkney 1536–1578* (London, 1975)

Fraser, Antonia, *Mary Queen of Scots* (London, 1969)

Goodare, J., 'Queen Mary's Catholic Interlude', *Innes Review*, 38, p. 154–70

Goodare, J. *State and Society in Early Modern Scotland* (Oxford, 1999)

Goring, Rosemary, *Homecoming: The Scottish Years of Mary, Queen of Scots* (Birlinn, 2022)

Guy, John, *My Heart is My Own: The Life of Mary, Queen of Scots* (London, 2004)

Henderson, Jennifer Morag, *Daughters of the North: Jean Gordon and Mary, Queen of Scots* (Muir of Ord, 2022)

Henderson, T. F., *The Casket Letters and Mary Queen of Scots* (Edinburgh, 1890)

Holmes, P. J., 'Mary Stewart in England', *Innes Review*, 38, p. 195–218

Hunter, Clare, *Embroidering Her Truth: Mary, Queen of Scots and the Language of Power* (London, 2022)

Lang, Andrew, 'The Household of Mary Queen of Scots in 1573', *Scottish Historical Review* (Edinburgh, 1905)

Lasry, George, Norbert Bierman and Satoshi Tomokiyo, 'Deciphering Mary Stuart's Lost Letters From 1578–1584,' *Cryptologia*, 47(2), 2023, pp. 101–202

Leader, J. D., *Mary Queen of Scots in Captivity: A Narrative of Events* (Sheffield, 1880)

Lee, Maurice, *James Stewart, Earl of Moray* (New York, 1953)

Lynch, Michael, *Mary Stewart, Queen in Three Kingdoms* (Oxford, 1988)

Marshall, Rosalind K., *Queen Mary's Women: Female Relatives, Servants, Friends and Enemies of Mary, Queen of Scots* (Edinburgh, 2006)

Marshall, Rosalind K., *Scottish Queens*, (East Linton, 2003)

Mignet, M., *Histoire de Marie Stuart* (Paris, 1852)

Oxford Dictionary of National Biography, online ed. (Oxford, 2008)

Reid, Steven J., *The Early Life of James VI: A Long Apprenticeship, 1566–1585* (Birlinn, 2023)

Sanderson, Margaret H. B., *Mary Stewart's People* (Edinburgh, 1987).

Scott, Jade and Alison Wiggins, 'The Afterlives of Mary's Letters', in *The Afterlife of Mary, Queen of Scots*, ed. Reid, Steven J. (Edinburgh, 2023)

Scott, Jade, 'Editing the Letters of Mary, Queen of Scots: The Challenges of Authorship,' *Women's Writing*, 2024.

Scott, Jade, ed., *The Life and Letters of Lady Anne Percy, Countess of Northumberland (1536–1591)* (Suffolk, 2024)

Warnicke, Retha, *Mary Queen of Scots* (Abingdon, 2006)

Weir, Alison, *Mary, Queen of Scots and the Murder of Lord Darnley* (London, 2008)

Weir, Alison, *The Lost Tudor Princess: A Life of Margaret Douglas, Countess of Lennox* (London, 2015)

Wiggins, Alison, *Bess of Hardwick's Letters: Language, Materiality and Early Modern Epistolary Culture* (Abingdon, 2017)

Wormald, Jenny, *Mary, Queen of Scots: A Study in Failure* (London, 1988)

Wormald, Jenny Court, *Kirk and Community: Scotland 1470–1625* (London, 1981)

Acknowledgements

———————⌘———————

MARY, QUEEN OF Scots has been a huge part of my professional life for many years now and I would be remiss not to offer her my enduring gratitude. As I've moved on to explore the lives of other women in early modern Scotland, England, and Ireland, Mary is there inspiring my research and reminding me that we always need to question the sources for women's history if we are to recover their agency, power and influence.

In the present, I have so many people from different disciplines to thank for supporting my research, offering insight and expertise, suggesting new methods and approaches, and generally making me a much better scholar by virtue of being in their company. I'd like to thank: Amy Blakeway, Danielle Clarke, Jane Dawson, Claire Elder, Elizabeth Ewan, Emily Hay, George Lasry, John McCafferty, Martin Macgregor, Andrew Mackillop, Roibeard Ó Maolalaigh, Peadar Ó Muircheartaigh, John-Mark Philo, Roslyn Potter, Jamie Reid-Baxter, Steven Reid, Ann-Maria Walsh, Alison Wiggins, Emily Wingfield, Ramona Wray, and Georgiana Zeigler. A special thanks has to go to the cheerleaders who have encouraged this book from the very start: Nicola Clark, Laura Doak and Helen Newsome-Chandler. No study of Mary would be possible without the immense scholarship undertaken by those who have gone before me and I am grateful to all the biographers of Mary whose work has shaped my own interests: Antonia Fraser, Rosemary Goring, John Guy, Michael Lynch, Rosalind K. Marshall, Retha Warnicke and Jenny Wormald. Similarly, I wish to thank all of the staff at archives and libraries who have helped me with the research for this book, especially everyone at The National Library in Edinburgh, The National Records of Scotland, The British Library, The National Archives, Kew, and at Hatfield House.

I am immensely grateful to my agents Amberley Lowis and Charlie Viney for their advice, guidance and enthusiasm for this project. And to everyone at Michael O'Mara Books, I cannot thank you enough for your fantastic efforts to bring the book to life. My editor Louise Dixon has been a steady hand, guiding me through the process of publication, and keeping my anxieties at bay. Alison Menzies has been incredible in her efforts to share the book with as wide an audience as possible. To everyone who has contributed, I can only say thank you.

This book would not have been possible without the support of family and friends. To everyone who pre-ordered a copy, let me ramble on non-stop about Scottish history, and gave me time to moan about the 'trials' of being a writer, I will be forever grateful. My parents have encouraged my love of history since I was a child and have supported me throughout my research career and I cannot begin to tell them how grateful I am. No one has been more supportive and encouraging than my husband, Stewart. He has never once doubted that I could do this and his enthusiasm and unwavering certainty in my abilities have kept me going. I'm sorry to say that there will always be other women in our marriage – my early modern favourites – but he accepts their company without complaint. This book would not have been possible without him. And the dogs of course! Without Archer and Winnie, our St Bernards, keeping me company, I'm not quite sure I'd have managed to write this book. To you all, I give my love and thanks.

Index